THE ARTISANS

A VANISHING

CHINESE VILLAGE

Shen Fuyu

Translated by Jeremy Tiang

ASTRA HOUSE • NEW YORK

Astra House
A Division of Astra Publishing House
astrahouse.com
Printed in the United States of America

Publisher's Cataloging-in-Publication data
Names: Fuyu, Shen, author. | Tiang, Jeremy, translator.
Title: The artisans : a vanishing Chinese village / Shen Fuyu;
translated by Jeremy Tiang.
Description: New York, NY: Astra House, 2022.
Identifiers: LCCN: 2021917170 | ISBN: 9781662600753 (hardcover) | 9781662600760 (ebook)
Subjects: LCSH Artisans—China—Jiangsu Sheng—History. | Artisans—China. |
Handicraft industries—China. | China—Social life and customs. | BISAC HISTORY /
Asia / China | SOCIAL SCIENCE / Customs & Traditions | SOCIAL SCIENCE /
Ethnic Studies / Asian Studies
Classification: LCC HD2346.C6 .F89 2022 | DDC 745.5/.0951—dc23

First edition
10 9 8 7 6 5 4 3 2 1

Design by Richard Oriolo
The text and titles are set in GaramondPro-Regular.

CONTENTS

THE ARTISANS

INTRODUCTION

FROM WHEN I WAS BORN, my family and I lived in a close-knit society. The people I knew in my hometown were either relatives or nearby neighbors, with several generations of affection between us. It's not like everything was sunshine and rainbows—we had misunderstandings and quarrels, and sometimes even came to blows. Still, we knew each other well enough that these never developed into lasting grudges. For several centuries, rules were formed around customs, ways of thinking and agreements, so although the village grew larger and larger, there was peace despite its many disputes.

My hometown is crisscrossing rows of white walls with dark roof tiles. It is ripples swaying through the wheat when the wind blows. It is the fallen ginkgo leaves that cover the ground. I'm middle-aged now, and have traveled from my village to the big city, from China to countries thousands of miles away, and though I've stayed in many places, none of them have made me feel as at ease as my hometown. Where I come from, people speak in loud voices with thick country accents, and their behavior is coarse. All these things are now dear to me, although they once filled me with loathing. As a young man, these signifiers of village life made me ashamed, and all I wanted was to free myself of them.

Until I turned eighteen, I couldn't stand what seemed to me like a dark future in the village. My father was obsessed with not losing face, and the non-stop stream of sarcastic remarks he directed at me were particularly hurtful. When I left the village, I was determined never to return. Now, though, I have gained some empathy. I return to my hometown so my father doesn't lose face, or for the New Year, or even for the birth anniversary of some long-departed ancestor. Even though I've been going back more often, the swift decay of the village still shocks me. There are no longer any young people there, not even children. Virtually every time I return, I see a newly added grave. Along with the declining population, one old house after another falls into disrepair and then disappears. What used to be farmland is becoming occupied by the factories of the encroaching city. My hometown is no longer my hometown.

Waves of anguish wash over me. I've realized that this is how hometowns work—the more energy you expend in getting away, the greater the force that pulls you back. And yet the road back has become overgrown with the weeds of time, and can no longer be seen.

When our hometowns vanish, we become rootless people, individual atoms existing in isolation within the ice-cold city. We who left our hometowns have nothing to rely on, and are anxiously absorbed by the prosperity of urban life. Surrounding us are the faces of familiar strangers.

Yes, I know that all around me are lost souls, drifting by as lonely and solitary as I am. We have shared memories. In these recollections are the people we were close to in our hometowns, once so full of life. We knew them as the carpenter, the gardener, the barber, the bricklayer, and so on. Apart from being artisans, all of them were also farmers. And now, the farmers are gone too.

This memoir only goes back a hundred years, the limit of my father's and grandfather's memories. The people they described to me, as well as the ones I've known, are mostly gone now. They exist only in family records, just a line or two each.

And yet each person, no matter how humble, contains an epic poem of their own. These villagers may be unknown to the wider world, but they reflect a hundred years of history, especially the enormous changes that have taken place in Chinese society over the last thirty years.

They constitute an era, and have also been swallowed by this era. A roughshod time, but also a tender one. And as long as this tenderness exists, so does my hometown.

ONCE UPON A TIME, EVERYTHING you needed in life could be found at the front and back of your house. Back then, life was straightforward, fresh, and warm as the palm of your hand. People treated each other with compassion and care.

At Gaogang in Jiangsu, the Yangtze River makes a large bend. A smaller river branches off here, extending eastward. Along it stands a line of ancient ginkgo trees. Follow these another twenty-odd kilometers east, and you'll reach Shen Village, where even more ginkgos grow. People call it the village of ginkgo trees.

Six hundred years ago, a man named Shen Liangsan came to this place from Changmen in Jiangsu. He fell in love with this low-lying, sandy piece of land and decided to settle here. In 1970, the seventeenth generation of his lineage was born—including me. Shen Village was now a large settlement with tens of thousands of people. No one could have expected that I and people my age were destined to watch our village decline and fade away.

In 2001, after more than a decade away from home, I returned to Shen Village, and saw, for the first time, a deserted house, its doors locked tight. That was the paper craftsman's home. His grave was at the back of the house, in a courtyard whose gate was fastened with a rusty lock. Weeds had sprung up among the green tiles of the roof. Since that day, every few years, I'd notice yet another house had been abandoned and was falling into ruin.

After so many years away, I was more familiar with places abroad than with my own hometown, but still felt a sudden jolt of bone-deep sorrow. The people I knew well were withering away, one by one. Soon, this village would no longer exist. As a kid, I'd run freely through the wilderness; now, half of it had been built over with factories. When the steel and cement of the city reaches Shen Village, with its six hundred years of history, it may well be reduced to nothing more than a mirage.

When I am in Shen Village, the faces of long-gone artisans appear before me. Time and again, they drag me back to bygone eras.

I am familiar with these artisans. I used to see them every day. I know every one of them through and through. They came and they went, leaving no trace at all. From ancient times, they have passed their skills on generation by generation—but now, the chain has been broken. They are not there, and the village I come from is, essentially, gone too. I am now an orphan, lost in the big city.

I've heard that when a person goes blind, they will eventually forget all the sights they have ever seen. I'm writing this now, because I'm afraid that the day will come, when I will forget what Shen Village looks like.

THE BRICKLAYER

M R. HE WAS THE ONLY DOCTOR in Shen Village. His home stood all alone on higher ground in the center of the village. At his front door was a fairly large yard, and each spring it transformed into a riot of greenery and blossoms. There was a profusion of ginkgo trees, and also persimmon, jujube, honey locust, and so on. A great variety, growing with abandon. Plenty of flowers too. On either side of the path from the garden gate to the front door, there were flowering crab apples, redbuds, roses, gardenias, and many others I didn't know the names of. In the center of the yard were medicinal herbs: wild asparagus, ranunculus, atractylodes, all attractive and delightfully scented. Everyone's favorites, though, were the peppermint, purslane, and green chiretta. Anyone who passed by grabbed a handful to take home. Peppermint can be baked into flatbreads or turned into a broth for noodles. Purslane, fried with eggs, leaves your skin silky smooth. Chiretta may not sound particularly appetizing, but eaten as a cold salad, it's good for digestion and detoxing. Mr. He smiled and said hello to everyone, and recommended more edible herbs. The more people helped themselves to his produce, the happier he was. He didn't charge a cent, naturally.

Mr. He's herb garden was on our way to and from school. We always stopped to hang out there—chasing butterflies, picking whatever flowers were growing that season. Just one or two, though. If we tried to take more, Mr. He would appear at the doorway of the greenhouse and gently cough, and we'd scatter like the wind.

After the rainy season this year, I made a trip back to Shen Village. On the way home, I had to pass by Mr. He's garden. He passed away many years ago, though the villagers left his thatched cottage standing for a long time, in memory of him. No one maintained his garden properly, though. Everyone just went in to plant and harvest whatever they needed. Each time I returned to the village I walked past his garden, and the fragrance of the medicinal herbs remained intoxicating.

On this last trip, though, the garden was gone. In its place, they'd built a church, with a cross rising high from the roof of the new building.

IN THE PAST, during the few days I was home, the bricklayer was a frequent guest.

My father is usually a great host, but he seemed frosty toward the bricklayer.

"That man's a Jesus-eater—he's stirring up all kinds of trouble in the village," my father said coldly, after he'd left.

A Jesus-eater is what the villagers call a Christian. The nickname probably comes from the Gospel of John in the New Testament, where Jesus says, "Whoever eats my flesh and drinks my blood has eternal life, and I will raise him up at the last day."

The bricklayer is old now, and walks with a limp. When he was young, all the girls for miles around had crushes on him. He was in the People's Liberation Army, and not only was he blessed with clean-cut good looks, he also played the erhu like a dream. He once gave me a five-pointed star, like we'd seen pinned to army caps. It was the greatest treasure of my childhood. On his occasional visits back, his house would be jam-packed with visitors. His future seemed full of promise. Unexpectedly, during the great demobilization he quietly returned to the village. After a few months at home, he became a bricklayer.

He didn't formally become anyone's apprentice, he just followed the other bricklayers around, assisting them and watching until he knew enough to pick up a trowel and start building walls himself. He was now a bricklayer, though his handiwork, to be honest, was mediocre. Just like that, his halo was gone. Still, although he must have been quite dejected, no one ever heard the bricklayer complain. He was perpetually smiling, busily building bridal chambers for newlyweds to move into. His voice was good, and he was articulate, so he was often called upon to "chant the blessing" at the start and end of each construction job. Strictly speaking, this task ought to have fallen to the most skilled craftsman, but few of our village artisans had his stage presence.

And what did it mean to "chant the blessing"? Before starting work, someone had to say auspicious things for the spirits to hear. These words had to be pleasing enough for the spirits to remember them and bestow blessings on the family. During the chanting, the other artisans would keep the beat: the carpenter whacking his ax against a plank, the bricklayer tapping his trowel against a stone, everyone using whatever tools they were holding, limbs swinging with enthusiasm. As the leader of the chant, the bricklayer received a thick red envelope of cash, and was given the seat of honor during meals. Only in these moments did the bricklayer's face glow.

THE BUSINESS OF building a church in Shen Village was spearheaded by a woman married to someone named Gao Gen, so everyone called her General Gao Gen. "General" means "wife" in our local dialect.

I was there when Gao Gen got married. He worked at the same foundry as my Second Uncle. Our families were close, anyway, so I got to go to the wedding, even though I was only in middle school at the time. It was a rowdy affair, though I don't remember the details. What left an impression was how pretty the bride was. When I heard people in the village talking about General Gao Gen, I remembered the beautiful woman lifting her red veil when she came out to offer a toast.

General Gao Gen was initially a believer in a religion called something-or-other Gong. After the government banned it, two fellow worshippers from another province hid in her home for a few days, until things got so dangerous that even Shen Village wasn't safe any longer. The three of them fled to the city.

When General Gao Gen returned to Shen Village half a year later, she'd surprisingly converted to Christianity. She was the first Christian in Shen Village, and the first missionary.

By then there were no young people in Shen Village—they'd all found jobs in the city, leaving behind the old and the infirm. General Gao Gen went household by household talking to those who'd stayed. Old people are lonely, and if they're unwell, they're suffering and in despair too. Minor and chronic illnesses were mostly left untreated. For anything major, you'd go into town and get some medicine from the hospital, then come home and dose yourself. Hardly anyone got admitted to the hospital, not even at the very end. Nothing was more important than dying at home. If you could be cured without taking pills or getting injections, so much the better. General Gao Gen went around telling the sick people of Shen Village that as long as you believed in Jesus, you would be healed of all that ailed you. They'd have tried anything at that point, and that's all it took to make believers of them. After all, it was just a matter of showing up every Sunday to hear a little speech, then sticking around to sing a song or two.

General Gao Gen gathered the old and weak from four villages in her home. Eventually, they ran out of space and needed a proper church building. As Mr. He was dead, she decided his garden would be the perfect spot.

When she set out to demolish Mr. He's thatched cottage, some of the older men asked the village chief to stop her, but he just sighed and said it was out of his jurisdiction.

General Gao Gen told her believers to petition the town council, who kicked the request upstairs to the county government. The county said it was best not to make a fuss about religious matters. Didn't they just want a small piece of land? So give it to them. And that's how Mr. He's garden became the site of our village church.

JUST AFTER THE New Year, the bricklayer went to Shanghai looking for work. At the train station, he ran into a couple of guys who said they had a job for him. Instead, they lured him to a deserted area where they took all his money, a few hundred yuan, and bashed him over the head with a blunt object. He made a police report and got sent back to Shen Village. His head throbbed so badly, he lay in bed for three days. His little brother Wokhead urged him to go to the county hospital, where a doctor solemnly told him, "These X-rays don't look good. You'll need to stay for observation." This examination alone cost more than a thousand yuan, so there was no way he was willing to be admitted. Wokhead, who'd accompanied him there, didn't escape either. The doctor said he didn't look great and insisted on giving him a checkup. It turned out Wokhead had high blood pressure, and if he didn't start taking medicine for it, he might be in danger. That scared Wokhead so much, he spent a few hundred yuan on pills. When they got back, the two brothers talked it over and decided, "What the hell, let's take it one day at a time." Wokhead didn't bother taking his pills, but instead joined a "slurry pump" team and headed off to Jiangnan to widen a river. The bricklayer's head hurt so much, all he could do was rest at home.

Just as the bricklayer was at his lowest, General Gao Gen came knocking at his door.

The day after the General's visit, the bricklayer limped over to the construction site of the church. His skills were needed here.

Faith really did seem to be effective. The bricklayer's headaches grew less severe, and by the time the church was built, they'd vanished altogether. He was the first person to be baptized in this church.

The bricklayer's conversion was a major development for Shen Village's Christian movement. His eloquence and physical strength made him stand out from the crowd. General Gao Gen sent him to study at the big church in the city. A couple of months later, he returned a new man. He'd set aside his trowel and was dressed in black robes, clutching a Bible. Now he stood in the humble, solemn church building, his voice resonant and stirring. Shen Village had lost a bricklayer and gained a priest.

At the end of that year, the bricklayer's little brother, Wokhead of the high blood pressure, returned to Shen Village with a large sum of money. He'd long forgotten about his diagnosis. At the New Year, he renovated his house. At first, he asked his brother for help, but the bricklayer was too busy with his ministering duties. Even if he'd had the time, he wouldn't have come—he no longer did construction work, as his earnings as a priest were pretty good. His congregation had almost doubled. Each week they put money in the offerings box. The amount didn't matter. Five yuan was fine, and so was ten—it's the thought that counts. The Gao residence was now a three-story house. At one point, Gao Gen had been unhappy with his wife, but now they were living in a mansion, he didn't say a word against her, just let her do as she pleased.

Wokhead was upset at his brother's refusal to help, but what could he say?

Soon, it was almost the New Year. On the last day of the old year, Wokhead showed up at the bricklayer's home with a generous array of offerings for their ancestors. According to local custom, the ancestral tablets lived in the home of the eldest son, who would then pass them on to his own eldest son, generation after generation.

The bricklayer barred his door to Wokhead. "I'm a man of faith, I don't hold with ancestor-worship. You should leave."

"You can believe in your God, and I'll go on worshipping my ancestors."

"If you do that, you're not entering my home."

Wokhead stood in the doorway, stunned, still carrying his basket of fish, meat, steamed buns, and cakes.

He walked away and went to see my father.

"Shan, we have a rebel in our family. The bricklayer says he believes in God, and won't let me honor our ancestors."

"He can believe what he wants, but why won't he let you honor your ancestors?"

"He wouldn't even let me through the door. Said he wouldn't stand for it. Afraid I'd clash with his Lord."

"You can't do anything about him believing in God, that's his business. How about this: move the ancestral tablets to your home. From now on, it's up to you to honor them. After all, if the eldest son dies without leaving any children, then his brother takes over. The way he is now, he might as well be dead."

Wokhead nodded. "That's how it will have to be. Everyone honors their ancestors at the New Year. Even the poorest household manages to put a good spread in front of their ancestors and pray for their continued protection. If I didn't do that, what kind of person would I be? I can be a decent person even if he can't."

But Wokhead couldn't get hold of the ancestral tablets.

The bricklayer said, "They're gone."

"What do you mean, they're gone?"

"I mean they're gone. Us believers know there's only one God, and we can have no others. Which means these things have no place in our homes."

"Those tablets are our ancestors. What have you done with them? It doesn't matter if you don't want them, I'll take them. If you don't give them to me today, I won't be celebrating New Year."

"I burned them."

Wokhead stared at his brother for a long time, unable to say a single word. Finally, he went home.

That night, Wokhead's family didn't have their usual year-end meal, nor did they set off any firecrackers. Wokhead sat red-eyed in his living room, murmuring, "Mom, Dad, your dishonorable son burned your ancestral tablets. Now it's the New Year, and I have no idea where you are. I can't make offerings to you. Everyone's celebrating, and you have nothing to eat or drink. What kind of curse are we bringing upon ourselves?"

ON THE FIRST day of New Year, like the rest of Shen Village, Wokhead went to the ancestral shrine to burn incense.

The shrine isn't particularly large, just three tile-roofed rooms around a courtyard. You walk in the main door, and there is a chamber to your left, from which sweet-smelling incense smoke emanates. Everyone goes there to honor the tree spirit.

On the wall facing the entrance is a mirror frame containing the picture of a withered ginkgo tree. The tree itself is dead, but you could see how magnificently tall it stood. Ten years ago, it was killed by lightning, a great tragedy for our clan. Six hundred years ago, our first ancestors planted that tree when they settled here. Everyone respected it, worshipped it, and felt its power. Perhaps we believed the spirits of our ancestors lived in its lush foliage.

The tree was a symbol of our village. From four or five miles away, you would catch sight of that ginkgo tree and know you'd reached Shen Village. As a child, I often passed beneath its branches on my way to Gramps's house. The reach of its root system was astonishing. Once, I was outside a little provision shop a few hundred yards away, when I noticed one of its roots protruding from the ground. It took quite a few of us kids, holding hands, to encircle its trunk.

Everyone in the village believed in the spiritual power of this tree. People often burned incense and prayed at its feet. After the lightning strike killed it, no one was willing to move it for several years, as if it might still revive. But no, it was truly dead. Finally, when the ancestral shrine was rebuilt, they had no choice but to chop it down.

The current shrine was built to replace the original one, which stood behind the ginkgo tree and was at the time the finest building in all of Shen Village. Then in 1937, the Japanese invaded the then-capital Nanjing, and the villagers tore it down. They were afraid that the Japanese would arrive and turn it into quarters for themselves. It was wartime, and anything that might be of use to the enemy had to be destroyed.

As a child, I felt fearful whenever I walked past the ruins of the shrine. Next to them was a little shed in which lived a violent, disturbed individual. He had no name, but because his head was unusually small, everyone called him Pinhead. He spent his days pacing around the enormous ginkgo tree, chasing after terrified little children. If you got scared and ran from him, that only encouraged him to come charging after you. Even knowing that, I couldn't control my fear. Clutching my mom's hand tightly, I'd wait till we were some distance away before turning back to look, and he'd still be standing perfectly still beneath the tree, tiny head tilted to one side, glaring evilly at me. If his scrawny mother caught him in the act of chasing a child, she'd let out a scream, and he'd freeze on the spot, docilely allowing her to grab him by the ear and drag him home.

Pinhead disappeared many years ago. Because his home was under the ginkgo tree, he knew from his earliest days that he could find his way back if he just walked toward that tree. After the tree died, he got some distance away and didn't see it when he turned back. Now he couldn't find his way home. His scrawny mother looked everywhere, but couldn't find him. He'd caused her daily aggravation, sorrow, and labor, but when he went missing and she couldn't track him down, she died. She wasn't ill, just too distressed by the loss of her son to eat, and eventually she starved.

On the ruins of the old shrine by Pinhead's home, they built a huge, glorious shrine. Right in the middle of the great room is a new wooden sign proclaiming: Southern Paragon Hall. This is the name left by our ancestors, the one our shrine has been known by for six hundred years.

"Song Gao," one of the Major Court Verses in the *Shijing*, says, "the King ordered the Lord of Shen to be a paragon for the Southern realms." King Xuan of Zhou gave a banquet for his uncle, the Lord of Shen, hoping he would return to the Shen Kingdom and make it the southernmost fortification of the Zhou dynasty. Our ancestors came up with the name "Southern Paragon Hall" to remind us that we are descended from the Lord of Shen.

In the great room of Southern Paragon Hall is a row of ancestral tablets, wooden slabs like small tombstones. Draped over each is a piece of red cloth, some of them so faded they've turned grayish. For the even older ones, there is nothing left but the naked wood. On each is written the name of the deceased, and the dates of their birth and death. Every small wooden tablet contains the spirit of an ancestor. Many Chinese people believe that when close relatives pass, they don't go far from us. All that departs is the flesh, while the soul lingers to watch over future generations. If the grave is the final resting place of the body, then these wooden slabs are where the soul resides.

THE CLANSMEN ARRIVED in droves, and among them Wokhead knelt before the tablets to pay obeisance. Right in the middle was the tablet of the first ancestor to arrive in Shen Village: Master Liangsan. In the early years of the Ming dynasty, Shen Liangsan left Changmen in Suzhou for Taizhou in Subei, and settled in Shen Village. That was more than six hundred years ago. After his death, he was buried northeast of Inkstone Pond, in front of Shen Village. The pond is still there today. A tiny body of water in the wilderness, so clear you can see all the way to the bottom. Now and then, a fish swims past. Grass grows thickly all around the pond, and standing amid this greenery is a stone slab on which is written, "The Grave of Master Liangsan." Not many people come here, and so the path by the grave is covered in moss. From there it winds its way toward Shen Village.

After Wokhead had honored his ancestors, many clansmen came up to him. They wanted to offer words of comfort, but no one knew where to begin.

The shrine was the place to worship the ancestors of long ago, everyone's common forebears. Parents and grandparents had to be provided for in your own home. Everyone knew about the bricklayer burning the ancestral tablets. This was unprecedented in Shen Village. What the villagers felt went far beyond shock.

Some in Shen Village believed in Taoism, others in Buddhism, and still others in Christianity. Yet nothing like this had ever happened before. No matter what people believed, they still honored their ancestors. They existed in a world where humans, ghosts, and gods had always intermingled. The laws of this world were more ancient than any religion. That's how they lived for over five thousand years.

In the countryside, the general belief is that when we die, there are two paths we can take. The first is to become a ghost, which is the fate of the majority, and the other is to become a god. Humans can turn into door gods, kitchen gods, earth gods, hill gods. There are also gods for carpentry and other crafts, and even toilet gods. These gods live in the world, alongside humans, but they're invisible. All you can see is representations of them, drawn on paper, sculpted from clay or carved in wood. Still, you need to deal with them every single day. There are also gods up above, looking down on humanity. They frequently soar down from the skies, and go for a stroll around our world, where they might interfere with mortal affairs at any moment. For instance, a lightning god might send a thunderbolt to strike dead an unfilial son or daughter, while a god-person might present an industrious individual with a magic paintbrush full of inspiration. Sometimes they take human form. Certain scholars who aced the imperial examinations may actually have been celestial beings of word and song come down to earth. A certain barefoot immortal managed to become an emperor in the Song dynasty. In special circumstances, an entire batch of gods might be reborn as people. At one point, 108 gods who made up a constellation were reincarnated as the heroes of the forest in the marshes of Mount Liang. All in all, these gods can enjoy a life of ease in paradise, but can also become mortal at any moment. They have freedom. They are ruled over by the Jade Emperor, who might look stern, but is rather simple-minded, and frequently gives the wrong orders. His rule relies on the expertise of the various immortals who assist him, and humans mostly ignore him—he rarely gets any offerings or prayers. People place much more trust in their own ancestors, because only our ancestors are certain to take good care of us.

Apparently, when people die, they instantly become ghosts. Ghosts don't live in hell, but rather in the netherworld, which exists alongside our own plane of existence. You might collide with it at any moment. Only the most wicked individuals are cast into hell to suffer torments. Most people's souls live in their graves, or in their ancestral tablets. When the living make offerings, they can enjoy the food and incense, and take the ghost money that's burned for them. Of course, they might also be reincarnated. Certain people may even retain a few memories from their past lives. People must keep a safe distance from ghosts. Get too close and disaster or illness strikes. If you accidentally come into contact with one, you must immediately perform various rituals entreating the ghost to depart quickly. Almost every child in the village has had to deal with a ghost at some point. I've had many such encounters myself.

One time, as I was heading home after a day of madcap fun in the fields, my head began to throb agonizingly. Back home, I slumped listlessly at the dinner table, refusing to eat. My mom brought out a bowl of clear water, set it in front of me, clasped a pair of chopsticks in both hands, and muttered: *Granny? Great-grandpa? Great-grandma?* As she called on each of them, she placed the chopsticks upright in the middle of the bowl and let go, to see if they would stand up on their own. When they fell, she'd chant the next name. Finally, the chopsticks remained vertical at a certain name. She hauled me to my feet and brought me to that person's ancestral tablet. We knelt and kowtowed. "Great-grandpa, please don't talk to this child." When we were done kowtowing, we went to bed. The next morning, my head no longer hurt. I asked my mom, "Why did Great-grandpa want to talk to me and make my head hurt?" She said, "You must have bumped into him while you were out. He saw that you were playful, and thought he'd have a chat with you. But people and ghosts can't talk like that. Now we've prayed, it's all right again."

The gods have too many humans to look after, and aren't likely to favor one family over another. Only our late ancestors will spare no effort in helping their descendants increase their wealth and avoid catastrophe. Ancestors look after their own.

The Chinese honor their ancestors at the Tomb Sweeping Festival, Winter Solstice, New Year, and on the anniversaries of their births and deaths. As soon as a Chinese person dies, they immediately gain much more power than any living soul. They aren't like dead people in the West, who merely lie in their graves, perfectly still. No, they're terribly busy, maybe even more than when they were alive. They have a future too, in which they could become gods, or else get reborn and be human again.

But now, Wokhead's ancestral tablets were gone. Which is to say, the family's contact with their ancestors was broken off, leaving him all alone in the world. As more people came over to chat with Wokhead at the shrine, some made sarcastic remarks mocking him. This babble filled Wokhead with unspeakable pain and rage.

He left the ancestral shrine and sprinted to his brother's home. In the hall as you entered the bricklayer's house was a hefty cross mounted on the wall. Wokhead picked up this cross and whacked the bricklayer hard across the legs with it.

And now, the bricklayer still goes to church every week, only he's lame in one leg and walks with a limp. The adults still refer to him as the bricklayer, but the children call him Uncle Hobble.

THE BAMBOO-WEAVER

IN THE WILDERNESS TO THE southwest of Shen Village stood a lonely thatched building: the village's pig shed. Cows were reared here too. After collectivization, the bamboo-weaver moved in here and became a dedicated livestock-feeder.

The pig shed was quite large, and consisted of five rooms: three for pigs, two for cows. The bamboo-weaver set up a bed in one of the cow rooms and passed the night there from time to time.

When the bamboo-weaver was a child, he went around begging with his father. Then when he was twelve, his father died, and someone recommended him for a job with the paper craftsman, whose family owned a few dozen mu of land. The paper craftsman's father had tried sending him to the schoolhouse, but nothing he studied sank in, though he did enjoy making human figures, horses and houses out of paper. His father tied him up and whipped him a few times, but that didn't do any good, so he gave up and let him have his way. The paper craftsman wasn't interested in anything except crafting paper. He needed a servant to take care of all the chores around the house.

The bamboo-weaver was not yet a bamboo-weaver, he was just a child. His duties, apart from cooking, laundry, and feeding the poultry, mainly had to do with raising the paper craftsman's son. The paper craftsman's wife had passed away, leaving him with a sickly son. The little boy was docile enough—as long as you brought him to the bamboo grove to play, he wouldn't cry or make a fuss. Actually, there was nothing to play with there, but he enjoyed sitting quietly and watching the birds: sparrows, mynahs, bulbuls, hopping around and chirping. This made him happy. It was Shen Village's largest bamboo grove, inherited by the paper craftsman from his father. Unlike the miserly paper craftsman, his father had been a benevolent person. People would frequently stop by to borrow his blade. "We'll just take a few bamboo stalks, sir." "Go right ahead." These visitors were always very careful, treading gingerly so as not to damage a single shoot. They would make sure to choose their stems from among the thickest clusters, and to take no more than two or three. These had various uses around the home. If they were making baskets and needed extra bamboo, they'd bring food to trade. When the paper craftsman's father died and he took over, he looked much less kindly on these requests. "Everyone's showing up and demanding stuff! How big do they think my bamboo grove is?" So people stopped asking. Instead, they waited for the paper craftsman to be out, and snuck in with their knives. What with them hacking away, the young shoots got trampled left and right. In just a couple of years, the bamboo grove became much sparser.

The paper craftsman noticed the bamboo-weaver was spending long hours watching his son in the bamboo grove, and said to him, "All our sieves and baskets are tattered. You're sitting around all day with nothing to do—why not try making some? The house has the knives and saws you'll need."

The bamboo-weaver was intelligent and good with his hands. He went to the home of a bamboo-weaver in another village and watched him do it a few times, then came back and replicated what he'd seen. Splitting a bamboo stem, removing the green and yellow fibers—that wasn't too difficult. Handbaskets were the easiest, large and roughly put together, no refinement about them. Then there were bamboo hampers, dustpans, and trays, which weren't particularly intricate either, you could throw those together quite quickly. The paper crafts-man was very happy to see how good he was and asked him to make a daybed, chair, and recliner. There was plenty of bamboo in the grove, after all. The bamboo-weaver got some old ones, studied them carefully, took them apart to see how they were made, and re-created them from scratch. After a year or so, he was turning out bamboo mats with patterns running through them. Finally, Shen Village had a bamboo-weaver of its own, and people no longer needed to go to other villages for their bamboo needs.

The first person to hire the bamboo-weaver was Mrs. Fifth Life. Mr. Fifth Life had died, leaving her a widow. Some guy tried to abduct her to be his wife, but he didn't succeed—she beat him up instead. Now she wanted to replace the bamboo mats at her home, to get rid of this bad luck.

After Mrs. Fifth Life commissioned him, other clients came knocking. So the bamboo-weaver quit his job with the paper craftsman to concentrate on bamboo-weaving. There was nothing the paper craftsman could do about it, except stand by his bamboo grove cursing his bad luck.

In 1955, Shen Village became an entry-level agricultural collective. The bamboo-weaver came from a poor family, so he didn't own any land. Right after enrollment, he was assigned to raise pigs and cows in the shed. Now and then, he would be asked to make bamboo baskets and trays. Taking care of this much livestock was more than one person could handle, so the brigade leader assigned the paper craftsman's daughter-in-law Qinxiu to be his assis-tant. The paper craftsman's son, the bamboo-weaver's former charge, had grown up, gotten married, and died. Qinxiu was his young widow.

After just a year at the pig shed, young Qinxiu died too. The same year, the old cow gave birth to a little yellow calf. Then came 1958, the year of the People's Commune. At the end of that year, there was a famine. The pigs required too much feed, so they were slaughtered. But a cow was needed for heavy work. The others had to be killed, but the little yellow calf was allowed to live.

The calf grew up quickly, and in just a few years, was ready to be set to work. Turning millstones, pulling carts, plowing the fields, it could do anything. It seemed in tune with human nature, and understood when the bamboo-weaver spoke to it. If he wanted the bull to do anything, the bamboo-weaver only had to say, and it would trot ahead, swaying from side to side. He never let anyone else lay a hand on it, not even the brigade leader. Whatever the job, he would lead it there himself. At night, the bull would slowly graze, while the bamboo-weaver slept by its side. He could only fall asleep to the sound of the bull chewing the cud.

Someone joked, "Hey, Bamboo-weaver, you should take that bull as your godson."

The bamboo-weaver laughed. "Get lost, a single one of its hairs is worth more than you."

The bamboo-weaver's wife died young. He had a son, Ren Xiao, now in his teens. His body was developing, which gave him quite an appetite. But this was 1959, and no one had a full belly. Ren Xiao wasn't the sort of person to keep his problems to himself. When he was hungry, he'd pester the bamboo-weaver. "Dad, I'm starving." There was nothing the bamboo-weaver could do, except give as much of his own rations to Ren Xiao as possible, but still the teenager clamored for more. One time, Ren Xiao came by when the bamboo-weaver was hard at work. He asked his son to chop up some hay and mix it with chaff, to feed the bull. When Ren Xiao put the bucket in front of the yellow bull, it ate a few mouthfuls, then raised its head and mooed. When the bamboo-weaver heard the bull crying, he came running and smacked his forehead. "Ah, I forgot the rusk. This idiot's picky about his food." He got a piece of bean rusk and cut it up with his knife. Bean rusk is what's left behind after the oil is extracted from soybeans. Compressed into a round biscuit, it makes excellent fodder. The bamboo-weaver tossed the crumbled rusk into the bucket and got Ren Xiao to stir it. Perhaps Ren Xiao really was unbearably hungry— he reached into the bucket for a chunk of rusk and popped it into his mouth.

Now that he was helping himself to the yellow bull's bean rusk, Ren Xiao's tantrums stopped. He didn't get any taller, but his body filled out. The bamboo-weaver felt bad about this and took to shoveling fresh grass day and night, to feed the bull with extra care. When the bull's work for the day was done, the bamboo-weaver would get his brush and go over its entire coat, removing every tangle, every speck of mud. The yellow bull was always beautifully clean.

In 1980, Shen Village began implementing the household contract responsibility system. The land was divided up according to the number of people in each household, and the production brigade's farming tools and buildings were all shared out. The yellow bull was twenty-four by now, fairly old. The brigade leader wanted to slaughter it and give every family a bit of meat. No matter what, the bamboo-weaver wouldn't agree to this. Now in his sixties, he showed up at the brigade leader's house every day dabbing at his tears. The leader's official position was soon being taken away, and he didn't want any more trouble. All he said was, "Just do your work. If everyone agrees not to, we won't kill it." The bamboo-weaver then went house to house, begging every family to show mercy.

"This bull has been with me more than twenty years. You can't kill it! Can't you do without this bit of meat? Set aside my feelings. Let this bull live, and you'll accumulate merit."

Some said, "Fine, it can live, if you buy it. You can't expect us to give you such a big beast."

There's no way the bamboo-weaver could get his hands on that much money. He thought long and hard, and finally said to the brigade leader, "Give me the bull, and I won't take anything else from the brigade. Name a price. I'll pay you back when I've sold this year's crop. If that's not enough, you can have next year's too, and the next." The brigade leader thought it over, and agreed.

When Ren Xiao got wind of this, he went home and screamed at his father. "An old bull who can't even work any more, and that's going to die any day now. And you want to bring it home? Why? Paying money every year on top of that?" Ren Xiao refused to agree to such a thing.

"Brute!" yelled the bamboo-weaver. "If not for this bull, you'd have starved to death long ago."

Shame fueled Ren Xiao's anger. "If you want the bull, you can go live with it by yourself."

The bamboo-weaver understood: Ren Xiao was saying they should separate their households. Because Ren Xiao grew up without a mother, the bamboo-weaver had always doted on him. But now the bamboo-weaver was old, and Ren Xiao was a spoiled brat.

When the villagers got wind of this, they came in droves to urge peace. Ren Xiao kept his head down, not saying a word. His wife was hopping mad, though. "The old geezer's losing his mind. If he sees anything tasty around the house, he feeds it to that bull. That's more than he does for our son. Go on, ask him—in all these years, has he bought so much as a piece of candy for his own grandson?"

The bamboo-weaver said sullenly, "Whatever money I have, I've given to you. Why are you saying these things?"

In the end, the bamboo-weaver and Ren Xiao split their households. The bamboo-weaver stayed in the pig shed. Most of the building was torn down, leaving just two rooms: one for the bull, and one for the bamboo-weaver. That was fine. In fact, he was happier living alone.

The land was split up so every household got some. They could do most things themselves, but what about tilling the soil? Once again, they called on the bamboo-weaver. He got his plow, hitched it to the bull, and set to work without another word. When he was done, whoever's land it was would invite him to dinner that evening. "Bamboo-weaver, this bull belongs to you. Whatever portion of it belongs to our family, we don't want it. When you pay back your debt, you can pay one less share."

Most of the households in Shen Village were kind and just. One family led the way, and the others followed. Who could be so petty as to refuse? Besides, the bamboo-weaver was an old man all alone in the world. How could anyone possibly demand money from him?

When Ren Xiao's land needed plowing, he sent his son to ask the bamboo-weaver, "Grandpa, could you come and help us with our field?"

"Run along home," said the bamboo-weaver.

First thing the following morning, he plowed Ren Xiao's patch of land. Afterward, Ren Xiao sent his son out again. "Grandpa, join us for a meal this evening?"

"I already have dinner plans."

Now that the bamboo-weaver had a lot more free time, he took up the craft he'd left behind many years ago. Whenever you passed by his doorway, you'd see him sitting in a bamboo chair cutting and scraping, weaving and twining. The old bull lay to one side staring at him, its mouth moving endlessly, chewing and chewing. On the walls of the bamboo-weaver's house hung all kinds of bamboo implements: sieves, baskets, trays, skimmers for getting wontons from the pot, back-scratchers shaped like little hands. Whenever there was a market, he'd carry these over on his back to sell them there. They always went very fast, not even lasting till the end of the day. Then he'd buy a flatbread for his grandson. These came stuffed with sweet sesame, bean paste, or shredded radish. The latter was most delicious, mixed with diced pork and shrimp.

On market days, his grandson came by the pig shed in the afternoon. The bamboo-weaver would reach into his basket and produce the flatbread in a grease-proof paper bag. He always broke off a little piece before handing it over. Not for himself, but to feed the old bull. Seeing his grandson and his bull eating away happily, he'd grin with pleasure, which covered his face with wrinkles and revealed his many missing teeth.

Two years passed. On the last day of the second year, the bamboo-weaver went house to house dispensing tens of yuan, a different amount to each household. This was the money he'd made selling bamboo goods. He'd worked it out: how much the yellow bull was worth, how much each family should get. Ren Xiao got his share too. They were living apart, after all, his was a different household. Everyone tried to turn him down. "Didn't we say we weren't taking our share? Now you're making us go back on our word." But even as they said this, they saw it was a substantial sum, and accepted it anyway. Ren Xiao and his wife were most unhappy about this. Who'd have thought the old geezer could have accumulated so much cash? Ren Xiao's wife said, "Shouldn't he have kept this money for his grandson? He's just giving it away. You think any of these people are going to appreciate that? He's getting more foolish the older he gets." She thought about it. "Ren Xiao, your old man seems better at earning money than you are. I reckon we should combine households again. Invite him over, and we can all live together."

The bamboo-weaver came to see his old friend, my grandpa.

"Carpenter, Ren Xiao came to see me—he wants to combine households. What should I do?"

"What can I say? No one would say you ought to stay apart, but you can't let other people make up your mind for you."

"You old devil, saying such things to me."

"So get back together. You're old now. What if something happens? You'd just be lying there, not even able to get a drink of water. Why else would you raise a son? In order for him to take care of you in your last days and give you a good funeral. You might as well combine households."

The bamboo-weaver was pleased with that.

Taking the bull with him, he moved back in with his son. One of the village men got married around then and needed a piece of land of his own. The brigade tore down the pig shed, leveled the soil, and gave it to the new couple.

Life went on, placidly. Seven or eight years passed with no problems at all, but the bamboo-weaver was aging, and the bull was getting older too. It couldn't do any work at all, but lay around listlessly, eating grass and basking in the sun. The bamboo-weaver kept plying his craft, mostly to pass the time, and still made it to every market. One market day, he was on his way home when a motorcycle suddenly roared past and clipped him, knocking him to the ground. The rider didn't stop. The bamboo-weaver couldn't get up. Passers-by called for Ren Xiao, and scrambled to get him to the hospital. When they took an X-ray, they found he had two broken ribs.

Ren Xiao and his wife took care of him to start with, bringing him food and cleaning him. At his age, an injury like this was enough to incapacitate him completely. A few months later, he was still unable to get out of bed, and he was losing more and more weight. Ren Xiao starting getting impatient. His wife said, "He's not going to kick the bucket anytime soon. He's your old man, you take care of him. I'm a woman, you can't ask me to wipe him down." Ren Xiao gave his father a sponge bath every few days and complained endlessly about it to anyone who'd listen.

An old bachelor who talked a lot of nonsense heard Ren Xiao grousing away over a game of mahjong, and thoughtlessly remarked, "That's easy enough to deal with! Don't give him anything to eat and he won't shit—that should help him stay clean."

A couple of days later, someone was passing by the bamboo-weaver's house and heard him hollering that he was hungry. When they asked Ren Xiao about this, he said, "Ignore him, he's confused. I've just brought him food, and he ate it all. The bowl is right there—see?"

The old bull was standing outside, and when it heard the bamboo-weaver howling, it started mooing too. More people came to ask Ren Xiao what was going on. By evening, he was so fed up that he stood in the doorway screaming,

"My old man's not in his right mind, and now you're all saying I'm a bad son. I've done so much for him, and still you treat me like this? If your tongues keep wagging, I'll sue you for slander."

A couple of weeks after that, the bamboo-weaver died.

After the funeral, Ren Xiao summoned a livestock buyer. The man examined the bull's teeth and prodded its hips, but shook his head. "It's too old—not worth slaughtering. I'd only get a few pounds of meat, and that'd be too tough to sell for much." Ren Xiao tried to haggle, wishing he could just stuff the rope into the man's hands. All of a sudden, the bull charged and, with a flick of its head, tossed Ren Xiao to the ground. It would have gored him if the man from the abattoir hadn't been quick enough to grab hold of the rope and drag the bull to one side, where it could be firmly tied up.

Ren Xiao was rushed to the hospital, where they found a lung injury. The doctor said even if they discharged him, he wouldn't be able to do any heavy work, so he might as well recuperate.

Ren Xiao stayed in the hospital, while his wife went home sobbing. She got a knife and wanted to slaughter the old bull, but the neighbors prevented her. They managed to calm her down and get her back inside.

The whole thing was a farce. My grandpa was there. He was about to turn eighty, and my father had been discussing with him how to celebrate. That night, he summoned my father.

"That bull accomplished what no human could have. That's a virtuous bull, and a virtuous bull can't be slaughtered."

"We shouldn't interfere with Ren Xiao's family. You know how brutal that couple can be."

"Someone needs to do something. Cancel my anniversary—use the money to buy the bull instead. Bring it back, and we'll take care of it." We only used "anniversary" when we were talking about dead people. Saying "anniversary" instead of "birthday" was fighting talk from Grandpa.

Dad was well aware of Grandpa's temper, so he didn't argue—he'd have lost, anyway. If he'd put up any resistance, who knows what the old man would have done.

The bull cost too much for Dad to buy it on his own. He thought about it and finally had to ask some prominent people in the village to use their influence.

The following morning, Mrs. Ren Xiao tried to get someone to wrangle the bull. But who'd be willing to do that? In the end, she had to do it herself. She tied it up sloppily, but it was still standing. She didn't dare raise the knife against it herself, so she asked the pig-slaughterer, but he refused.

Around noon, a stranger showed up. He named a price, which wasn't a ton of money, but reasonable for what the bull was worth. Mrs. Ren Xiao accepted the cash and let him take it. Even as the bull lumbered away, she ran after it and thwacked it on the rump with a bamboo pole, making it stumble.

The buyer turned and spat vehemently on the ground. "Crazy woman!" he shouted.

A couple of days later, Dad ferried Grandpa on his bicycle to a village far to the west, to visit the old bull. A couple in their fifties, honest and trustworthy people, had taken it in. Their son had left their village to find work, and they weren't doing badly. The husband used to rear cattle, so he knew what he was doing and was fond of livestock.

In a single evening, a few dozen households in Shen Village had pooled their money to buy the bull and give it to this couple to take care of it as it lived out its final days.

THE TOFU-MAKER

THE TOFU-MAKER CARED MORE THAN anyone in Shen Village about reputation and placed a lot of emphasis on ritual. He taught me my first lesson on the importance of table manners.

I was six years old at the time, and someone in the village was having a milestone birthday. According to custom, every family would send one person to each of the five celebration meals: breakfast, lunch, and dinner on the day of, and breakfast and lunch the following day. I went along to one of these, probably because all the grown-ups were busy, and was seated next to the tofu-maker.

Grown-ups ate in a roundabout way. They kept stopping to toast back and forth, and it took forever to get through a meal. I was done with my food before long, placed my chopsticks on the table, and headed for the door, eager to get back to playing. The tofu-maker shouted, "Hey, Fishy, get back here. You're not going anywhere."

"What is it?" I didn't know why he was looking so stern, but came back slowly to my seat.

"You can't just drop your chopsticks after a meal. Hold them together, like this, in both hands, flat sides out. Starting with me, go round the table and tell everyone to enjoy their meal. When you're done, put the chopsticks across your bowl, not upright. That shows you've finished eating, and you're waiting for everyone else. If the grown-ups are still eating, you can't go. When the grown-ups stand, take your chopsticks and put them on the table. That's the rules. If you don't know the rules, you shouldn't be allowed at the dinner table."

Everyone at the table was nodding along with the tofu-maker's words. Kids ought to be taught the rules from an early age. That's basic etiquette, which you need to learn to be a respectable person.

Seeing how solemnly everyone was taking this, I felt alarmed. I picked up my chopsticks, placed them across my bowl, and sat there quietly, listening to them talk about things I didn't understand. I stayed there for the rest of the meal. From then on, I knew that the tofu-maker was a serious, upright person who never joked around. I'd seen tofu-makers in other villages hawking their wares. Before you got anywhere near them, you'd hear them shouting, "Tofu! Tofu, oh!" but ours never shouted. He rode along sedately on his Model 28 "Eternity" bicycle, with two large wooden buckets hanging off the back rack, one on either side. Every once in a while, he rang his bell a couple of times. This, too, was unhurried. When people heard the bell, they knew the tofu-maker had arrived.

I often went to the tofu-maker's house. His son Buckethead was my good friend. I was afraid the tofu-maker would yell at me, so I never dared go inside. Instead, I would clack a couple of stones together some distance away, signaling to Buckethead to sneak out.

Around the time we were in second grade, Buckethead and I beat a snake to death, a white one. We'd heard that snake meat was delicious, but we'd never tasted it. We carried the dead snake into the wilderness, gathered some branches, lit a fire, and hung the snake over it from a wooden pole. The branches hadn't been seasoned, so they released huge quantities of smoke, which attracted the attention of the bamboo-weaver in the pig shed. When he saw what we were doing, he gasped, snatched the snake away and flung it aside, then stamped out the fire that had taken us so much effort to make, roaring at us all the while. Buckethead and I ran. My father and Buckethead's father—the strict tofu-maker—went all the way there to look at the mess we'd left. The tofu-maker said, "Our Buckethead is a trouble-maker. This must have been his idea." My father said, "You don't need to cover for Fishy. You think I don't know what he's like? Every time there's mischief, he's involved somehow. You have to beat kids at least once every three days, or they'll start raising hell." Both men were throwing their own sons under the bus, to prove they weren't the sort to deflect blame, otherwise they'd never be able to hold their heads up high. The upshot was, Buckethead and I both got a good thrashing.

After the snake-eating incident, the grown-ups began calling us "soul-lacking dull-wits," which meant something like "foolhardy idiots." The tofu-maker instructed Buckethead: no more playing with that soul-lacking dull-wit Fishy. To be fair, I had indeed been the one who'd instigated the snake-eating. Buckethead was just following my lead.

For this and many other reasons, I was not fond of the stern, inflexible tofu-maker. Not liking him didn't do me any good, though. At the New Year, we still had to ask him for help. Not just my family—every household in the village needed him.

As far back as I can remember, it was customary to serve three dishes on the last day of the year: tofu with vegetables, pork bones, and fish on a platter. The fish wasn't there to be eaten, it was just an auspicious display, because the word for "fish" sounded like the one for "prosperity." It was put away untouched at the end of the meal, to be served on the second day of the New Year when relatives came to visit. Everyone got a large chunk of pork bone. When that was eaten, you weren't allowed to look like you wanted more. Us children usually got the biggest pieces to start with, and if we stared too long, our parents or even grandparents might offer us their portions, which would be unseemly.

So of these three dishes, tofu was the only one we could eat as much of as we wanted. If we finished our serving, there was always more available. Every household made their own tofu, a bucketful at a time. The day before, we'd put the soybeans in water. Then when Buckethead shouted, "Fishy, it's your family's turn," Mom and I would heft the bucket of soaked beans to his house.

The tofu-maker's home had two rooms filled with tofu-making equipment.

First was the grinding. Ladle by ladle, we poured the beans into the mill. Then Mom and I would turn the millstone by pushing on a wooden handle. "Slow down, slow down, no need to run so fast. You have to pace yourself," the tofu-maker would yell as he removed the leather cap from the top of the mill and trickled water in.

By the time we were done, I'd be too exhausted to move a muscle. Now it was the tofu-maker's turn. He'd set two wooden sticks flat in a cross shape and put a metal ring around them, and hang that from the rafters. A square of muslin got tied to the four ends of the sticks, creating a little cradle that the bean slurry was poured into. The tofu-maker manipulated the two sticks, twisting them back and forth, so the white soy milk poured into an earthenware urn below, first quickly and then more slowly. Finally, only bean mash was left in the muslin, a round glob of the stuff. This didn't get thrown away—cooked with salt, it made a good accompaniment to congee.

The soy milk from the urn was scooped into a pot. Normally, this was enough for a family—it was a really big pot. We had to bring our own firewood, and the tofu-maker's wife kept an eye on it as it cooked. When it had boiled long enough, it was poured into another urn, for the tofu-maker to brine.

Brining was the most important step—whether a batch of tofu turned out good or bad depended entirely on this. The tofu-maker held a scoop of brining liquid in his left hand, and a long-handled ladle in his right, with which he kept stirring the soy milk, slowly dribbling the brine in. Sometimes he stirred more quickly, sometimes more slowly. Bit by bit, the soy milk began to coagulate in the urn, and you could see yellowish liquid around the curds.

"It's done!" the tofu-maker would call out.

Next to the urn was a square platform with a trough on all four sides, and a wooden spout on the innermost side leading down to a wooden bucket.

Mom and the tofu-maker's wife would place a large sheet of thick gauze flat over the platform, holding on to the corners. The tofu-maker scooped the curds onto this cloth, and when he was done, its four corners were brought together and tied to form a bundle. A heavy wooden lid went over this, and rocks were piled on top. It was then left alone. A yellowish liquid would trickle down the spout into the bucket. When the dribbling stopped, the process was complete.

Move aside the rocks, lift the wooden lid and untie the bundle, and inside would be a huge block of tofu. The tofu-maker got out his special knife, slashed horizontally then vertically, as if he was drawing a chessboard, and when he was done, the tofu would be in blocks. These went into a bucket of clear water and would last you till the fifteenth day of the New Year. I couldn't wait. Back home that evening, I'd put a piece of tofu on my plate, sprinkle it with soy sauce, pick it up with chopsticks, and shove it in my mouth. Then I'd reach for another piece.

A few days before the New Year, the tofu-maker would be busy making tofu for every household in Shen Village. This was a completely voluntary service he provided. In return, everyone in Shen Village would, at some point in the coming year, pick a day when the tofu-maker was free to invite him over for a meal. This would be a special dinner, with him as the guest of honor. Anyone else who was there, whether it was the village head or another prominent figure, could only take a secondary seat. This was when the tofu-maker was at his grandest. He normally didn't touch a drop of alcohol, but on these occasions he would allow himself two drinks. Just two, so as to avoid greed and drunkenness.

Usually, the tofu-maker smoked instead of drinking. His pipe was specially made, long and coarse with a copper bowl and mouthpiece, joined with a mottled bamboo stem. The whole thing was a meter long—I'm not sure why, maybe because it looked cool. The way he lit his pipe was also interesting: he did it with a dry hemp stalk. Our village was full of these, and you could pluck one pretty much anywhere. Almost every household grew hemp, spun it, wove it, and turned it into fabric. In the summer, we wore clothes of hemp linen. If you stuck one of these hemp stalks into an oil lamp or the stove so it caught fire, you could take it out and blow out the flame, and it would keep smoldering for up to an hour. Everyone also grew their own tobacco. The quality wasn't bad—fragrant with a bit of a kick. More refined folk rolled their tobacco leaves in a square of white paper and held it between their fingers. The tofu-maker kept his in a gray cloth bag, from which he would pull out a pinch, just enough to fill the bowl of his pipe. With the long pipe hanging from his lips, he'd touch the lit hemp stalk to the tobacco, breathe in, and expel smoke from his nose. Then he'd move the mouthpiece aside, raise his head, and let out a long exhale into the void. As the smoke swirled above his head, a smile of satisfaction spread across his face. Generally, after he'd taken a couple of puffs, all the tobacco would be reduced to ash. When he blew hard into the pipe, the ash would arc through the air and land on the ground. If he didn't blow, but rather lifted one leg and tapped the bowl on the sole of his shoe, that meant he was done smoking and ready to do some work. Having tipped out the ash, he'd tuck the pipe back into his belt.

Once, Buckethead stole his father's pipe. While the tofu-maker was busy making tofu, Buckethead and I hid behind the house, playing at smoking. We were in high school then, even better friends than before, and more mischievous. Tobacco was easy to get hold of—the blacksmith had some drying on a bamboo tray on his roof. We didn't know how to light it with a hemp stalk, but I'd stolen some matches from our stove at home. We put the tobacco into the bowl, and while Buckethead puffed, I lit it for him. Then I smoked, and he returned the favor. We kept choking and coughing, and our eyes were streaming, but afterward we were grinning foolishly with bliss. The tobacco wasn't completely burned out when we tipped it out, and the pile of hay it landed on caught on fire. Buckethead and I made a run for it. A mute guy was standing nearby, and he saw the whole thing. As the hay burned, he got a copper basin from his home and banged frantically on it. This alerted the whole village, and they rushed over with brooms and water buckets. They stopped the fire before it could spread, so only the small heap of hay by the blacksmith's house was burned down.

The tofu-maker strung Buckethead up and beat him half to death. I only heard about this later, because my father had also tied me up and hung me by my arms from the rafters. He whipped me with a hemp rope, but only managed a couple of lashes before the blacksmith and bamboo-weaver grabbed hold of him—Grandpa had sent for them. You can't stop a member of your own family from beating a child, only outsiders can intervene. The blacksmith and bamboo-weaver were Dad's elders. One of them pulled him aside, and the other untied me and set me free.

"Are you trying to beat him to death? It's not like he's a bandit or murderer," the blacksmith rebuked my father.

After that vicious beating, my father starved me for a day. From then on, Buckethead no longer played with me. Soon, we'd graduated from middle school. I transferred elsewhere for high school, while Buckethead was sent by the tofu-maker to work as a welder at a factory in Wuxi.

I was busy studying for my college entrance exams when Buckethead died. He was eighteen, the same age as me. I heard the cause was a boiler explosion. When the tofu-maker rushed over there, the foreman told him Buckethead's work had nothing to do with the boiler, but he was fiddling around with it for fun, and it blew up. He wasn't even eligible for a cent of compensation. A pointless death.

By the time the tofu-maker got back to Shen Village from Wuxi, it was the small hours. At the village entrance, something glowed by the side of the road—probably a discarded cigarette butt. Exhausted from his long walk, the tofu-maker got out his pipe, filled it with tobacco, bent over, and touched the bowl to the flame. He inhaled a few times, but couldn't get it to light. Losing his temper, he smashed the pipe into the fire. "I'll beat you to death, you stupid thing!"

The flame skimmed along the ground for a bit before soaring into the air and vanishing. It was a will-o'-the-wisp.

Two days after he got home, the tofu-maker fell ill. No one knew what his illness was, and he refused to get treated. Two months later, he died. Buckethead's ashes were sent back from Wuxi. Now father and son are buried in the same place, behind the northwest corner of their house.

THE LANTERN-MAKER

GRAMPS, MY MOTHER'S FATHER, LIVED alone on a hillock outside the village. His front door faced east and looked out on a major north-south road. This was unusual—almost all the houses in the village faced south. I'm not sure why that was. My grandmother died young, and my three uncles had all married and gotten started with their own lives and careers, so none of them lived with Gramps. I would go stay with him for a few days every New Year. That's when he was at his busiest, the time I found most fun: when he was creating decorative lanterns for the Lantern Festival, the fifteenth day of the lunar year.

One New Year, on the second day, my little brother and I visited Gramps with two packets of snacks: one of glutinous rice puffs, one of peach cookies. It was over twenty kilometers to his place, but we horsed around all the way there, so it didn't feel that far to walk. The aroma of the rice puffs wafted into our noses. I said, "Let's have one each. He'll never know." My brother agreed, of course. One each, then two, then three, and soon we'd finished half the packet.

You can't give someone half a packet of snacks as a New Year gift—that's rude. Normally, Gramps would have to give us a packet in return, so we decided to just finish this one and not exchange gifts—it would work out the same.

Gramps had lost all his teeth, so his mouth had collapsed in on itself, which was especially unattractive when he smiled. He was kind, though. When he saw we'd only brought a bag of peach cookies, he just smiled his gummy smile and handed us a bunny lantern each to go play with.

There were three rooms in Gramps's thatched hut: his bedroom on the left, a living room in the middle, and his workshop on the right. There was also a separate shed, which he used as a kitchen. The house was surrounded by trees: mulberry, persimmon, ginkgo, peach, jujube. In the summer, his hut was dappled with shade. With wilderness all around him, he allowed the chickens and goats he reared to roam freely. No one saw where they went, and no one cared. A little yellow dog was supposed to look after them, but the dog was mischievous too, and not particularly serious about its duties.

Gramps's workshop was filled with all kinds of paper, bamboo strips, and lanterns. He doted on me and my brother, and we were allowed to play with any of the lanterns. Even if we ruined them, that was fine. There was only one that we weren't allowed to touch: an eight-sided carousel. It had a frame of pear tree wood, carved with various weapons, and the sides were covered with translucent paper. Inside were figures of people on horseback, one of whom had a black-and-white design across his face—this was meant to be General Xiang Yu. Inscribed on the base of the lantern was: AMBUSHED FROM ALL SIDES. This lantern hung from a rafter all year round, and no one was allowed to touch it. Only on the sixteenth day of the third month, the temple day of Dongyue the Great, did he take it down to hang before the sacred figures in the Dongyue temple. When he lit the candle, the figures in the lantern would revolve. From the outside, it looked like countless mounted soldiers were galloping after Xiang Yu. This was the most dazzling lantern in the whole village. Gramps created it. Every year, when it came to Dongyue Temple Day, I would say to all my little friends, "Look, look, that lantern that moves—my gramps made that."

He started in his twenties, and made lanterns for forty years. Then, at the age of sixty-five, he abruptly stopped, and went into a different line of work: a blind-guide.

What kind of job was that? It wasn't really a job. I don't know where the blind man came from, but all of a sudden, there he was. He held a little gong in his right hand, and every few paces, he would strike it with a clang. In his left hand he had a long bamboo pole, which guided him as he walked. And holding the other end of that bamboo pole was Gramps.

The blind man went around all the nearby villages, hitting the gong to advertise his fortune-telling. Gramps introduced this annoying man to everyone he knew. Everyone for miles around knew the honest, stolid lantern-maker, so they tried to support the blind man too.

I was in elementary school, at an age when appearances mattered a lot. The blind man's gong frequently sounded as he passed the schoolhouse, which happened to be at a busy crossroads between four villages.

"Isn't that your gramps? He's guiding the blind man."

"The blind man cheats people of their money."

"Blind-guide! Blind-guide!" they chanted each time they saw me.

As a result, I got into quite a few fights at school. The more I lashed out in anger and shame, the more of a joke it seemed to them. Every time we fought, they would use "blind-guide" as a taunt.

I bumped into Gramps almost every week, as he led the blind man around. As soon as he saw me in the distance, he'd holler, "Fishy!" I'd pretend not to hear and run in the opposite direction. Even so, he shouted my name every single time.

I complained to my mother. "Mom, why doesn't Gramps make lanterns anymore? I hate that he's a blind-guide. The blind man just cheats people of their money."

"Who told you that? They don't know what they're talking about. He only tells fortunes for people who believe in it. They go into it willingly—so who's getting cheated? Stop and think about it. If he wasn't telling fortunes, what else could a blind man do?"

"Fine, so he can go ahead and tell fortunes, but why does Gramps have to lead him around? It's embarrassing!"

My mom stopped threshing the vegetables and shouted at me, "Go pluck some ragweed!"

The last time I visited Gramps was on the third day of one New Year. He still lived in that dilapidated thatched hut, but I was older now and could zoom along on my bicycle. He heard me pulling up and came out to greet me. I called out a hello and brought the snacks I'd been carrying on my handlebars into the living room, where I set them on the table. Gramps had cleaned the house thoroughly, inside and out, in honor of the New Year. From the rafter hung a large chunk of pork—I almost bumped my head on it.

I didn't sit, nor did I want to. "Gramps, there's still a lot to do at home. I'll head back now."

"What do you think you're doing? This hardly counts as a New Year visit. At least stay for lunch. Look, there's all this pork, and I have some fish too."

"No need. I really am needed back home."

He tried to argue a bit longer, but when he saw that I was determined to leave, he told me to wait a moment and went back inside, muttering to himself. A moment later, he came back out and stuffed a couple of yuan into my hands. This was New Year money and couldn't be refused. Two yuan was a huge sum to both of us. In previous years, he'd only given me fifty cents.

I hopped back on my bike and flew away. When I got to the main road, I looked back. Gramps was still standing by the front door of the thatched hut, watching me.

"See you next time!" he shouted.

I never saw Gramps again. I attended high school in another town and didn't come back often. I didn't even want to see him at New Year and sent my brother instead. Then eventually, as an adult, I heard about Gramps's shameful past.

Gramps was an army deserter.

One of my high school classmates came from the same village as Gramps. We got on well at first, and then we quarreled over something or other. Now that we were no longer friends, he went around telling everyone that Shen Fuyu's grandfather had run from the army.

My father had always known, but if I hadn't asked, he might never have told. I was always especially interested in stories of war. That's how it was with kids in my time, we all wanted to grow up and become soldiers. The area around Shen Village had been a revolutionary base for the New Fourth Army, and I would often hear their stories. Apparently, Commander Su Yu once stayed in our village.

"Gramps was in the New Fourth Army?" This was when I was still little, and we were cooling off outside one summer. Waving a palm leaf fan, Dad was giving a spirited storytelling performance to the courtyard full of people. It wasn't true storytelling, because he was mixing true things in with made-up tales. But no one seemed to mind—they were having a grand time.

When I asked this question, Dad turned and glared at me. "Go to bed." We'd had a fun evening, but now it was time to part unhappily.

Afterward, I didn't probe any further.

Only when my classmate started talking about it did I realize there was more to the story. I was in high school, old enough to ask about it. When I got back from school, I put the question to Dad.

In 1940, the village cadres mobilized Gramps to join the New Fourth Army. That October, the Huangqiao Battle took place. They went against Han Deqin's troops. During the Battle of Taierzhuang a couple of years before this, these same soldiers had had several formidable skirmishes with the Japanese in Subei. They did so well, it was said Chiang Kai-shek personally commended them. Everyone knew not to cross them. Luckily, Su Yu was an excellent commander and always led his men into battle himself. After three days of fighting, they were victorious. But Gramps's nerves were shattered. On the night of October 7, two days after the victory at Huangqiao, he abandoned his rifle and slipped away from the camp.

Not far away, he was caught. All of a sudden, a sentry stepped out from behind a tree, gun pointed at Gramps. They were only a dozen meters apart. Gramps stood frozen. They were comrades from the same squad. They stood like this for more than a minute, then the sentry put down his weapon and let Gramps get away.

He made it back to our village, but didn't dare stay at home—if anyone found him here, they'd tie him up and deliver him back to the army.

On a hillock some distance from the village, he built a thatched hut. To the east of the mound was the only road to and from the village, running north-south. The end of the road was visible from his hut, and so he could see whenever anyone entered the village. There were wide-open fields behind the mound, crisscrossed with ditches that he could disappear into. Perhaps the only useful thing Gramps learned from being a soldier, was how to flee for his life.

Gramps was never caught. And so he went on living on the hillock. First, he expanded his thatched hut. Next, he married and learned a profession: making lanterns.

So that's who I had for a grandfather, an army deserter. Never mind the blind-guiding, who knew what other bizarre things he might get up to. I didn't want to see him again. As for Gramps, he eventually stopped leading the blind man around our village. Perhaps he'd realized how ashamed we were of him.

After high school, I went to Wuxi for work, and then to Guangzhou, Zhuhai, Beijing, and Nanjing. By the time I got back from my wanderings, Gramps was no longer around.

Mom told me the news. When he was ill in bed, my uncles wanted to bring him to their village, but he refused. Mom and Dad asked him to come to Shen Village, but he said no to that too. And so everyone took turns to go to the thatched hut to take care of him. The blind man was there too, keeping him company every single day.

"The blind man he used to bring around?"

"Yes, the same one. They were in the army together."

"In the army together? I thought he ran away after just a few months?"

"They met during those few months. He only escaped thanks to the blind man. He wasn't blind, back then. He was a sentry, and he let your Gramps go. If not for him, your Gramps would have been shot dead."

"The blind man was in the New Fourth Army too?"

"Yes. He lost his sight in a bomb blast."

Gramps was sixty-five when he met the blind man again. He was eighty-one when he died, having been his companion for sixteen years.

At Gramps's funeral, Mom asked the blind man if he could tell my fortune. I'd been in the outside world for several years by then. Where was I? What was I doing? She had no idea. The blind man cracked his knuckles. "Don't worry, young lady. You'll hear from him soon."

Three days after this, Mom got a letter from me, mailed from Zhuhai. I was letting her know that I'd found a job, and everything was going well.

I'd been a mover for a furniture company in Huangqi, Foshan, but then I thought there was no future there, so I went to Zhuhai instead. When I wrote the letter, I'd just gotten a job servicing computers at Zhuhai's World Trade Exhibition Center.

That might have been the last fortune the blind man told. When she got my letter, Mom gave him five yuan as a thank-you. He took the money and said he wasn't going out again.

"I'll just stay at home and wait to die."

The winter after Gramps passed, so did the blind man.

THE CARPENTER

A HUGE SAW HUNG ON OUR living room wall. Sometimes, in the middle of the night, it would emit a very loud zing, as if it were going to snap in two. Everyone would be startled awake, and we'd get out of bed right away. We knew this meant someone had died, and their spirit was warning us that Grandpa needed to make a coffin.

Grandpa was the best carpenter within a hundred-li radius.

GRANDPA HAD BEEN dead for more than a decade, but according to local custom, we still had to celebrate his hundredth birthday.

We'd cleaned up Grandpa's grave at the Tomb Sweeping Festival, so even though long grass had grown over it since our last visit, it still looked neat and tidy.

When we got back from the cemetery, I went to the loft and found Grandpa's magical saw. It was two meters long, and though the blade was rusty, when I blew the dust off the oak handle, it gleamed darkly, polished to a glossy sheen by years of use. When I gently bounced the blade, it let out a resounding hum, a warm response to this unexpected visit. The hum didn't fade right away, but drifted out through the window, causing the dust motes in the sunlight to vibrate in sympathy.

The saw had lain there since Grandpa's death, accumulating more than ten years of dust. It seemed as if no one remembered there had once been a famous carpenter here.

In fact, Grandpa stopped being a carpenter in 1958—he didn't do a single day's carpentry after that. He didn't do any farmwork either. He was only forty-six at the time, but decided to wash his hands of everything and be a completely aimless person. Nineteen fifty-eight was when the People's Commune was established, and everyone's possessions were confiscated—land, livestock, furniture. Even the ginkgo trees around their houses were moved to the side of the road, where they could belong to all humanity. The ginkgo tree by the front door of my family home was one of those.

In the fall of 1958, the production brigade sent two people with ropes and shovels to dig up this ginkgo tree and bring it to the public road some distance away. Grandpa stopped them. He said, "Don't do that, you'll kill it. Let me. I'll come with you, and we can replant it together." And so this silver ginkgo, along with the ones belonging to our neighbors, was moved to the side of a dusty, unfamiliar road. In 1962, the tide turned, and everyone hurried to the roadside to retrieve their trees. A bunch of them had died when they were first transplanted, and a bunch more died when they were moved back. Grandpa went along too, with my eighteen-year-old father, who helped him carry our tree back. In the three years it was gone, it had gotten skinnier. It took a full thirty years to regain its full stature.

Grandpa had brought this ginkgo tree from his master's house, back when he was an apprentice. Perhaps because it was a memento from his youth, he always took especially good care of it. Each New Year, he would paste an upside-down "fu" on the trunk to summon good fortune, hoping this would help it grow big and tall. And sure enough, its branches now rise above the highest roof in the village, and its crown is lush enough to shelter the whole family. But Grandpa's no longer here to see it.

Collectivization took away Grandpa's motivation to work hard. Everything he'd painstakingly acquired now no longer existed and had nothing to do with him. As a result, he refused to take part in any communal activities. On a few occasions, the village cadres sent people with ropes to tie him up and force him to labor, but in the end they let him be, due to the reputation he'd once had as a carpenter. They cut off his rations and let him go hungry. At every meal, the family scraped together a bowl of barley gruel for him, so thin you could see through it. When he was done eating, he sat on a little stool in the corner, got out a small wooden block, and whittled a "drunken eight immortals" scene with a tiny knife. The original image had been given to him by his good friend Dong Xi, who lived in the Earth God Temple to the west of the village and was a well-known sculptor himself.

When I was a kid, I looked in Grandpa's toolbox and found one of the immortals, Zhang Guolao, riding a donkey backward, waving and chuckling. I kept that tiny figurine as if it were a treasure and asked Grandpa to carve some more, but though he usually gave in to my whims, he ignored me this time. After 1958, he stopped making eight immortals.

What dreams did Grandpa once have? I asked Dad, but he didn't know. Mom said, "What dreams could he have had? He was just lazy. He even had his breakfast in bed." Dad said, "That's not laziness, you two never saw him work. He knew how to suffer. Going at it day and night. By day, he was a carpenter in people's houses, and by night, he would labor in the fields. His whole body was filled with so much energy, he could never run out. He supported all of us, such a big household, all by himself. Your grandma was sickly from when they were married, and she could never work. The whole family depended on him."

I didn't believe it. As far as I could see, Grandma was the most industrious person in the world. I saw her cooking for him every day, bringing his food over to him and even placing the chopsticks in his hand. If Dad had said it was Grandma supporting Grandpa, I might have bought that.

Grandma died when I was ten, in 1980. I stood beneath the ginkgo tree in front of our house, as she was carried out on a bamboo stretcher. Dad followed behind, sobbing. They put her on a bed in the ancestral shrine, and I sat beside her, keeping watch. She was wheezing hard, unable to speak. Grandpa sat at her feet, warming her icy legs. Bit by bit, she stopped breathing. Grandpa didn't move, just stayed there with his arms wrapped around her legs, warming them against his chest.

In the thirty years after that, whenever I thought of Grandma, I felt warm and happy. She was always smiling, never mind that she'd lost all her teeth. Every wrinkle on her face was a smile too. When she wanted to scold Grandpa, she'd call him an old fool. I used to hide under the table and shout, "Old fool" at him, and he just laughed. He didn't mind. Grandma would giggle too. My brother and I were very protective of Grandma. We refused to help Grandpa, but we'd do whatever Grandma asked us to. Grandma often sat in the sun, removed the silver hairpin from her bun, let her dappled white hair down, and slowly ran a gap-toothed comb through it, telling me stories about Grandpa all the while. I couldn't keep still, and after listening for a while, I would scamper away to poke blades of grass into the little holes in the dirt walls of our house, where wild bees lived. Grandma would call, "Stop that, my little one. If you keep messing around, you'll collapse the whole house."

Our house was built by Grandpa when he was young, and our family lived for forty years in that thatched cottage with dirt walls, until I was in my teens, when Dad built a new place with brick walls and a tiled roof. Even so, the house Grandpa built was an astonishing accomplishment. Back then, no one was allocated a property plot—you had to buy your land with Big-Head Yuan silver coins. This was when Grandpa was still known as Honger the Carpenter, and was renowned for his handiwork—everyone in the vicinity wanted to hire him. He had more work than he could cope with. Each day, he and his apprentice would carry that enormous saw back and forth. The same saw that later hung on the wall of our living room. When I turned eighteen and left home for my travels, it was still there.

The big saw carried a huge amount of symbolism. It represented Grandpa's prime. He had work to do every single day, and everyone admired his craft. But in order to be a good carpenter, Grandpa went through an unimaginably awful ordeal.

When Grandpa was eighteen, he caught the eye of a highly skilled carpenter named Zhengxin from a village to the north, who wanted to take him on as an apprentice. Grandpa's father, Wanli, wouldn't let him. He was a man of few words with a stubborn personality. Better to be a farmhand and provide labor in someone else's fields, he said, than to train as a carpenter. It took three years to learn carpentry, and during that time you would live in your teacher's house, effectively as his servant. There were a large number of complex skills that had to be learned, and only a quick, intelligent person would be able to master them all. Even after that, acquiring a full set of carpentry tools would be another onerous burden.

Great-grandpa Wanli's family hadn't actually been that poor to start with, but the year Grandpa was born, their house caught fire, and they lost everything. This was in the winter of 1911, when Grandpa was just a few months old. Wanli didn't even stop to dress him, just wrapped him in a blanket and charged out of the burning building. It turned out to be a case of arson. This fire changed the course of my family's destiny. As for the arsonist, a Taoist priest made a prediction one hundred years ago that came true: his family would be affected by mental disability for the next three generations.

I have no recollection at all of my great-grandfather, the man named Wanli who fled an inferno with Grandpa in his arms. He died in 1946. My only memory of him is that every year at Tomb Sweeping Festival, Grandpa would bring me to his grave to kowtow three times. In our ancestral shrine at home, there was a long table called "heads of the household," and on it was a tablet with Great-Grandpa's name. These tablets are tiny tombstones of inscribed wood, and each represents an ancestor's resting place. At Tomb Sweeping, Winter Solstice, the New Year, and their death anniversaries, we kneel and pay our respects to them. In addition to Wanli's tablet, this table now holds two more for Grandpa and Grandma. Grandma's is a bit more elaborate—Grandpa made it for her when she passed away and added a carved wooden frame around it. This was the last thing he made, after allowing his craft to lie fallow for decades, and it took him a month of carpentry. Each day, I'd get home from school to find him sitting in the doorway, chiseling and carving. Because of overuse in his younger days, his hands trembled a little, and he had difficulty raising his arms.

In the period right after Grandma passed, I would fix her a bowl of food each day, place it before her wooden tablet, and holding back my tears, I'd murmur, "Eat, Grandma." As the wind blew the warm aroma of the meal toward the tablet, I'd sense her within it, smiling benevolently at me. I was ten when she died. With her gone, there was no one left to cover for me, and Dad could whip me as much as he liked. Perhaps because Dad was so out of control after that, my teenage years were filled with longing for my late grandmother, who'd doted on me so.

Grandpa died when I was twenty-three. I was living in Zhuhai at the time, languishing in lockup on some bullshit charges. The day they released me, I got a letter from my little brother: *Grandpa is gone*. It happened to be Mid-Autumn. I sat alone by the sea, and all night long I listened to the ocean roar in the darkness.

Six weeks or forty-two days after their deaths, we stopped placing bowls of food and chopsticks before their tablets, inviting them to come back and eat. The more time passed, the more distant they grew from us. Now, only at Tomb Sweeping do I occasionally go back home to clear the weeds from Grandpa and Grandma's graves, add a few shovelfuls of fresh soil, and drag my daughter back from wherever she's run off to so she can kowtow to them. My most resonant childhood memory of Tomb Sweeping is Grandpa leaving the house with his shovel first thing in the morning, to tend to his parents' and grandparents' graves. I'd follow him and do as he did, kowtowing to their renewed resting places.

IN 1929, AGED eighteen, Grandpa became Carpenter Zhengxin's apprentice over his father's objections.

His apprenticeship was a terrifying time. Zhengxin was a skilled craftsman but a bad teacher. Everyone feared his explosive temper. Grandpa had only been there a month when, one day, he was planing a piece of wood, but had neglected to sharpen his planer and it skipped. Zhengxin flung a wooden block so hard, it drew blood from Grandpa's hand. Grandpa ran back home. Zhengxin's new bride, a beautiful and virtuous woman, had to come and plead several times before Grandpa consented to return with her. Another six months passed, during which he suffered many kicks and punches. Then he somehow aroused Zhengxin's temper again and got an ax flung at him. Grandpa didn't manage to duck in time, and the ax hit him on the head. Blood pouring down his face, he fled home again, weeping and refusing to go back no matter what. Unfortunately, the contract he'd signed when he took the apprenticeship stated that for three years, the apprentice would accept his master's beatings and scoldings, and there would be no consequences even if he died. Carpenter Zhengxin sent someone to promise that there would be no more assaults, and Grandpa had no choice but to return.

A year and a half into the apprenticeship, Zhengxin took ill and, after a month in bed, died. Grandpa returned home, breathing a sigh of relief, but also disappointed. He hadn't learned the craft, and these eighteen months of suffering had all been for nothing. Now that Carpenter Zhengxin was gone, his wife gave some of his tools to Grandpa. These mostly weren't worth much, but the large saw was quite something, and Grandpa was pleased. In his eighties, a full thirty years after he'd stopped being a carpenter, he still took it down from the wall every New Year and wiped it clean with a cloth. He'd ask me to cut him a piece of red paper, write "Godlike Carpentry" on it with a brush, and paste it to the saw.

This saw was his most beloved treasure. When it was taken out of the house for work, no matter how far away, it had to be brought back by evening. Dad said the saw could make its power felt. It did so when Grandpa was in his prime.

Not long after Grandpa returned from Zhengxin's home, Second Carpenter from North Village took him on as an apprentice. Second Carpenter was a good-tempered man, but didn't do much teaching. Instead, he got Grandpa to follow Master Hua, his hired assistant. Master Hua was a marvel. He didn't seem like a carpenter, being literate and well-mannered, yet his skills were exceptional. By shadowing him, Grandpa learned a lot about carpentry, as well as literature. Master Hua taught him about important books like *The Three Character Classic* and *The Book of Family Names*. Two and a half years after this, Master Hua abruptly disappeared. Grandpa was the only one who knew he was a Communist and, many years later, sought refuge with him.

NOW THAT GRANDPA was fully trained, he returned home and hung out his shingle. Soon, he was making a name for himself. The next step was getting married and establishing himself in the world.

Grandma was from Beixinjie, and her family used to be quite prominent, until her father gambled away everything they had. That's how she ended up marrying a carpenter. I imagine Grandma must have been pretty when she was young, though Dad described her as sickly and sallow-faced, only in relatively good health when Grandpa was at the height of his powers. In 1958, when there was nothing left to eat, she dug up a jar of rice she'd buried and made congee. When they'd gotten through the rice, she gathered edible leaves and dug up wild vegetables, like a magic trick. "If not for her," Dad said, "some of us would have starved to death." Grandma found a way to take care of every single person, while she herself went hungry and her health suffered. Dad remembered how she often sat on the low stool in front of the stove, one hand on her stomach, the other raising her faded blue apron to wipe the sweat and tears from her face. She put that tattered apron on as soon as she got up in the morning, and kept it on till she went to bed that night, even at the New Year. She cooked for the entire family and always managed to put something on the table. Dad said she died of stomach cancer. "We brought her to the hospital, but when the doctor cut her open with the scalpel, he took one look and told us there was nothing he could do. Her insides were rotten, like tofu mush."

In the second year of her marriage, Grandma gave birth to Uncle Qinglin. Grandpa had managed to save up enough money from his carpentry to buy a piece of land, but didn't have any left over to build a house, so he decided to move the one they were living in. This wasn't difficult. First, they tied wooden poles in place to support the important parts of the structure. Next, they pushed the dirt walls over so they fell to the ground, leaving only the frame and thatched roof. Grandpa's younger brother went round every household hitting a gong and yelling, "Moving—house—" All the men in the village immediately stopped what they were doing and came over, a few hundred of them. At a signal, they heaved the house off the ground, and carried it over to the plot, which had been leveled in preparation. Once it was in place, earth could be packed around the frame to form thick walls.

It took a few days to make these walls, but two or three strong men could do it. You placed two wooden boards a short distance apart, filled the space between them with carefully chosen soil, and hammered at them with long-handled mallets, until the earth was sturdy and compacted. Then you raised the boards and repeated the process: more earth, more hammering, until the wall was high enough. The roof needed fixing too, after its move. Luckily, Grandpa was good at roofs. The rafters didn't need changing. They were made of proper timber, stuff you couldn't buy. All you could do was repair them where they were damaged. They were covered in reed mats, with straw on top. Sparrows loved houses like this. The thatched roof was a great place for them to build nests. They were free to do that—no one tried to stop them.

Grandpa worked even harder now. A few years later, he was able to buy another piece of land to the east of the house and expand its two rooms into four. The cost of purchasing property and building the extension was alarmingly high. Grandpa spent all the silver coins he'd worked day and night to save up, plus several years' worth of harvests. When the building work was complete, though, he was very satisfied. He put everything he had into his work. He left the house before the sun came up, and only returned when it was dark. His reputation grew more and more resounding—he was known as the best carpenter within a hundred-li radius.

Then one day, out of the blue, something astonishing happened. Late at night, as the house lay silent, the saw on the wall let out a few hums as if someone was flicking it. The family startled awake. At first they thought something had fallen, but when they got up and looked around, everything seemed in order. A short while later, there was another hum. They got out of bed again, but still saw nothing. At daybreak, someone came knocking at the door to say there'd been a death the night before, and could Grandpa please come and make the coffin.

Grandpa was the best coffin-maker for several villages around. He immediately sent Dad and Uncle out to find helpers. When something like this happened, the coffin needed to be finished within a day. Any carpenter who got summoned would have to abandon their work, no matter how important it was, and come running. They were happy to do this, because they got paid double, though it wasn't just about the money. Anyone who refused would find some mysterious tragedy descending upon their head. Making coffins was a carpenter's most important task.

The mystical thing was, from then on, whenever the great saw sounded in the middle of the night, someone would show up at first light to report a death and invite Grandpa to make the coffin.

"Often it happened very late. When the saw started humming, we'd all get out of bed. Your grandma would fix some food for your grandpa, while your uncle and I would go to the neighboring villages to find helpers. On rainy nights, we'd get soaked through. There was a reason we had to go looking so urgently. A poor person's coffin took five or six people a whole day to make. For a rich family, it had to be fancier, which meant seven or eight people. But it had to be finished that same day. That's why we needed so many other carpenters. If we got there too late, the carpenters would already have jobs for the day, and it would be harder to pull them away. Besides, we didn't have time to waste." Dad and Uncle told me this story several times. They had to repeat it because it was so improbable. Even so, I only half-believed it, though I did develop a fear of the great saw that hung on our wall, and never dared to touch it. It wasn't just me, no one in our family ever disturbed it. That's why it remains there to this day, more than ten years after Grandpa's death, in good condition unlike the rest of his tools, which have either fallen apart or gone missing.

The saw stopped humming after collectivization, when people stopped hiring carpenters—they could no longer afford coffins, or indeed furniture.

IN 1958, THE People's Commune was established. It was said the soil needed to be tilled extra-deep to produce unheard-of amounts of crops. Someone invented a machine called the jiaoguan, a wooden device like an enormous millstone with four wooden poles protruding from it. You pushed these to turn the wheel, which set in motion some long, thick ropes attached to a huge plow. Plows like these, specially designed for deep tilling, were too massive for oxen to move—only the human-operated jiaoguan could budge them. At a shouted signal, workers would set the jiaoguan in motion, and the plow would dig deep into the ground, throwing up yellow earth. This was hard on the ropes and poles, which often snapped. The jiaoguan were made of wood, and frequently fell apart. Grandpa was required to stay nearby and fix them when needed.

As far as Grandpa was concerned, this was the most ridiculous thing he'd ever heard of. He pretended to be ill and didn't show up. As time went on and food began to run out, people no longer had the strength to move the jiaoguan anyway.

Next came the building of the "ten thousand pigsty," a hundred pig sheds that had to be finished in a very short time—the Commune would be coming to inspect them at the end of 1958. Grandpa and Uncle Qinglin, along with two other villagers, had been struggling day and night. They'd chopped down almost all the remaining trees. In this year, some of the village's trees had been moved to the side of the public road, others had been cut down to make farming tools for the collective, and now the few remaining ones were meeting their end too. There wasn't a single tree left in the village, not even saplings whose trunks were no thicker than the mouth of a bowl. This pained Grandpa. "It's not right. If we just waited a few years, these trees would be much more useful." But that's how it was, and there still wasn't enough wood. The production brigade secretary insisted that the hundred pig sheds had to be finished according to schedule. Getting them built would count as a victory. Not finishing on time would be counter-revolutionary. Grandpa didn't want to be a counter-revolutionary, so he came up with a plan: he collected sunflower stalks to serve as pillars and rafters. Carefully covered with a thin layer of thatch, these actually did look like sheds from a distance. They quickly completed a hundred in this way. The brigade secretary was so delighted, he rewarded each of them with a pound of rice. Grandpa hefted his share back home and sighed, "But all the trees are gone."

Within a few days of the inspection team's visit, more than half the sheds of the "ten-thousand pigsty" had collapsed, and Grandpa said to Uncle, "Those are the ones you built!"

After 1958, when all land and possessions were collectively owned, the village no longer needed a carpenter. Or when they did, it was to put up some jury-rigged structure that would have been an insult to an artisan like Grandpa. He began refusing to leave the house and wouldn't take part in any communal activities. On his own, he found some bits of scrap wood, which he assembled into a chair. After getting up each morning, he brought this chair outside and set it under the ginkgo tree by our front door. Sometimes he stayed there an entire day, not moving a muscle. I don't know what he thought about, but he sat there till dusk.

In 1993, on the twentieth day of the sixth lunar month, my grandpa Shen Tongshou, a carpenter who'd been on strike for thirty-five years, died of old age. I, his eldest grandson, wasn't by his side. I was being held at Jida police station in Zhuhai. By the time I got home, all that was left of Grandpa was a row of inky black words on the tablet he'd carved himself, next to Grandma's name.

THE BARBER

"THE OLD BARBER'S COMING!"

Seeing him approaching in the distance, I ran yelling into the house. Grabbing a chair, I brought it out and set it under the ginkgo tree by our front door. The barber always began with us kids.

Under his arm, the barber carried a long, slender wooden box. He had a brisk walk and booming voice.

"Carpenter!" he called to my grandfather by way of greeting, and placed the box on the chair. Grandpa had appeared, alerted by my hollering, and was smiling from our doorway.

The box was made of peach tree wood, and had ferocious-looking heavenly generals carved on the front and back, one wielding a mace and the other a sword, riding strange beasts. This box made you think of martial arts warriors with monstrous, deadly skills.

There was nothing monstrous about the barber, though. He chuckled all day long, cracking jokes with adults and kids alike.

"Hey, Fishy, how are your family's goats? Want to run around with them for Ol' Barber to see? How about it?"

I ignored him. The whole village was teasing me because I enjoyed racing goats. A little over a month ago, I'd gotten a small goat so tired it died.

The barber clicked the latch and opened the lid. Inside were two razors, a neatly folded sheet, scissors, a narrow strop, a pig-bristle brush, a little bamboo tube of ear-cleaning implements, a broad wooden comb and a slimmer one, a rather cloudy mirror, and freshly oiled clippers. Before the barber did anything, he always clacked the clippers in the empty air, perhaps to make sure they were working, or to sound a warning so you could prepare yourself.

It didn't take long to cut my hair—no sooner had I got a good look at each of his tools than he was done. He brushed my face and neck clean, untied the sheet from my front, and shook it out with a crisp *thwack*. I scampered off.

Grandpa went last. He didn't just get his hair cut, but also had a shave and ear-cleaning. He was probably at his liveliest when getting shaved.

First, the barber wrung out a hot towel and laid it over his face. Next, he unrolled his strop and looped the string that hung from one end onto his stool. Holding the other end, he pulled it taut and sharpened his razor back and forth, *schwuh schwuh*, like striking a flint to make fire. When the blade was ready, he smeared a thin layer of foam over Grandpa's face. It was probably soap, what Grandpa called "Westerners' lye." The barber's movements were a lot gentler now. The razor passed over his skin with a faint scraping sound, and Grandpa's aged features gradually reappeared, looking cleaner. His eyes were almost closed, and he let out what sounded like little moans of pleasure. These shaves always took longer than expected. The blade passed over the forehead, down both cheeks, to the lips, the chin, the throat. Finally, he was done. Grandpa leaned back in the chair, looking sound asleep. The barber went over his face twice with the hot towel, then removed the sheet and shook it out into the wind with another *thwack*. Only now did Grandpa slowly awaken.

"How was that, Carpenter?"

"Mm, mm," was Grandpa's only reply, which seemed to please the barber.

The barber was a few years younger than Grandpa, but they were of the same generation. He left Grandpa for last every time, so they could chat afterward. Sometimes they kept going till eight or nine at night.

The barber lived at the rear of the village, by the river. Just him in a thatched hut with two rooms containing barely anything. Out the back door and down a few dozen steps was the river and his boat, which was propelled by a long bamboo pole. On the northern bank of the river was a large general store where you could get fancier goods. From time to time, when someone from Shen Village wanted to go there, they'd ask the barber to ferry them across the river. Everyone kept score of who had done what for whom, so there was no need to return the favor right away.

The barber made a round of our homes each month, which took him five days. If you happened to be out when he arrived, you'd find out where he was headed next and hurry there to get your hair cut. He never doubled back. During those five days, he had his lunch and dinner at his customers' homes. If he had lunch with us, then dinner would be with our immediate neighbor, and the following day would find him at the next house along. That was the cycle. Some families fed him a little better, some a little worse, but he never minded. As long as his belly was full, he didn't utter a word of complaint. Even so, everyone broke into their stash of meat or killed a chicken for him—it was just once a month, after all, and you had to put on a good show.

The days leading up to the New Year were his busiest. Everyone wanted a smart haircut to bring them good luck in the coming year.

"Ol' Barber, are you here to cut year hair?" I asked, when I bumped into him by the roadside.

"What's 'year hair'?"

"Hair for the New Year."

"There's no such thing. Yer hair's looking grimy, though. Come here, I'll shave it off."

On the last day of the year, the barber didn't leave his home. He swept the yard spick and span, pasted a spring couplet on the front door, dusted the rafters, put up pictures of the deities of prosperity, happiness, and long life, and wrote "fu," the character for "good fortune," on a square of red paper, which he stuck on the side of his boat. All of this had to be accomplished in the morning. Come the afternoon, he'd put a chair outside his front door and sit there puffing on a gurgling water-pipe. This was when he awaited his reward for a year of hair-cutting.

Every family in Shen Village would pay him a visit on this afternoon. Some brought freshly steamed buns, some tofu, fish, or meat. Others gave him rice or noodles or oil, or else sausages or duck eggs they'd preserved themselves.

No matter what they presented him with, how much or how little, the barber never minded. He always acted like he couldn't accept. "Oh no, this is far too much."

Grandpa was always the last to come. He would inspect the gifts as the barber pointed them out one by one, his face glowing with pride. When he'd seen everything, Grandpa would head back home to fetch whatever items the barber still lacked to celebrate the New Year. If nothing was missing, he would put some cash in a red envelope. Grandpa wasn't the only person who gave the barber a red envelope, but the others were mostly prominent or wealthy individuals.

The artisans of Shen Village didn't all collect their wages like the barber. Grandpa accepted money or provisions. Others only took cash. Did anyone ever not pay up? Yes. But as long as they said, on the last day of the year, "I'm really sorry, I'll take care of it next year," any artisan would reply, "No problem at all, there's no hurry." If they didn't even do that much? That was rare, but it did happen. Those kinds of people would find it difficult to get anyone to work for them again.

The reverence Shen Village had for the barber was a little over the top. They respected him more than the village head, and more than other artisans like Grandpa. I only found out why when I was in high school. By then, the barber was in his seventies, and his hand shook as it held the razor. Nonetheless, Grandpa and others his age insisted on letting him work on them. Fortunately, nothing ever went awry.

As a young man, the barber had worked at a big monastery on the north side. There was a special name for his job: scripture-bearer. When the monks sallied forth to carry out a ritual, they needed various scripture scrolls and other worship implements. Someone had to carry these, but the monks never did manual labor, so they had to bring in a worker from outside. After he'd been bearing scriptures for more than a year, the abbot noticed that this kid was kind-hearted, good with his hands, and able to put up with harsh conditions—and so he taught him to cut hair. Shaving monks' heads is no easy business, and he was still learning two years later. Before he could complete his training, the Japanese army arrived.

One day, the Communist Party's county committee secretary led a delegation to have a meeting at the monastery. The Japanese got wind of this, and surrounded the building in the middle of the night. The secretary rallied his delegation to break through the siege. Everyone else got away, but the secretary was bringing up the rear, and when he realized he wasn't going to make it, he shot himself.

All the Japanese had to show for their trouble was a dead secretary. In a fury, they dragged all the monks out and demanded the abbot tell them which way the Communists had gone. But how could the abbot possibly know that? After questioning him for some time, they lost patience and bayoneted him to death, then set the monastery on fire. The other monks and handymen were forced to leave with them, carrying ammunition and medicine for the troops.

A few days after that, the Japanese soldiers bivouacked in a large town. What with the chaos of war, they hadn't bathed in several days, so their bodies stank and itched. Now they could finally soak in hot water. Once they were clean, they began thinking how good it would feel to have a trim and a shave. Someone recommended the barber.

Though he wasn't fully trained, the barber was pretty good at his job. The Japanese soldiers gave him a try and were satisfied with his handiwork.

Now that they'd set up camp, the other captives were turned loose. The barber wasn't allowed to leave, though. They needed his skills.

Eventually, even the platoon commander and his deputy were getting groomed by the barber.

One afternoon, the platoon commander sent for the barber. The commander was staying in an old house with a front and back entrance. The soldiers lived in the front portion, while the back was the commander's bedroom and office. The barber had been here quite a few times by this point, and he knew everyone here, not just the commander, having given them all haircuts.

After the commander's shave, he'd always be so relaxed he would lean back in his chair for a snooze. When this happened, you weren't supposed to wake him, but should instead quietly gather your things and tiptoe out.

The commander was sitting in the middle of his office. When he saw the barber, he smiled and offered him a cigarette. The barber accepted it and bowed from the waist by way of thanks. He tucked the cigarette behind his ear for later.

When he was done cutting the commander's hair, the barber dipped a towel in hot water, wrung it out, and gently placed it over the commander's face. Next, he got out his razor and stropped it a couple of times. Removing the towel, he ran the razor along the commander's skin, gliding along gentle as a touch. The commander's eyelids drooped. He took a breath in, and when he breathed out, his whole body slackened with bliss.

The razor passed over his forehead, his nose, his lips, his chin, his throat. A quick slash. The commander didn't make a sound as his blood gushed freely.

The barber gathered his equipment and left, carefully closing the door behind him. Outside, he took the cigarette from behind his ear, asked a soldier for a light, bowed in thanks, and departed.

He made his getaway in a little boat. Probably he'd had his eye on it for some time.

A few days later, the barber arrived back in Shen Village, after many years away. He tied his boat up by the bank and hired someone to build him a thatched hut nearby.

And this is where he passed away, decades later, at the age of seventy-eight.

THE POT-MENDER

AFTER HANGING OVER THE FLAMES for some time, a blackened layer forms on the bottom of a pot. You have to scrape this away on a regular basis, otherwise you'll waste firewood. This was usually a morning job. At the crack of dawn, the shrill sound of metal on metal filled the air. Several families would be doing it at once, generating an almighty racket. You took the pot off the stove, placed it upside down on the ground outside your front door, and ran a metal spatula over it again and again, removing the ashy residue. When you were done and lifted up the pot, a black ring would be left on the ground. At this point, you'd have to put a cross inside this circle. The villagers believed mischievous little imps were attracted by the sound of scraping, though you couldn't see them. They'd wait for you to be done and steal your pot. That night, you'd think your pot was safely in its place on the stove, but actually an imp would have made off with it. He'd find someone walking alone and drop the pot over their head, leaving the hapless pedestrian unable to see a thing, so they'd never find their way home. A cross within the circle was a string tied across the mouth of the pot, rendering it useless to imps—they wouldn't be able to get it over anyone's head now.

In the morning, I'd wake up to the sound of Mom scraping the pot, get out of bed, and go study by the river outside our front door while I waited for her to make breakfast, before heading to school. This racket accompanied me till I left home at the age of eighteen.

Even when I was too young for school, I still scrambled out of bed when I heard Mom scraping the pot, eager to go out and play.

One time, I tried to help Mom, but I used a shovel and put a crack in the bottom of the pot. Dad heard Mom screaming and came running. He was jumping with rage at what he saw, until Grandpa said, "What's the fuss? Just get the pot-mender to fix it when he comes by in a day or two."

YOU COULD HEAR him from a li away, a sharp voice calling, "Pots mended—" Grandpa walked out to the river and shouted just as loudly, "Pot-mender!"

"Coming!"

The pot-mender arrived walking along the river bank, doubled over from the weight of his burden. He was very old, even older than Grandpa. He was a small, scrawny man, but his constitution was good. Placing his bundle under our ginkgo tree, he laid out his tools one by one.

First were the bellows. They had a pipe at one end that connected to the bottom of his coke stove. On the stove was a crucible, into which he placed little metal rods and sheets he'd prepared earlier. The stove wasn't lit yet.

Grandpa brought out our pot.

"Wow, that's quite a crack."

"Fishy's fault, the little menace."

I assisted the pot-mender, handing him tools and holding out coke. My hands got all black, but I didn't mind. I smeared them over my face until all you could see were my eyes blinking in the dark. All the grown-ups burst out laughing at the sight.

The pot-mender picked up the pot and studied it carefully. Only then did he light the fire.

"Just look at your face. All right, help me push the bellows." I did as he asked.

The metal pieces slowly became molten. Holding a small ladle in a pair of long pliers, the pot-mender scooped up a little and swiftly poured it onto the crack and the holes on either side of it. He pressed down on it with some asbestos, and the crack was sealed. There was now a raised scar that had to be smoothed away with coarse sand, then polished with sandpaper. By the time he was done, it was perfectly flat and gleaming.

The pot-mender lived on the north side of the river. There was a causeway in front of his house: a couple of stone arches with slabs across them. For some reason, there were no railings, which is why we called it a causeway rather than a bridge. It wasn't very high and got submerged whenever the river flooded. You had to tread very carefully if you tried to cross at these times.

This causeway, which you could only just about walk across, took several years to build. Shortly after it was completed, the villagers heard music in the night, blaring and banging as if someone were passing by with a celebratory troupe to pick up their bride. When they came outside, though, they didn't see anything out of the ordinary. The noise went on for several nights, until the river surged and the causeway collapsed. They rebuilt it, but the same thing happened. Unsettled by these strange events, the villagers sent for several yin yang masters, but none of them could explain it. Then they heard there was a guy in Dongtai county with yin yang eyes, which meant he could see past and future lives. The clan elders sent him a hefty gift and invited him to the village.

The yin yang master looked around, set up an altar on the riverbank, wrote a charm, and burned it. His eyes rolled back in his head, as he sat cross-legged on his reed cushion. After a pause, he stood up and laughed. "This is a great omen. Who lives by the river? That house over there—whose is it?"

The riverside house belonged to an honest farmer named Fisthead. As his name suggested, he didn't have a single skill and could only earn his living through the honest toil of both hands, working on the land. His wife was six months pregnant.

"Do you know what that blowing and banging is? The advance retinue of him above. You can't build a causeway here—that'll destroy your good fortune. Shen Village is about to bring forth an exceptional individual."

The yin yang master's words sent a wave of excitement through Shen Village. What you have to know is, in the five or six hundred years since the Shen forebears first settled here, we'd produced a few top scholars. From a feng shui perspective, the village is low-lying like the bottom of a pot, on an exceptionally flat piece of land. The villagers were prosperous, but only in a small way—there were no tycoons, and no great personages.

The yin yang master walked around Fisthead's house with his geomancy compass, nodding the whole way. "That's right. The exceptional individual will land in this child's body. When he's grown, he's sure to be as great as a marquis."

Joy descended upon Fisthead as if from the heavens, and he threw a banquet that very night. The clan elders and yin yang master had the table of honor, with both village schoolmasters keeping them company. There was another big table for all the neighbors. Everyone showed up to celebrate with him, and no one mentioned the causeway.

Fisthead was poor, so the other villagers pooled their money to present the yin yang master with a few silver dollars. The master got completely smashed that night. Afterward, Fisthead had to push him home to Dongtai in a wheelbarrow.

Half a month later, the yin yang master had some trouble with his eyes. First they got red and swollen, then tears kept streaming and his vision grew blurry. He gave himself a reading, with alarming results: he'd inadvertently revealed a celestial secret, and his vision might be in peril.

Another couple of weeks later, the yin yang master returned to Shen Village and sought out the clan elders. "You can build your causeway—I've had an idea."

Once again, he set up an altar on the riverbank and placed on it a platter each of beef, pork, and mutton. He then lit some incense, chanted a spell, wrote a charm, burned it, and emptied the platters of meat into the river. He sat back down, removed his straw shoes, took a knife from the pouch at his waist, and sliced the shoes to pieces, screaming the whole time, "Why aren't you leaving?" When he was done, he walked over to the water and flung the shoes in. Then he knelt and scooped up some water to bathe his eyes with.

"It's done." He courteously took his leave, refusing to accept a single cent in payment.

The villagers built the causeway again, and this time it went smoothly. It stayed standing, and they didn't hear drums and gongs and woodwinds in the night. They were overjoyed and proclaimed the yin yang master a true marvel.

Not long after the causeway went up, Fisthead's son was born. Because of the yin yang master's prediction, he was given the name Marquis. The baby came out scrawny and covered in fine down, so everyone called him Little Monkey, rather than using his grand real name.

Little Monkey got to the age of twenty-eight without becoming educated or skilled. All day long, he roamed around idly, or helped his parents with rough farmwork, showing no signs of greatness at all. His family was poor, and his looks unprepossessing—his head was pointy—so he didn't even manage to get a wife. His parents finally gave up their grand hopes for him and got hold of the necessary tools so he could learn to mend pots.

During the year that Little Monkey was learning this trade, his father made some inquiries and realized that the yin yang master of Dongtai might have destroyed his family's fortunes.

The old folk of the village said the yin yang master had revealed a celestial secret, and fearing that his sight would be taken as punishment, he'd thought hard and come up with a way of breaking the curse. He'd returned to Shen Village claiming he wanted to help build the causeway, but actually came to ruin the feng shui. By cutting up his straw shoes, he'd banished the spirits who'd been making noise at night. This allowed him to keep his sight, and Shen Village returned to its placid, mundane existence.

In doing so, he'd made a monkey of the man who should have been a marquis, the pot-mender.

After they'd learned the truth, the pot-mender's parents died one after the other. The pot-mender, who used to go around smiling and laughing, underwent a huge change in personality. Not only did he become a man of very few words, he looked at everyone with the frostiest of gazes. He was always alone now. Luckily for him, he was the only pot-mender in Shen Village, otherwise everyone would have avoided him. The villagers disliked no one more than a person who never smiled.

Because of his perpetual long face, the villagers made up a little rhyme about the pot-mender, which they used to frighten small children:

The Pot-Mender comes after lights off,
Carrying a big sack on his nights off,
He'll snatch kids and sell them right off.

You can tell from this little ditty that people did not think well of the pot-mender—rather like the pot-stealing imps. The more this went on, the more ferocious the pot-mender was with children. All the kids in Shen Village feared him. When someone cried out that the pot-mender was coming their way, kids would scatter and peep out at him from a distance.

I wasn't scared of him, though. It didn't matter how he glared at me, I followed him around everywhere. It wasn't that I was particularly brave, but ever since I was little, my family would joke that I wasn't actually theirs, but had been found on a fishing boat. Hence my nickname, Fishy. I believed them. And then I thought, if the pot-mender snatched me and sold me, that might actually be for the best—perhaps I'd even end up with my real parents. Who can understand what's going on in a child's mind? Anyway, I wasn't frightened. There was nothing the pot-mender could do about it, except offer to take me on as an apprentice. And so I got another nickname: Little Pot-Mender.

This nickname clung to me for many years and brought me all kinds of trouble. I didn't like it. It made me sound dirty and nasty. As a result, I got into plenty of fights with the other children—I punched anyone who called me that.

People stopped calling me Little Pot-Mender after I started high school, which is when the real pot-mender died. After this, Shen Village didn't have a pot-mender. What did people do when their pots broke? I have no idea.

In the early years of the Ming dynasty, Shen Liangsan set out from Changmen in Jiangsu and founded Shen Village on this spot. The old folk say in over six hundred years, the only prominent figure who might have emerged from this place was the pot-mender, if only the yin yang master hadn't ruined his feng shui. It seems near impossible that Shen Village could produce anyone eminent now—only the old and ill are left there, while the young have all gone to the cities for work. Some have brought their elders with them, abandoning their family homes. The Shen Village elementary school has shut down, and its roof has fallen in. The walls will probably collapse too—just give it a couple of years. The whole village now has an aura of defeat. Never mind producing a great personage, the village itself might soon vanish.

No one in Shen Village knew what the pot-mender meant to the village. When he was still alive, thanks to his background, we would mock him behind his back, time and again: "Marquis? Monkey, more like!"

THE SCULPTOR

1.

The *Shijing* speaks of "sharing a carriage with a lady, her face like a hibiscus." The hibiscus is also known as the rose of Sharon.

Rose of Sharon shrubs grew in front of the Earth God Temple, one on either side of the entrance. Beneath the left-hand one was a well, so old there were grooves in its stone wall, worn through by countless ropes. From the distant village came the faint sound of a cock crowing, as dawn tinged the sky. With a creak, the temple door opened. The sculptor emerged with a wooden basin. He went to the well and drew some water to wash his face, then looked up to see the budding roses of Sharon. Now he remembered it was the first day of summer.

After breakfast, the sculptor braided a streamer out of silk strings in five colors, and draped it from the branches of the shrub on the right. This streamer was known as a long-life thread, and you were supposed to tie it around the arm of the person you loved on the first day of summer. The sculptor was twenty-six years old and lived alone in the Earth God Temple. To mark the beginning of summer, the villagers would come here in the afternoon to pay their respects. He swept the temple hall clean and dampened the courtyard soil. Next, he fetched the statues of the Earth God and Earth Goddess and placed them on a table in the yard, then carefully wiped them down with a clean cloth. Both of these figures were freshly carved from oak wood, with craftsmanship so exquisite you could make out every strand of their eyebrows. As he worked, he heard a voice calling from the other side of the wall, "Sculptor, do you have any dried chrysanthemums?"

It was the carpenter. "Yes, here," he replied. He carried the figures into the temple and set them down on the altar, then went into the western chamber for a carved wooden box. He lifted the lid and offered it to the carpenter.

"Help yourself, take more," he urged hospitably. The carpenter only took a small handful, which he placed in a lotus leaf he'd grabbed on the way here, from the East Shan River. "I don't need much," he said, "it's just for the symbolism."

The carpenter was planning to burn the chrysanthemums. If you scattered chrysanthemum ash on your wheat stacks on the first day of summer, your wheat wouldn't get infested.

"Carpenter, don't let the chrysanthemum ash drift into the East Shan River."

"I know." As the carpenter left, he caught sight of the long-life thread in the rose of Sharon bush.

2.

The carpenter was my grandfather, Shen Tongshou. He died at the age of eighty-three. If he were still alive, he would be a hundred this year.

When Grandpa told me about the sculptor tying the long-life thread to the rose of Sharon shrub, I asked, "Was there a Mrs. Sculptor?" Grandpa replied, "He didn't want one." "Why not?" "He just didn't." "So why did he tie the thread to the tree?" Grandpa said, "You're still a child, you wouldn't understand. I'll explain it to you when you're grown." I said, "Why wouldn't I understand? I bet I would. I'm ten, you know." Grandpa turned away, ignoring me, concentrating on the knife in his hand as he continued whittling Grandma's memorial tablet. It had been several months since Grandma passed, but he was still carving her tablet, adding more and more attractive decorative details.

Now that I knew about the sculptor hanging a long-life thread from the rose of Sharon shrub, I went to the Earth God Temple for a look at the start of every summer, and it was there each time. On a table beneath the branches would be a bucket of cool peppermint water. I'd scoop some up in the wooden ladle, drink it, and kowtow to the Earth God. You couldn't go to pay your respects empty-handed, you had to bring some rice stalks from your family's fields, which you placed reverentially on the altar. The Earth God and Earth Goddess both looked delighted. As I kowtowed, the sculptor stood to one side, hands clasped to acknowledge the kowtow. He was thin and not particularly tall, and a smile seemed perpetually on the verge of appearing on his face. When I was done kowtowing, he would always say, "Don't allow the chrysanthemum ash to drift into the East Shan River." And I'd reply, "I know, Ol' Sculptor. If the chrysanthemum ash falls into the river, the frogs will stop croaking, and if that happens, we'll have a poor harvest." The sculptor would smile, but the following year, he'd remind me again, as if the Earth God was making him say it.

3.

The sculptor had fought in the Korean War. He had nowhere to live when he got back, so the village head arranged for him to stay at the dilapidated Earth God Temple, which was missing its Earth God and Goddess. The village head told Grandpa to lead a team there and refurbish the place.

The sculptor had been away with the army for six years. The day he returned to the village, he went straight to Qinxiu's home.

The East Shan River flows from south to north, cutting the village in two. There was a little wooden bridge across it, and Qinxiu's house was on the east side. You walked across the bridge, and there it was on your left, the one with a large mulberry tree by its front door.

Qinxiu's husband was gone, leaving just her and her father-in-law, the paper craftsman. The sculptor was there because of Wellwater, whom he'd gone to war with. Now the sculptor had returned, but Wellwater hadn't. He'd died on Triangle Hill in Korea.

The sculptor's two older brothers were both married. Being a bachelor, he'd learned the trade of sculpting. The person in charge of recruiting troops was the village's fanshen leader, Blacksmith Cao. "Fanshen leader" was a new term—it meant leading the poor people to fanshen, or roll over, and take charge. The blacksmith came to the sculptor and said, "If you join up, there'll be monthly rations—that's far more than you'll ever get as a sculptor." And so the sculptor agreed. His two other brothers took turns hosting three days of banquets for him.

As for Wellwater, he was the fourth son in his family. He'd studied at the village schoolhouse for three years and had a very logical mind. He honored his parents as he should and was also very respectful of his three older brothers. Whenever anyone asked him for help, he'd agree right away—just call for him and he'd be there. So there shouldn't have been any trouble recruiting him, yet when Blacksmith Cao asked, he refused point-blank. His parents sobbed each day as they tried to persuade Wellwater. His three older brothers all had families, they said, what if something happened to them? What would become of their widows and fatherless children? Wellwater wept too, but wouldn't say anything.

On the day the army was due to leave, the blacksmith and his men searched everywhere, but they couldn't find Wellwater. The blacksmith flung the army uniform at Wellwater's father and said, "Being a soldier is a glorious business, but your family seems to treat it like a hot potato. Wellwater's name is on the list, and there's nothing I can do about that."

Wellwater was hiding in Qinxiu's home.

Qinxiu's husband had died the year before. She was from a wealthy family and had skin like snow and a melon-seed face. She smiled when she saw you and looked like she wanted to speak but was too shy. After he'd married her, her husband treated her like a precious pearl and never let her do a moment's work in the fields. Then he died and the villagers said it was her fault for being too beautiful—her husband was weak and she'd made him over-exert himself every night, shortening his life.

Wellwater lost his soul at Qinxiu's wedding banquet. In the two years after that, his parents found him five prospective brides, but he turned them all away.

Wellwater's trade was cotton milling. The winter after Qinxiu's marriage, her husband hired him to make them two new quilts. Wellwater's work on these was exceptionally fine, and Qinxiu could tell they were special. Eight pounds of cotton went into each quilt, and Wellwater made sure there wasn't the smallest imperfection on a single tuft. His bow was so taut it sang, harmonious as a stringed instrument. When he spread the quilts in their living room, fine cotton fibers danced through the air like flowers. Qinxiu came out to pour tea, but when she noticed the gleam in Wellwater's eye, she hid in the bridal chamber and didn't dare to show herself again. Even so, she could hear the zing of his bow.

The next time Wellwater saw Qinxiu was a full year later, again in the winter, after her husband's death. His body was laid out in their living room, and Wellwater had come to give his condolences. Qinxiu was in a white silk mourning dress, her face streaked with tears. Wellwater felt a twinge in his heart when he looked at her, as if he might start sobbing too. But when he got home and lay in bed, wrapped in his quilt, it was joy that filled his mind.

The only person who knew about Wellwater's infatuation was his second brother, an honest man who barely spoke a sentence or two each day—he mostly kept his head down and worked. Now he said to their father, "I'm afraid Wellwater is hiding in Qinxiu's house."

Their father went and dragged Wellwater out. Wellwater clung to the mulberry tree in the courtyard, howling so loudly neighbors came from all around. The blacksmith stood to one side, uncertain what to say. He thought he would wait for Wellwater to cry himself dry, then they could get going. The sun was beginning its descent, and still Wellwater had his arms wrapped around the tree.

The sculptor was already dressed neatly in his uniform. The neighbors admired his clean-cut appearance, and someone offered him a water-pipe. The sculptor was shocked to find out what had been going on between Wellwater and Qinxiu. So the cotton miller had taken advantage of the village head and others? He couldn't help mentally hurling a few choice epithets at Wellwater.

All of a sudden, Qinxiu flung open her front door and hurried out to embrace Wellwater—but her arm stopped in mid-air. Instead, she dabbed at his tears with the back of her hand and murmured, "Go, I'll wait for you." With that, she went back in, and the door slammed shut behind her.

4.

In the six years the sculptor and Wellwater were gone with the army, no one in the village heard a word from them. It was only when the sculptor returned that they found out about Wellwater's death.

The sculptor went to Qinxiu's house. Many people watched as he crossed East Shan River, creaking his way across the wooden bridge, in his faded army uniform. He told Qinxiu, "Wellwater is dead," and she fainted. He had to pinch her philtrum to revive her.

A few days later, the sculptor returned to tell Qinxiu how Wellwater died. It was dark when he showed up. The dog barked wildly at him, and no one came out to shut it up.

The sculptor took his courage in his hands and went inside. The first thing he saw was an array of paper goods scattered across the floor, people and horses, houses and furniture, some finished and others half-formed. Qinxiu's father-in-law was the only paper craftsman for miles around. The eight immortals table was covered in his tools: knives, scissors, glue, and all manner of paper. In the center of the table was a shaded lamp, very bright. The paper craftsman sat at the table facing west, not looking up from his work. Every now and then, he took a swig from the liquor bottle—just drink, no food. Qinxiu sat across from him. Her head was down, and she was slumped back in her chair, as if someone had removed all her bones. The sculptor sat at the table with his back to the door, facing the north wall.

An altar stood against this wall, and on it were the memorial tablets of the dead, an incense burner, and candle holders. On the limewashed wall was an enormous portrait of Mao Zedong. So really, the whole time, the sculptor was speaking to Chairman Mao.

5.

The shelling had only just stopped, after going on all day. The sculptor reached his position with his squad leader, who was Wellwater—he'd gotten promoted not long after they reached Korea. From this vantage point, they couldn't see a single living person. The squad leader told the men to split up. Probably out of nervousness, the sculptor undid his flies and pissed at a smoldering tree, thinking he could put out the embers. Suddenly, he felt a chill. When he looked around, there was a rifle pointing at him. He froze, hands still holding up his trousers.

The person holding the rifle, an injured soldier, realized he was on the same side as the sculptor and let his eyes drift shut again. He let out a moan and lowered the rifle.

"Squad Leader!" the sculptor shouted, and Wellwater came running. He ripped open the soldier's blood-soaked coat and bandaged him. The sculptor took the rifle from his hands and opened it, only to find it wasn't loaded. He turned and spat hard on an empty piece of ground.

"Bring him back down," said Wellwater, waving at the sculptor.

The sun began to set as the sculptor carried the injured soldier down the hill.

The sculptor walked fast, stumbling a little, but the injured man on his back kept screaming from being jolted. So he slowed down and said, "Stop shouting, comrade. If you attract the enemy, we'll be done for." The soldier did his best to be quiet.

It got dark, and the enemy shelling started again. The sculptor started to worry. He'd walked half the night and rested eight times, but there was no sign of the hospital. It was as if someone had put a spell on him. His legs began to wobble, and he had no choice but to stop and sit by the side of the road. "Comrade," he said to the injured soldier. "Just hold on a bit longer, we're almost at the hospital." Afraid the soldier would freeze to death, he took off his coat and covered the other man with it. The soldier was exhausted too and didn't even have the energy to grunt in response.

When the first light appeared in the sky, the sculptor saw the hospital in a dip just five hundred meters away. "There we go!" he shouted, lifted the injured soldier on his back, and started running.

At the hospital entrance, he put the soldier on a stretcher and shouted for help. A youngish doctor appeared, but as soon as he touched the soldier, he looked up at the sculptor and said, "He's been dead for some time. What did you bring him here for?" The sculptor's face turned stark white in an instant, and he muttered, "I'll just go, then."

"Catch your breath first, have something to eat." The doctor gestured, and two female soldiers carried the stretcher away.

The sculptor had a couple of bowls of congee, and having regained his energy, he jogged back. What would he say to Wellwater? He'd spent all night getting an injured soldier to the hospital, but the guy died on him anyway.

Back at the front, he stood there stunned. The tree he'd pissed on the previous evening was still smoldering. He looked downhill, and the entire squad were splayed across the ground.

They must have run out of ammunition and gotten bayoneted by the enemy. Some had gaping holes in their backs, with more corpses piled beneath them. Others had been peppered with bullets before getting close enough to engage. He searched, but couldn't find Wellwater.

Then right at the bottom of the hill, there he was. All that was left of him were his head and shoulders. Around him were enemy corpses. Wellwater had pulled the pin from a grenade and flung himself into an enemy cluster just before it exploded.

The sculptor carried Wellwater's head back to their trench. After searching for a while, he managed to find a couple of grenades in the hands of late comrades, who'd died before they could pull the pins. There wasn't any ammunition left. He sat in the trench, back to the wall, the rings of the grenade pins around his fingers, and waited for the enemy to come. Then the gunfire stopped, and the shelling stopped, and there wasn't a sound to be heard.

6.

The sculptor returned alive.

He went to Qinxiu's house every day. Word was that Qinxiu had asked him to come—she wanted to hear all about Wellwater. He ate dinner there every evening. Qinxiu's father-in-law put up with this for a few days, but finally flew off the handle. "A grown man like you, coming round to our house at the drop of a hat—what do you think that looks like?" The sculptor knew he was fond of a tipple, so he used his demob money to buy him some booze. Now that the paper craftsman had a drink in his hand, he stopped complaining and sometimes even shouted at the dog to be quiet when it barked at the sculptor.

Qinxiu worked in the pig shed, helping the bamboo-weaver take care of the pigs and cattle. The sculptor worked on the land with the other commune laborers, so he never bumped into her. Only in the evening, when they were both done with work, did he come by for an after-dinner chat about Wellwater. Because Wellwater had saved his life, he felt he had to take good care of Qinxiu. Wellwater had talked about her every single day. During their years together in the army, whenever there was a spare moment, Wellwater would bring up Qinxiu.

The sculptor now knew as much about Qinxiu as Wellwater had. After getting to Korea, Wellwater seemed to know there was no way he'd return alive, so he took every opportunity to tell the sculptor about her. How he'd hidden under her window, singing. How he'd accompanied her part of the way when she went home to see her parents. How he used to buy all kinds of delicious things and leave them on her windowsill when she wasn't looking. How even her dog had grown fond of him, so he only had to pat it on the head for its tail to wag with joy. The story continued until he finally got to enter Qinxiu's bedroom. Wellwater dredged up every detail he could remember and passed it on to the sculptor. The sculptor listened attentively and afterward stared distractedly into space. Wellwater would smack him and say, "Hey, dog-fucker, you're going to die in this place too."

Whenever it heard someone creaking across the bridge, Qinxiu's dog would run out and bark, but if the visitor turned out to be the sculptor, it would wag its tail and run ahead of him as if guiding the way. At the doorway, it would crouch and gaze up at the sculptor. The door would be ajar, with light seeping out from inside. The sculptor would bend down to give the dog a pat on the head, then he'd gently push the door open and go in. Qinxiu and the paper craftsman would be sitting across from each other at the table. They'd glance up at the sculptor and then go back to what they were doing.

The paper craftsman took swigs of liquor as he glued his paper furniture together. Papercraft was just a hobby at this point—no one hired him anymore. When someone died, they just burned a bit of hell money and called it a day, not like before, when you had to get paper houses, paper beds, paper stoves, paper furniture. Life was now so hard for the living, they didn't have time to care for the dead.

Qinxiu was stitching shoe soles as she listened to the sculptor speaking to Chairman Mao. Now and then, she'd shoot him a fleeting look. In this brief glimpse, the sculptor saw the flicker of a smile in her eyes, and he was satisfied. After sitting there awhile longer, he'd return to the Earth God Temple where he lived, his heart full of joy.

7.

Naturally, the sculptor didn't let on to Qinxiu how much he knew about her and her late paramour. Wellwater had told him more than once about virtually every moment he'd spent with her. By the end, the sculptor had no idea which stories were true, and which were just Wellwater getting carried away with bragging.

The sculptor only talked to Qinxiu about Wellwater's time in the army. She didn't like to hear about the fighting, but enjoyed stories of the men joking and horsing around. Later on, the sculptor told Qinxiu about how Wellwater had tried to desert.

The sculptor and Wellwater had been brought to Qintong and enrolled in the same squad of the New Fourth Army. The squad leader had been the fan-shen leader in one of the villages on the Lixia River. When the New Fourth Army headed north, he was afraid he would get killed by reactionaries if he stayed in the village, so he fled north with the troops. When he returned, he was made the squad leader. He was tall and slender, and his hips wiggled like a woman's when he walked. Although his voice was strident, he wasn't fierce, but frequently wore a warm smile. The squad leader led four new recruits and some press-ganged civilians to deliver rations to the front line. As they traveled, he showed the recruits how to use their rifles. They didn't do it for real, just went through the motions—they didn't have gunpowder to waste, so it was fine as long as everyone understood the theory.

They reached a river and had to wait for the ferry. Then an enemy plane passed overhead and started dropping bombs, later strafing them with a machine gun. The squad leader shouted, "Hit the ground!" And everyone flung themselves facedown.

The sculptor and Wellwater stayed on the ground for a very long time. When they couldn't hear a single sound, they climbed to their feet. There was no one in sight. Several of their carts had caught fire and were still burning. The squad leader was dead—he was lying faceup, eyes staring. Next to them, gibbering in fear, was one of the recruits who'd joined up at the same time as them. The fourth recruit was nowhere to be seen—he'd fled. The civilians were gone too. Those who hadn't managed to escape were on the ground, dead.

"Now what? We might as well go back," said the sculptor. The sight of all these corpses had frightened him. "They'll shoot us if we don't reach the front."

Wellwater said, "If we go back now, they'll shoot us anyway."

The two of them were caught in Supang Village. A captain with a Mauser pistol knew at a glance that they were deserters: despite being dressed in civvies, they were still wearing their puttees and didn't have travel permits. The captain summoned a couple of conscripts, who tied their hands behind their backs. Wellwater said, "We're on the same side—we're New Fourth Army too." The captain kicked him. "Despicable! If you were Nationalists, at least we could liberate you, and then you could join us." He gestured to the conscripts. "Lock them up. Tomorrow they'll face the firing squad."

The sculptor and Wellwater were locked up in a warehouse piled high with farming tools. They sat with their backs to the wall. The door was locked, and a civilian conscript sat on a stool outside, smoking a gurgling water-pipe.

Neither man spoke. In the middle of the night, Wellwater began choking and sobbing.

"Hey, are you thinking about Qinxiu?" said the sculptor.

Wellwater said nothing, just sobbed. The guard opened the door and came in, shining a lantern at them. When he saw the tears on Wellwater's face, he went back out without saying anything, shutting the door behind him.

No longer crying, Wellwater sagged heavily back against the wall and sighed. Then, abruptly, he jerked upright, leaned over to the sculptor, and whispered, "It's an earth wall. Help untie me."

Wellwater and the sculptor dug a hole in the wall with a shovel blade and escaped.

In the wilderness a good distance from the village, they got into an argument. Wellwater wanted to go home no matter what, while the sculptor wanted to find their squad. Either choice was fraught with danger. The sculptor said, "If we go home, for all we know the village head will deliver us straight to the firing squad." Wellwater said, "I'm just going to sneak back in for a short while, and then I'll escape far, far away. I'm sure I'll find somewhere to hide myself." The sculptor said, "That's nice for you, the two of you will be able to live in bliss. But what's in it for me? I'm not going back." Wellwater stared into space for a while. In the end, he decided to go with the sculptor.

After a day's travel, they caught up with the supply team. Luckily, three or four of the civilian laborers could vouch for them. The new squad leader didn't ask too many questions. All he said was, "New recruits?" They nodded. The two older soldiers next to him sniggered.

Wellwater got injured after they'd crossed the Yangtze River.

When they sounded the charge, Wellwater advanced with the rest of the men. Bullets zipped wildly through the air like locusts. All of a sudden, he heard someone shouting, "Comrade, they got you!" He stopped and touched his leg; his hand came up red. He wobbled and crashed to the ground. Five or six soldiers rushed over to carry him. The platoon commander shouted, "Two fuckers can take him. The rest of you, keep going!"

The sculptor went to see him in the hospital. Wellwater's face was radiant. "My leg's busted. I can't walk." The sculptor glared at him. "What's so great about your leg being busted? You think Qinxiu will want a cripple?" Wellwater just chuckled.

During a break in the fighting, the platoon commander came from the front line to the hospital, to fetch Wellwater and the other injured soldiers. Wellwater came out moving awkwardly on his crutches. The commander was in the small hospital courtyard, under a ginkgo tree that looked at least a hundred years old. Leaning on his crutches, Wellwater half-stretched out a hand for him to shake. "I'm really going to miss you all, Commander." Only when the commander took his hand did Wellwater notice how dark his face was. The commander grabbed one of his crutches and flung it away. Wellwater lost his balance, stumbled a couple of steps to one side, and landed clumsily on the ground. The commander took the other crutch from his side and hit him viciously with it. "You're faking! I knew you were faking!"

Wellwater tried to desert three more times after that. Twice, the sculptor caught up with him and persuaded him to return. The third time, they nabbed him before he even got out, because the sculptor had reported him. This was for his own good. If he'd actually managed to desert, they'd have caught him and shot him dead. Even if he made it all the way back to Shen Village, they'd have sent him back because he didn't have discharge papers. The sculptor couldn't stand by and do nothing.

When they arrived in Korea, Wellwater truly lost hope. Now he became friends with the sculptor again, letting go of his grudges from before. He fought without fear for his life, and said to the sculptor, "Let's die here together."

The sculptor believed that he would die in Korea too. Yet, even at the very end, he didn't tell Wellwater what was in his heart. How could he? There was no way to get the words out. Time after time, he stopped Wellwater from deserting. He said it was to keep him from the firing squad, but that wasn't the only reason. He simply didn't want Wellwater to get back to the village. When did he start feeling this way? If he thought about it carefully, it was probably when Qinxiu came running from her house, embraced Wellwater under the mulberry tree, and murmured, "I'll wait for you."

Now Wellwater was dead, and that feeling was nightmarishly tormenting the sculptor. He kept telling himself he had to take good care of Qinxiu, for Wellwater's sake.

8.

It was no longer possible for the sculptor to take care of Qinxiu on Wellwater's behalf.

The sculptor was still visiting every day, but hadn't brought the paper craftsman any booze for almost two weeks. The paper craftsman said nothing, but he knew the sculptor's demob money had run out, and he was just another poor bastard again. Besides, rumors were running rampant in the village.

On the last day of the year, the sculptor visited with a couple of fish. Entering the courtyard, he came face-to-face with Qinxiu holding a little basket of quicklime, which she was sprinkling in a white circle on the ground. This was known as "hitting the grain store," and represented an abundance of staples, so much you had to fill granary after granary. You did this on the last evening of the year. When she saw the sculptor, Qinxiu straightened and came toward him smiling.

"Have you had your dinner?"

"Yes." By moonlight, Qinxiu's face looked like a painting, mesmerizing. She smiled gently, took the fish from his hand, and said, "Come in and have a seat."

The paper craftsman was on the bench where the sculptor usually sat, facing outward, puffing on a water-pipe. When the sculptor came in, the paper craftsman looked up at him, took a pinch of golden tobacco leaves from his box, pressed it into the bowl of the pipe, lit it with a smoldering hemp stalk, took a breath that gurgled through the water, and expelled a long stream of smoke through his nostrils. Then he blew lightly, and with a small thud, the ashes in the bowl leaped out onto the floor. "You should stop coming here after the New Year. You care about your reputation too. You can't have people gossiping behind your back."

The sculptor flushed bright red, and for a while he couldn't speak. Qinxiu had been about to bring the fish into the kitchen, but when she heard the paper craftsman's words, she flung them to the ground, flounced into her room, and slammed the door shut.

The fish were flopping around on the floor, though they couldn't get very far as their mouths had been tied together with straw. The paper craftsman picked them up and handed them back to the sculptor. "We're all in the same small village. You'll be right there under people's noses. Don't make me say any more than that."

The sculptor took the fish. When he got to the East Shan River, he turned back and looked at Qinxiu's window, which was lit up. Someone was standing there. The sculptor walked along the bank until he was right across from the window. The fish in his hand kept writhing, and his eyes remained fixed on the backlit silhouette.

The light went out, and like the house, the window became no more than a vague outline in the dark. The sculptor headed back across the bridge, which creaked under him. When he got to the middle, he turned back, and once again there was a light in Qinxiu's window, just for a moment, before it winked out again. The sculptor stood on the bridge. After some time, he untied the straw and dropped the two fish into the river, then he stumbled back to the Earth God Temple.

A month into the new year, all the men in the village went off to work at the Guma River irrigation project.

It was spring now. The workers stripped off their padded clothes and worked in light shirts and trousers. Only the sculptor insisted on keeping on his army greatcoat, which was so filthy you could hardly bear to look at it. Everyone was making fun of him behind his back, because of that coat.

Ever since the sculptor came back, he'd worn that greatcoat as it slowly changed color from khaki to black. My grandfather the carpenter, who talked to him more than anyone else, couldn't resist saying, "Sculptor, it's such a warm day. Why do you still have your coat on?"

The sculptor led Grandpa into the shed, where they could talk without being overheard. "I can't help it, Carpenter. Ever since coming back, I haven't bought a single thing for myself." He unbuttoned his coat; under it, he wore only a tattered pair of shorts. Taken aback, Grandpa said nothing. When he got home that evening, he had a pair of his own trousers and an undershirt of my uncle's sent over to the sculptor.

The next day, the sculptor left off his coat and came to the site in his undershirt. He carried two full baskets of earth from the river bottom up onto the bank, chanting as vigorously as everyone else as they worked.

That night, the sculptor had a deep conversation with Grandpa.

The sculptor said, "Wellwater saved my life. I want to treat Qinxiu well to pay him back, but the paper craftsman won't let me set foot in their home."

Grandpa said, "Forget it, then. Does she even need your help?"

"But then I'll be letting Wellwater down."

"What can you do for her? You have no money, all you have is strength. What good is strength? I think you'd better think about what's going to become of you."

The sculptor sighed. "I'm a useless person."

Grandpa heard the sculptor sigh like this almost every night and knew what he was thinking—but these thoughts could never be spoken out loud.

Before the Guma River project ended, news arrived that Qinxiu had suddenly taken ill and died.

9.

Qinxiu was laid out in her living room in an old-fashioned funeral outfit made of coarse, crimson fabric. On her head was a round black hat with a soft brim, in which was tucked a piece of yellow paper that covered her face. This was meant to symbolize that she was too ashamed to see anyone. A strange custom—apparently it originated with King Fuchai of Wu.

The sculptor shed tears, but couldn't sob loudly. Instead, he kowtowed three times by her head, burned a couple of handfuls of ghost money in the pot on the ground, and left.

Qinxiu was cremated the next day. After what had happened with Wellwater, she was unchaste, and the paper merchant refused to have her ashes in the house. Instead, they were scattered in the East Shan River.

The sculptor sat on the riverbank that whole night. Some night owls said hello as they passed by, but he ignored them. He looked as if he was in shock.

10.

The sculptor came to borrow Grandpa's carpentry tools: ax, chisel, utility knife, file. He'd lost his own set long ago. Grandpa asked what he was planning to make. The sculptor said, "I live at the Earth God Temple, but the Earth God's missing, and it's hard to feel at peace. I want to make an Earth God to worship." Grandpa said, "That's a good idea. It's been years since we honored the Earth God, no wonder harvests have been so bad. Make sure you do a good job." Grandpa brought out a piece of oak he'd been holding on to. "This is excellent wood. Hard to work with, though. They say oak is hard as steel. But that's exactly right for the Earth God."

The sculptor thanked Grandpa and left. He spent the next few months working on this.

First he made the Earth Goddess. Everyone who saw her said she was wonderful. Who'd have thought that after all these years, the sculptor's skills would be just as sharp as ever?

The Earth God Temple was on an overgrown slope to the west, separated from the village by a mulberry forest. The sculptor lived there all alone, and when he had nothing better to do, he worked on the Earth Goddess, whom he modeled on Qinxiu—although she was smiling, which Qinxiu had rarely done. Besides, her clothes and hair were in the ancient style, so unless you looked closely, you probably wouldn't notice the secret of her origins. Grandpa knew, though. When the sculptor finished, Grandpa said, "She looks familiar." The sculptor said, "Don't tell anyone, Carpenter. Once she's painted, no one will be able to tell." Grandpa said, "I won't breathe a word." Then he added, "It's a good thing, I guess."

"Why did he have to scatter her ashes in the river? She's dead, let her rest in peace in the earth. He could have buried her. Why feed her to the fish?" the sculptor blurted out to Grandpa one day.

"He had to, what else could he have done? The paper merchant couldn't have let her into the ancestral grave, not after what happened with Wellwater. And if she were buried somewhere else, she'd have ended up as a wandering ghost, which also isn't ideal. Might as well scatter her in the river."

"Now her soul doesn't even have anywhere to rest."

Grandpa and the sculptor had been sitting at the doorway of the Earth God Temple as they chatted. Now Grandpa glanced at the altar where the Earth Goddess stood, still unpainted.

Having finished the Earth Goddess, the sculptor turned to the Earth God. Naturally, his likeness was modeled on Wellwater.

"Carpenter, do you remember what Wellwater looked like?"

"Yes."

In this matter, the sculptor hid nothing from Grandpa. And right up to his death, Grandpa helped him keep the secret—the only person he told was my father. Grandpa said both these people were wandering spirits, a tough existence. Now the sculptor had given them a resting place, which was good.

11.

After the Dragon Boat Festival this year, Dad came to visit me in Nanjing with a basket of dumplings that Mom had made.

The next morning, I got up to find him in the living room, where he'd clearly been sitting for a while. On the table was a white porcelain platter with three cooked dumplings on it.

"Are these still wrapped in East Shan River bamboo leaves?" I pulled one open, revealing snowy white glutinous rice.

"Yes, the same. And look at the string they're tied with—that's not the plastic stuff you people get in the city, it's young bamboo leaves from the grove behind our house. I can't eat dumplings with that artificial plastic taste."

I looked at the leaf wrappers I'd discarded on the table. "When I was little, us kids always got sent to pick these bamboo leaves. We'd take the opportunity to play in the East Shan River, catching freshwater clams and river snails."

"I'm the one who picks them now, and your mom wraps them. Right now, her dumplings are the neatest in the whole village."

I nodded in agreement. I hadn't seen my mother making dumplings for many years now. The wrapping usually happened one afternoon before the Dragon Boat Festival. She would sit on a low stool in the doorway, next to a low water-filled wooden basin in which bamboo leaves had been soaking for some time. Beside the basin would be a bamboo container filled to the brim with glutinous rice. Like a magic trick, Mom would turn each bamboo leaf into a cone, scoop some rice into it with a little wooden ladle, tamp it down, then finish the wrapping and tying. I remember most clearly how she'd bring the finished dumpling to her mouth, and with one end of the string between her teeth, pull hard on the other end so a sturdy pyramid with clearly defined points would appear, just like that.

I ate a whole dumpling as I recalled this image, and soon the kettle had boiled. I got up and made us both a cup of white tea, then leaned back on the couch. We didn't speak for a while, just stared at the pale tea leaves drifting upright in the glass.

My father said simply, "The sculptor is dead."

12.

The day before Dragon Boat Festival, the sculptor drowned while picking bamboo leaves by the East Shan River.

His ancestral tablet is in the Earth God Temple.

The spring the sculptor turned twenty-six, Qinxiu died at the age of twenty-five, and her ashes were scattered in the East Shan River. At the age of eighty-three, the sculptor died in the same river. He'd been alone all his life and left no family. The village elders took care of things. He was cremated the same day, and his ashes were placed in a box he'd made himself. For the last twenty-odd years of his life, he'd supported himself by making these funeral containers. Why had he chosen this line of work? Perhaps only Dad and Grandpa knew the answer to that. He'd spent his life dwelling on Qinxiu not having a resting place. Her ashes shouldn't have been scattered in the river, he thought. They ought to have been placed in a box and buried. And so he spent the last two decades of his life making these boxes. At the time of his death, there was a pile of them stacked up against the wall of the Earth God Temple's main hall, some finished, others not. The elders chose the best one, which had flowers carved on its lid. They burned the others.

The box containing the sculptor's ashes was placed on the altar in the middle of the temple, in front of the Earth God and Earth Goddess, with candles and incense. In front of it was a low table on which the villagers could place their offerings: there was meat and fish, but most left dumplings.

Everyone who came to pay their respects, whether old or young, knelt on the reed cushion in front of the table and kowtowed thrice to the sculptor's box. No one was there to acknowledge them. The sculptor had spent his life alone. Getting up after this, the first thing they saw was the gently smiling couple. The Earth God and Goddess had been carved when the sculptor was in his twenties, and by now they'd been sitting here smiling for almost sixty years.

Now that the sculptor was dead, his dwelling could be turned back into an actual Earth God Temple. After some discussion, the village elders decided the box of remains couldn't live there permanently, otherwise the villagers would end up inadvertently praying to the sculptor as well as the Earth God—which wouldn't be appropriate.

"It would be best to let him rest in the earth. We'll find a place in the courtyard to bury him."

By now, the sculptor's only true friend, my grandfather the carpenter, had been dead for many years. Before he passed, he'd told my father these stories from the past, and now my father suggested burying the ashes under the rose of Sharon.

13.

"Do you still remember those rose of Sharon bushes?" asked my father. I nodded.

"And you remember how on the first day of summer each year, the sculptor would put a long-life thread on one of them?"

I nodded again. We both fell into a moment of silence.

"Do you remember the temple's Earth God?" my father said. I sensed he wanted to tell me something, so I answered, "Yes, I remember. He was always smiling."

"Did you notice anything unusual about him?"

"Wasn't he modeled on Wellwater? The sculptor told Grandpa that, right? And no one else in the village knows?"

"No," said my father. He was still holding his cup of tea, but hadn't drunk any.

"The sculptor meant for the figure to look like Wellwater. But when he was done, your grandfather and the sculptor both realized that the Earth God statue didn't resemble Wellwater at all," said my father. "It looked like the sculptor himself."

THE GARDENER

1.

I was the one who brought the gardener to the city. His name was Rufa, and he'd been in elementary school with me. Each morning, I'd pass his home on the way to school. He wasn't the gardener back then, but the gardener's son. Their family had a huge courtyard whose walls were covered with blooming roses in spring. The bamboo gate stood perpetually open, and when I got there each morning, I'd shout, "Rufa, it's time for school!" while sticking my head in to admire the flora. Rufa's home was like something from a fairy tale. Thanks to him, I learned to identify a few dozen plant species.

Every time I shouted for him, Rufa came running. His hands were often stained with soil that he hadn't had time to wash off. He helped his dad with the gardening. Not far off was a little stream, where he cleaned his hands carefully, making sure to get all the dirt out from between his fingers. His dad had had him relatively late in life and treated him like a little treasure. A braid dangled from his head, to signify he was the lone shoot of his family. Our classmates frequently teased him for this, and would tug at it when we were horsing around. When he was ten, the gardener threw a banquet and finally cut off the braid. I breathed a sigh of relief when that happened.

By the time I graduated from high school and left the village, Rufa had already been a gardener for three years. He gave me a crabapple tree. When I returned twenty years later, that tree was more than two meters tall.

Rufa paid me a visit.

"Fishy, the gardener's here to see you."

As my mother spoke, Rufa appeared at our front door. He wanted me to help find him a job in the city. He had no children, his wife had just died, and he didn't want to stay in the village any longer. A bit of distance would be good, as long as he could support himself.

2.

In the blink of an eye, the gardener had been working at a university in Nanjing for five years. Everyone liked him. He was a simple, cheerful soul, with a smile for everyone. He was good at his job too, and all the plants in the sizable campus flourished.

Sometimes I'd drop in to see him if I was passing by. He lived in a small house at the bottom of the hill. Despite its size, there were plants everywhere, inside and out. No matter when I showed up, it felt full of life. Before I left, he'd present me with a pot of something: lantanas or jonquils, a serpent tree or pistacia.

Then the day came when I visited and saw right away that something was wrong.

3.

The gardener hadn't slept well for several days now. He'd gone to bed early the night before, but in the middle of the night, he'd felt a stabbing pain in his heart that jolted him awake. He sat up and drank a glass of water. He felt the sharp object pull out, leaving a wound that made it hard to move. Sitting on the edge of his bed, he gently pressed on his chest and breathed slowly. The pain gradually faded into a pervasive sense of discomfort.

It was the small hours of the morning, but he wasn't sleepy at all.

This was the third such terrifying event. After the second time, the gardener began to fear he would die suddenly. He went to the municipal hospital, where a doctor asked him a lot of questions, listened to his chest through a stethoscope, and sent him for an EKG before saying, "You're okay. A touch of autonomic nervous system dysfunction, but that's no big deal. Try to relax and you'll probably be fine." Even without a firm diagnosis, the doctor prescribed him quite a lot of medicine and wanted him to wear a gadget on his back for twenty-four hours to measure something or other. The gardener got the pills, but refused to put on the device.

After a couple of days on the meds, he began to feel dizzy. When he read the labels carefully, he realized they all had fairly severe side effects. They say medicine is three parts poison, especially the Western variety, and it was hitting him hard. Feeling anxious, the gardener made the decision to stop taking the pills. Sure enough, the dizziness stopped, and his appetite improved a great deal, though a faint, persistent discomfort lingered in his heart.

Once you get past forty, any sort of pain or twinge immediately sets your mind racing, until you're convinced it might be a terminal disease. What's more, this was the sort of thing that actually might lead to sudden death. The gardener was afraid not to take this seriously. After much thought, he went to the traditional medicine center and got an appointment at a well-known clinic.

The kind-faced doctor who examined the gardener was in his seventies and spoke slowly. After taking his pulse and studying the coating on his tongue, he said, "You've been worrying too much, unsettling your nerves and giving you terrors. A few sessions of acupuncture should give you some relief. You'll still need to see a specialist about your heart. But loosen your collar, don't work too hard."

The gardener nodded non-stop at the old doctor's words.

He spent the whole day surrounded by plants. If you'd asked what was troubling him, he wouldn't have been able to answer. And yet, during this time, he was indeed troubled. There'd been a lot of talk recently around the school, saying the new university president was planning to fire a bunch of migrant workers like him, and hire students to do their jobs. Although a change of scenery wouldn't be a bad thing, after several years here, he had formed a relationship with every tree and plant in this place and didn't want to leave them. Then his father, the old gardener, called to say he was having dizzy spells again, asking his son to buy a few bottles of six-flavor dihuang pills and mail them back. With all these things troubling him at the same time, the gardener felt a sort of blockage in his heart.

Only a dozen days after the acupuncture, he had another late-night attack of heart palpitations. The gardener was very anxious now. It wasn't that he was scared of death, but he didn't want to die without understanding what was going on. He wouldn't have minded getting ill—at least he'd know if his condition could or couldn't be treated, and he could be prepared. What he feared was suddenly keeling over, without warning. As he thought about this, the sky began to brighten. First the birds began chirping incessantly, then human noises started and the birdsong vanished. Next he heard vehicles and machinery, and soon he was back in the noisy tumult of day. He didn't need to look outside—just by listening, he knew what time of day it was.

I came to see the gardener after he'd had another sleepless night of heart pain. I tried to comfort him, though of course that didn't have any effect. As we chatted, I mentioned the Taoist Priest Zheng Yi at Crane Temple. The gardener suddenly grew enthusiastic and insisted that I take him there.

4.

When we arrived at Crane Temple, Zheng Yi was in the courtyard making tea.

Crane Temple was on a hill behind the college where the gardener worked. I sometimes came here for a chat with Zheng Yi. If it was a mealtime, I would occasionally get invited to join them for a bowl of vegetarian food. I hadn't been here for a few months, though.

Perhaps because it was raining, we hadn't seen a single other person on the way there. We entered the complete silence of the Hunyuan Hall, bowed to the deity Taishang Laojun—who held a yin yang ring in his hand—and headed to the rear courtyard. In the middle of this courtyard was an octagonal bagua pavilion, spacious and airy, with a tea table. Against a curtain of rain, Priest Zheng Yi was making tea. Seeing us approaching on the flagstone path beneath an umbrella, he darted closer and, smiling beneath the eaves, bowed in salute with his hands clasped. "Long time no see. I didn't expect you on such a rainy day." I said, "The rain is cleansing, a good time to come for advice." The gardener bowed deeply. "Greetings, your holiness." As we went into the pavilion, I folded my umbrella, shook it out, and left it leaning against a pillar.

The priest invited us to sit across from him, pulled a little porcelain cup from the boiling water with wooden tongs, and poured us some tea. "I went to Huzhou last month, and while I was on Guzhu Mountain, I picked some purple bud tea. Try this, and see how you find the aroma." I brought the bowl to my nose, sniffed gently, and smiled. "The tea-master Lu Yu praised this kind of tea—now you've managed to get hold of some, you shouldn't waste it on cattle like us." Zheng Yi chuckled. "Don't be humble, you're quite the expert." Now that we were done making small talk, I said to Zheng Yi, "There's something I'd like to ask your advice about."

Zheng Yi really did have supernatural Taoist powers. I'd heard that even officials from other provinces would visit to ask for his blessing. I wouldn't say I was close to the priest, but we were familiar enough. At our first meeting, I said to him, "The 'Zheng' in your name, 正, is a good character. It contains 上 for 'up,' 下 for 'down,' and 止 for 'stop.' 'Up' for the heavens, 'down' for the earth, and 'stop' for knowing our limits—because this knowledge will bring us certainty, and hence peace. Thus heaven, earth, and humanity are all contained within. As for 'Yi' or 'one,' that is even more straightforward. One gives rise to two, two gives rise to three, and three gives rise to all creation. A good name." Zheng Yi was delighted by my analysis and looked at me with a certain regard after that. Every time I visited, he offered me tea.

He led me and the gardener to the Three Purities Hall at the rear of the temple. The gardener kowtowed three times to Venerable Jade Purity. Zheng Yi had him sit at a table and gave him a bagua reading. He used the ancient yarrow method, which was fairly complex. We didn't understand it at all.

Zheng Yi had started out looking solemn, but his features gradually relaxed. He looked up at the gardener. "This is the well. 'Six-four, well walls, no harm.' The well is being repaired, and no misfortune will come to you. There is a significance here that you understand. You don't need me to explain. A dark cloud floats between your eyebrows. That's negative energy. Tai Sui is coming for you this year, and you have a difficult hurdle ahead. If you manage to get over it, you will have twenty years of good luck."

The gardener said, "Can you tell me a way to get across this hurdle?"

Zheng Yi gave this a moment of deep thought. "You have to be careful in all things, avoid arguments, yield as much as you can. Also, you should get a cat. Cats know the future and can repel evil. An old cat would be best."

5.

When the old gardener got the phone call from his son, he hurried from Shen Village to Nanjing the very next day with their cat, who was twenty-three, a hundred in human years. After such a long time together, the old gardener found it hard to be parted from his companion—but for his son's sake, he brought the cat to the city.

The father carried a small cloth bag with his possessions, while the old cat squirmed between his legs.

The night after his father brought the cat, the gardener slept reasonably well and felt much better when he woke up the next day. He knelt enthusiastically by the old cat and reached out to give it a pat on the head. The cat reared and retreated a few steps, glaring at him, ears pulled back and tail up. Man and cat froze for a second. The gardener met the cat's eyes, which looked to him like the bottomless emptiness of two mirrors facing each other.

The cat didn't recognize him at all.

He'd left home five years ago, and though he returned several times a year, he'd never paid much attention to the cat on these visits. The cat only made an appearance when the old gardener called its name. Normally, it spent its time roaming around the village. All the villagers knew the cat—whenever they saw it, they'd say, "Oh, there's the gardener's cat," and offer it a snack. Not that it ever ate these morsels. After a disdainful glance, it would stalk away. It only ate what the old gardener fed it, or what it caught itself. There weren't many mice around anymore, so it only occasionally got to feast on one. When the gardener was back home last New Year, the cat caught some mud loaches from god knows where, and laid them out by the well at their front door. The old gardener cleaned the fish, cooked them, and served them to the cat. It ate a couple, then took a break, cleaning its face with its paws. Their neighbor Uncle Tiehead's dog couldn't resist the temptation and came by to steal one. The old cat swatted the dog in the face, making it yelp and run far away.

The gardener said, "What a fierce cat!"

There was a hint of smugness in the old gardener's laugh. "Every dog in the village is scared of that cat. When it walks by, they go into hiding."

More astonishingly, the cat could catch birds too. It would climb up a tree and hide among the branches, perfectly motionless. Eventually, a bird would perch in front of it, and the cat would pounce. That's why the gardener had always thought of it as half feral.

When the gardener's father saw that his son couldn't get near the cat, he came over and patted the animal on the head. "He's family, Old Cat. Not an outsider. Family."

He picked up the cat and held its nose to the gardener's face. "Remember. Family."

The cat understood. Its body relaxed, and the gleam in its eyes softened. The gardener gently stroked its fur. The old cat's paws had lost their shine and were dull and dry. It licked its fur where the gardener had touched it, then the back of his hand. The old gardener chuckled. "The cat will remember who you are now."

The gardener happily took the cat from his father. The cat struggled, leaped to the ground, and walked away. His father said, "Don't worry, once it gets to know you, everything will be fine. Don't get too close, though, it's a grumpy old thing and doesn't like to be carried. It stays away from people."

His father left without mentioning his own dizzy spells.

The gardener waved goodbye at the college gates, as his father had said not to see him to the station. When he got back home, he opened the front door, and the cat—who'd been crouched behind the door—jumped out and ran away.

There was no way the gardener could catch up. He ran out into the street, but the old cat was nowhere in sight.

6.

This cat had been with the family for twenty-three years—he couldn't lose it. The gardener searched fruitlessly for three days. He was fairly certain that the cat was somewhere on the campus, though. As long as it was on school grounds, he'd find a way.

What the gardener hadn't realized was just how many stray cats there were on campus. Some had been abandoned here, and others, alas, were the result of their procreation. There were fat ones and skinny ones, large ones and little ones. Right after getting up each morning, the gardener went to the market and returned with a bag of little fish. He made round after round of the campus, tossing fish to the cats. As soon as a cat got hold of a fish, it would dart away to enjoy its spoils in private. Those that didn't manage to grab one would follow him at a distance. They never got too close and remained wary—any sudden movements and they'd instantly scamper away among the trees. The gardener counted the cats. There were more than a hundred, but none of them were the one he was looking for. Fortunately, someone mentioned that they'd seen the old cat, so he didn't completely despair.

Soon, the whole school knew the gardener was looking for his cat. When he bumped into someone he knew, their first question would be, "Have you found it yet?"

By noon, the gardener would have distributed all the fish in his bag. He'd find a bench by the campus lake and stare blankly at the lotus-covered water. This late in the summer, the lotus flowers were gone, and though the leaves were flourishing, the lake still looked a little forlorn. Even the ripples seemed sluggish. When the wind blew, leaves fell from the parasol tree onto his shirt. He brushed them off and unconsciously tightened his collar. His father called twice. To keep him happy, the gardener told him the old cat was doing well, and the tightness in his chest was much better.

A large brown cat popped out from under the holly tree and stared unblinkingly at the gardener, as if there was something on his face. The gardener stared back. This cat looked like the rough sort—there was something aggressive and reckless in its eyes. The gardener didn't give way. At first, he hadn't believed his father when he said cats had a spiritual side, then not long ago, he'd read an article about Steere House, a nursing home in Rhode Island that had a black-and-white cat named Oscar who could foretell when a patient was about to die. After more than fifty successful predictions, people were calling Oscar "the four-legged angel of death." Reading this put the gardener on his guard around cats. Finally, the brown cat realized it wasn't going to win this staring match and grudgingly turned away. The gardener let out a sigh of relief. Then he had to laugh at himself. He wasn't even seriously ill, yet here he was believing this mumbo-jumbo.

The gardener fed the cats every day, then sat here on this bench. Each time he did this, a different cat would show up and stare at him from a distance. Some kindly, some timidly, some with a patrician air. The relationships between one cat and another seemed complex. They all went around alone, but some of them were fairly close, while others were indeed loners, and still others frequently got into fights. The gardener became more and more interested in their world, and they got used to him feeding them, so they showed up for him almost every day. There was still no sign of the old cat. He suspected it might have left the campus, but he couldn't stop worrying. There was no way he could broaden his search. He placed all his hopes on the school grounds. If the old cat really were a creature of the spirit, surely it would come back to see him.

7.

As usual, the gardener gave out all his fish, shook the empty bag at the cats, and walked along the lake shore to the parasol tree. On the wooden bench was a bulging black plastic bag. The gardener ignored it and sat down. Someone would probably be back for it.

Strangely, not a single cat came by. Usually, he couldn't come to the lake without a couple of cats dogging his steps. The cats had gotten used to him quite a while back, and no longer kept their distance. They wouldn't allow him to pick them up, but twined themselves between his legs. He felt a glimmer of tenderness when they did this, and sometimes thought vengefully: *We had you for twenty-three years, Old Cat, and you've abandoned us just like that. I thought you were a spiritual creature? Turns out you're nowhere near as good as these strays.*

He felt somewhat crestfallen not to see any cats around. After sitting there blankly for a while, he got bored and stood up to leave. Looking around, there weren't any humans in sight either. Now he started to wonder about the bag. "Whose bag is this?" he called out. Its owner had probably forgotten it, thought the gardener. Perhaps he ought to see what was inside.

The gardener opened the bag and, with a scream, flung it away. Inside was a dead cat.

The cat had been beaten to death. It was covered in blood, and its head had been practically squashed flat by something like a club or a brick.

The gardener stood by the bench, feeling first nausea, then rage. How could anyone be so cruel, so psychopathic? To beat a cat to death, and then to—to put it in a bag and leave it on a bench. Why this bench? The gardener had a sudden notion: *This was put here for me to find. This person knows I'm fond of cats, and I'm searching for mine. That means I'm responsible for this cat's death. Does the killer hate me or cats?* The gardener felt a sudden surge of twisted fear. He looked around. No one. Or perhaps the cat-killer was hiding somewhere, watching him.

Now the gardener could see that the dead cat was the large brown one he'd had a staring contest with. Such a strapping cat, its life cut short. The gardener had once thought this must be the king of the cats in this place. And now it was just a dead cat with a squashed head.

The gardener carried the cat away and went home to get a shovel to bury it under a magnolia tree. He was fond of magnolias—they were the first to bloom in the spring, so their branches were covered in flowers without a single leaf, as if all of life were hanging from each tree. They had much in common with the brown cat, but now the cat was dead. As he walked along, he gradually calmed down and promised himself he would track down the despicable person who'd done this.

He dug a small pit and placed the cat in it, feeling regretful. If he hadn't fed this cat, it would have continued avoiding humans and wouldn't have gotten killed so easily. He felt it was his fault, which only fueled his anger against the murderer. He clasped his hands in prayer: *Cat, I hope in your next life you get to be a tiger roaming the hills.* Then he thought better of it. There are practically no tigers left in China, apart from those caged in zoos. Maybe it would be better to be reborn as a cat, one that stayed far from people. The thought filled his heart with sorrow, not just for the cat. The gardener went to the security post to tell them that there was a cat-killer on campus.

For the rest of the day, the gardener felt icy chills down his spine, as if a frosty gaze was fixed to his back. This went on even after he returned home. As if someone was crouching downstairs, glaring up through his window.

The gardener didn't sleep well that night. In fact, he barely slept at all.

8.

The next morning, the gardener bought fish as usual. When he saw a cat, he'd fling a fish as far as he could. If the cat took the fish in its mouth but didn't leave, he'd chase it away. He didn't want any cat to come near him again. He'd intended to stop feeding them, but somehow or other, first thing in the morning, he found himself back at the market. *Since I'm here, I might as well buy some fish. But this is the last time,* thought the gardener. *If I keep feeding them, I'll only be hurting them.* Despite these thoughts, the feeding continued, but his emotional state got lower and lower. Perhaps sensing the gardener's change in mood, the cats no longer followed him around with as much enthusiasm. Sometimes he'd reach the lake and still have three or four fish left, jumping around in his bag. He didn't sit on that bench again. He'd glance at it, and phew, it would be empty, nothing to worry about. With a sigh of relief, he'd release the remaining fish into the lake.

As he walked around the campus, the gardener kept his eyes peeled for any cat movements. More than ever, he missed the old cat his father had brought him. Sometimes he felt there might be a mysterious connection between his fate and the cat's. His initial idea had been to become thoroughly familiar with all the campus cats by feeding them, and in doing so discover traces of the old cat. Now an evildoer had completely disrupted his plan.

Three or four days passed uneventfully. The gardener got some fish food, and after patrolling the grounds, sat by the lake to feed the fish. He no longer knew whether he wanted to find the old cat, or how to go about doing that. Sometimes he wondered if he ought to tell his father. And yet, though he felt the words rising to his lips, what actually came out was, "Everything's fine. The old cat keeps me company every day."

As the gardener stood by the lake, Chen Gaoge came by and said, "Gardener, another cat's been killed." Chen Gaoge, a security guard, was quite friendly with the gardener.

The gardener hurried over. This cat had been found by a student who was walking past the air-raid shelter when she saw the body. It had been hacked to pieces. One of its ears was dangling by a shred. A few girls were huddled nearby, staring at it. One of them had her face in her hands, sobbing and trembling.

Chen Gaoge put the cat in a bag, and the gardener followed him looking for a vacant piece of land where they could bury it.

The gardener felt a deep discomfort in his heart. Without saying much more, he returned home.

He stayed home for the next three days, resting. When he went back to the school to tend to the plants, Chen Gaoge called out as he walked past the security post. "Gardener, come in for a moment, would you? Have a seat."

Inside, Chen Gaoge said, "Some strange things have been happening around the college. Including the two that you've seen, thirteen cats have been killed recently."

The gardener was shocked. "Thirteen?"

Chen Gaoge nodded. "In really nasty ways. Some were beheaded or had their tails cut off, others were skinned. It must be some sort of pervert. The security department got us to investigate, but we didn't find a thing."

A plump, older guard crinkled his brow. "Even the security cameras didn't see anything. It's someone who knows where the dead angles are."

"The students are losing their minds over this. People online are saying there's a psycho at large in the school."

"Thirteen cats," said the gardener. "Did you call the police?"

They all laughed. "What for? It's just a few dead cats, the police aren't going to care."

The plump security guard was still frowning. "To be honest, there are far too many stray cats around here. They scream all night long. It's awful—I can hardly get any sleep."

The gardener shot him a look. "How can you say that? So there are a lot of cats—does that mean it's okay to kill them?"

"Don't talk nonsense, Wu," said Chen Gaoge. "Try to be a bit more humane."

Wu glared at Chen Gaoge. "Don't pretend to be all high-minded."

The gardener left, downcast.

When he was far enough away not to hear, Wu turned to the other guards and whispered, "Do you think it was the gardener himself? He's always walking around the campus for no reason, hanging out with those cats. I haven't seen him for a while, and suddenly a dozen cats are dead."

9.

They still hadn't found the cat-killer, and the rumors about the gardener were growing. Whenever he walked around the school, everyone looked at him differently.

It was Chen Gaoge who told the gardener about the rumors.

"Do you know what they're saying behind your back?" he said, accepting a cigarette from the gardener.

"What are they saying about me?"

"Those dogfuckers are wagging their tongues, saying you're a cat-killer. Such dogshit." Chen Gaoge spat thickly into a patch of grass by the side of the road.

The gardener was stunned. "Why do they think I would do that?"

"I told you, it's dogshit."

The gardener went home.

He'd once thought about setting out to catch the cat-killer, but never followed up on that. Now that so many cats had been slaughtered, he feared for the old cat. What he wanted was for the security guards to do their jobs, although naturally they weren't taking this too seriously. The gardener called me and asked if I could speak to someone at the police station. I said, "That's not going to achieve anything. Killing a few cats isn't that big of a deal. No point bothering the police. Besides, even ten times the manpower wouldn't produce any results. This time of year, they're busy catching drunk drivers. Just stay home and have a rest."

A few days later, he called again. "Someone's killing cats on our campus. In really cruel ways. Everyone's on edge. Why don't you come by and do some interviews."

"Are you feeling better, Gardener? Why do you care so much about this? There's no point reporting this. No journalist would pay any attention." I thought he was really getting into the weeds.

"These cat killings are making everyone panicky. If you people came and wrote a report, that might draw some attention, and they'd catch the psychopath."

"Fine, all right. We can get together when we have time." I hung up.

The gardener hadn't expected to become a suspect in these cat killings. It wasn't right. He walked back and forth along the shady paths on the school grounds. It wasn't right. How could this have happened? Why were they pointing fingers at him? He felt he had nowhere to run. They'd backed him into a corner.

The gardener had a flashlight with him and a little trowel. He'd thought of bringing a knife, but that might be hard to explain if he got caught with it. The trowel was a work tool, but if it came to a fight, at least he'd have a weapon. If anything were to happen, he could call it self-defense. The gardener was the sort of person who thought things through.

The gardener went to the security post. The chief of security was a pale, middle-aged man in rimless glasses. He knew the gardener, and though he'd heard the rumors, he hadn't paid too much attention. He was aware of a good number of oddballs in this school, the sort who couldn't stand the slightest shock—they might not be responsible for their actions. Anyway, there was no evidence it was the gardener. And even if it was, killing a few cats wasn't against the law. The more disturbed this sort of person was, the more careful you had to be around them. So when he saw the gardener, the chief of security turned and said politely, "Oh hello, can I help you?"

"Hi, Chief Huang." The gardener kept his voice calm. "Have there been any more cat killings?"

"Not too bad. Just one or two."

"So I was thinking, this person who's killing cats. If they're capable of that, who knows what else they're capable of? Having someone like that on campus is a ticking time bomb. The security department ought to be taking this more seriously."

"We're taking it very seriously."

"I just wanted to let you know that I'll be investigating too. From today, I'll join the patrols. I have an idea. Could you issue me a walkie-talkie? That way, if anything happens, I'll be able to get in touch with you."

"We have rules here—walkie-talkies can't be issued willy-nilly. But how about this—I'll give you my cell phone number. Call me if anything happens. Is that okay?"

"Fine." The gardener put the number into his phone.

The gardener went, leaving Chief Huang a little confused. He didn't know whether the gardener was a psychopath, or just a little touched. Probably touched.

10.

Chen Gaoge said he'd heard cats screaming a few times. Probably their death cries. Going by this, the gardener was certain the killer operated in the middle of the night.

The campus cats tended to gather in a few places, all of which the gardener knew well. After this spate of murders, their nerves were on edge. Never mind twining between your legs, if they so much as heard a human footstep, they'd vanish instantly. There'd once been cats everywhere on this large campus, but now they were nowhere to be seen. Some had departed for greener pastures, others were lying low. The old cat had probably left, thought the gardener. Chen Gaoge, who was in charge of burying the corpses, had told the gardener the old cat he'd described hadn't been among the dead.

The gardener was up a ladder against a tree, working his pincer pliers to pull a length of wire from where it had been deeply embedded in the trunk. "Look, Gaoge, a perfectly good tree, but someone had to put a metal wire around it. As the tree grew the trunk absorbed the wire, and it worked its way in deeper and deeper. Look, it's gone right in, and the injured tree is swelling out around it. The tree's trying to heal. Can it? Not with the wire there. You know, seeing this makes my heart ache just as bad as if it were around my neck. People damaging trees, people killing cats. Back in Shen Village, we'd have beaten them half to death by now."

Gaoge said to the gardener, "Are you really going to catch the dogfucker?"

"I won't sleep until I do. For all I know, he'll club our old cat to death one of these days. And you know if I don't catch him, everyone's going to think I'm the culprit."

The gardener spent a few nights patrolling, but saw nothing at all. Perhaps with fewer cats and the survivors on alert, it wasn't as easy to strike. Or perhaps the gardener's presence had not gone undetected by the killer. Like a grizzled old detective, the gardener regarded everyone with suspicion—students, teachers, passers-by strolling through the campus. Many found this odd and called him nuts behind his back. Eventually, the word on the street was, "There's a crazy gardener in this school who goes around murdering cats. Apparently he lost his mind after his wife died."

11.

It was turning colder with each passing day. Cats were still getting killed from time to time, and there was nothing the gardener could do to stop it. He lost more and more weight. Everyone feared him—he was a crazy cat-killer. Quite a few people got in touch with management to complain.

The gardener didn't realize people thought he was the very psychopath he was searching for, but he certainly sensed their remoteness and fear. Sometimes he'd smile and nod at a student, but before he could say a word, the student—particularly if she was female—would turn pale and quickly walk away. After this happened a few times, the gardener began avoiding people. He had no idea how he'd ended up in this situation. The only thing he could do now was apprehend the villain. Only thing was, the killer might as well have been a ghost. Twice now, the gardener had heard a cat shrieking, but when he rushed toward the noise, all he saw when he got there was a dead cat, with no one anywhere in sight. These cats' dying cries were the only sound the killer produced.

Chief Huang had received complaints about the gardener, but didn't want to take action without proof, so all he could do was keep a close eye on him from the surveillance room. Sometimes, in the small hours of the morning, the gardener would still be making round after round beneath the murky street-lights, like a wolf in a cage.

A little after eleven one night, not too late, Chief Huang was playing Fight the Landlord on his computer while keeping an eye on the gardener on the security monitor. The gardener was walking along, then abruptly froze, as if he'd heard something. Without warning, he began to sprint. Chief Huang shouted into his walkie-talkie for a guard to hurry there too.

In a dead angle not covered by the cameras, a cat was writhing on the brink of death. The gardener was standing next to it. The guard said into his walkie-talkie, "He's killed another one."

Seeing the guard, the gardener called out, "The killer can't have got far!" He ran as he spoke, shining his flashlight across the surrounding trees. The guard followed behind, eyeing him coldly.

Naturally, there was no sign of the killer. The gardener stood dejectedly beneath a streetlight and reached into his pocket to grip the trowel tightly. His jaw was clenched, and the muscles in his face were twitching a little. The security guard shuddered and beat a hasty retreat.

The guard told Chief Huang, "This guy's completely nuts. He obviously killed that cat himself, but still went running around looking for the culprit. I think he really had no idea what he'd done. Either he's a sleepwalker or he's possessed."

Chief Huang nodded and looked away from the security footage. "I saw."

As soon as he started his shift the next day, Chief Huang had a very long phone call with the head of the facilities department.

12.

The next time I saw the gardener, I realized he was seriously ill. He'd lost so much weight that he scarcely looked like himself.

I took him to a Hunanese restaurant on campus called Snow Garden. He seemed like a completely different person from the last time we'd met. He was stick-thin, his skin was sallow and waxy, and there were more wrinkles on his face. His expression was wooden, even a little perplexed. He seemed happy to see me, though, and chattered freely.

"Maybe in other people's eyes, I'm a lunatic." He sighed and put down his chopsticks. "Female students run away from me. I think I should go back home. I don't think I can stay here. But if I don't find the old cat, how will I explain myself to my dad? What do you think is going on with these cat killings? Someone must be out to get me, don't you think?"

I grabbed a piece of flesh off the fish head with my chopsticks and popped it into my mouth, only to unexpectedly bite into a chili. Taking a sharp breath, I dabbed at my watering eyes and mumbled, "Have you offended anyone?"

"I thought of that too, but I'm a gardener, who could I possibly offend? Even when people shout at me, I just smile back. I've been here five years now, and never given anyone cause to get upset. I'm a humble laborer. Never mind the professors or staff, I can't even afford to annoy the students."

As we talked, I felt someone kick my leg. I glanced at the gardener, who was saying, "How could anyone hate cats?" My leg was kicked again, and then once more. I looked down. His leg was far from mine. This was strange. What was going on with the gardener? Could there really be something wrong with his brain? First he had his fortune told, then he got tangled up with some sort of cat killer, and now here he was kicking me repeatedly. What did this mean?

The gardener noticed I was looking at him strangely and broke off. Looking me in the eye, he said, "Do you also think I'm losing my mind?"

Another jolt against my knee. My hand shot out and found something soft there, under my trousers. I jumped to my feet.

A mouse darted out.

It had climbed up my trouser leg. Luckily I had on thick long underwear, so it was between two layers of fabric.

I shouted for the restaurant owner, an attractive middle-aged lady with a heavily powdered face.

"I had a mouse in my pants. What kind of restaurant is this?"

"A mouse?" She stared at me.

I pointed. The gardener had stood up too, and when he saw where I was pointing, he moved. The owner pulled the table aside and came closer.

"Over there, over there!" the gardener screamed, pointing.

She stomped hard, then calmly said to the waiter, "Go get me a plastic bag."

Obviously, we abandoned our meal. When I went to settle the bill, the owner said, "We'll give you a 12 percent discount. There didn't use to be any mice here, but now there's some psycho killer going round the school. He's scared all the cats away."

When we got to the gate, the gardener said, "I'll say goodbye here." I shook his hand, which was icy cold. A gust of wind blew dirt in my face. I covered my mouth with one hand as I waved to the gardener. We both felt strangely agitated as we parted.

13.

About three days after our lunch, Chief Huang showed up at the gardener's home with Chen Gaoge and another guard. They said they'd discussed the matter with the administration and wanted to bring the gardener to the hospital for a checkup. The gardener said, "I've been, they didn't find anything."

Chief Huang said, "Why not let them have another look? Don't worry, we're paying."

They brought the gardener to a mental hospital. After a thorough evaluation, the doctor said, "You have a fairly serious condition known as clinical depression. When it's this severe, it's very dangerous. You may not be able to control your own actions. You may not even be aware what you've done. This requires medication, and I'd recommend in-patient treatment."

The gardener looked at the diagnosis and finally believed that he really was ill. Depression. He'd always thought only intellectuals with comfortable lives got that kind of sickness. Who'd have thought a gardener could be afflicted too? Good thing Chief Huang had said the school was paying, otherwise he'd really be screwed.

They led him down a corridor of wire mesh to his ward. The gardener happened to arrive at dinner time, and people were hanging out in the passageway, eating off their food trays. As they chatted, one patient smacked another in the face with his tray, and they started fighting right away. The doctor shoved the gardener into his room and hurried over to break up the fight. The room door was locked from the outside.

The gardener lay down, tossing and turning. He believed the doctor. He kept turning over the thought: *Was it me? Did I really kill all those cats without realizing it? Do I have a mental illness? Really? If not, how could I have thought getting an old cat could ward off evil? That wouldn't have happened a few years ago. This is all because of my heart palpitations.* He decided he would take any meds they told him to and get well as quickly as possible. He was scared. Scared of himself. Sometimes he thought: *Could the cat killer really be me? I did it and had no idea?*

14.

It was a retired professor who made the report. Her son had had polio, and because she'd taught here, he had a guaranteed place at the school. Each day, she pushed him to and from school in his wheelchair. Everyone on campus knew who she was. She told the security department that she'd seen several dead cats in the basement of their building, frozen in the water.

Chief Huang hurried over with four or five guards.

"It's usually shut," said the retired professor, opening the door to the basement. "When I passed by this afternoon, I saw that the door was ajar. I went to close it, but when I looked inside, there was water everywhere, frozen solid. Look—"

The basement had been flooded, and a thick layer of ice had formed. In it were the bodies of four cats, partly encased and sticking up into the air. Someone had killed them and tossed their bodies in here. Then the water came, and they froze.

The water must have seeped in from outside. There'd been a storm about a week ago. A thick layer of torn-up cardboard boxes had been piled against the wall: a makeshift bed. There was nothing on it now, but you could see the imprint of a body where someone had lain. Now this cardboard bed was frozen beneath the ice too. There was nothing else in the basement.

Chief Huang went back to the security post and looked carefully through the video footage.

There were three clear shots of the guy. He looked a little rough, a little violent. Around forty, five foot seven, splayed-foot walk, baseball cap. He wasn't a member of the teaching staff. No one remembered seeing or speaking to him. Going by the security footage, he'd walked out of the school gates about a week ago and hadn't returned since.

15.

Sure enough, there were no further cat killings. Some people said it was because the murderer had gone elsewhere, but even more people said it was because the gardener was in the mental hospital.

Quite a lot of time passed. The college hadn't hired a replacement gardener, and many of the plants died. A few days before an important conference, the president realized what had once been the most beautiful campus around was looking somewhat bedraggled. Only when he asked about this did Chief Huang remember that the gardener was still in the hospital.

By this time, he knew the cat-killer was this stranger, not the gardener.

The gardener was discharged from the mental hospital and came back to the college. He found the campus full of "wanted" posters. There'd been a bank robbery a few days ago. The culprit had shot someone dead and made off with two hundred thousand yuan.

As soon as he got home, the gardener phoned his father, who said, "I heard there was a murder in Nanjing?"

"It was a robbery," said the gardener.

"Have they caught him?"

"No."

"Be careful when you withdraw money. People are in a frenzy these days. If they want to steal money they should just do that, but no, they'll shoot you dead first. Look around you when you take money from the bank. It might be all right for now, though. I heard he made off with quite a bit of cash. Probably he'll spend that before he strikes again."

The gardener was silent.

"How's your health?"

"I've completely recovered."

"That's good. I'm coming to Nanjing in a couple of days. Is the old cat all right?"

"Um." The gardener hesitated, looking out the window. There were soldiers patrolling with rifles on their backs. "Don't bother coming, Dad. I'll be back home in a couple of days. And this time, I'm staying for good."

THE BLACKSMITH

CAO XIE'ER, THE BLACKSMITH, LIVED by the East Shan River not far from our home and died in 1985 aged eighty. His sons quietly buried him in their back garden. When the village secretary found out, the body was exhumed and cremated. As they dug him up, the corpse stench infested the whole of Shen Village.

The village secretary directed the laborers he'd hired from another village to wrap the rotting remains in a plastic sheet and lift it onto the back of a tractor. I was fifteen at the time, already out of middle school. Along with more than a hundred other villagers, I stood at a distance, silently watching this tragic scene.

IN THE EARLY summer of 2014, I went back home for a visit, along with the artist Zhu Yingchun and his wife. The afternoon we arrived, after it had stopped raining, I took them on a walk. When we got to the East Shan River, an old man was tilling the soil on the bank. He was walking backward, straining as he pulled a steel plow that cut deep into the earth. When he saw us approaching, he stopped to say hello. I offered him a cigarette, and he settled in for a chat, leaning against his plow. He was Cao Xie'er's son, Hongrong. Now eighty-one, Hongrong had a full head of white hair and heavily wrinkled face, which always had a smile on it. We said it must be hard for him, living alone at such an advanced age. A woman passed by just then with a shoulder pole and laughed to hear that. "He's not alone, he's got a nanny at home!" Hongrong chuckled and said, "Nonsense, off with you!" It turned out the "nanny" she was referring to was the nanny-goat Hongrong was rearing. For many years now, the old man and old goat had been bound together.

Hongrong is the second son. His elder and younger brothers both passed away some time ago. He's alone in the world and never married. Every time we return, we see his old goat leading several kids to graze by the riverbank. When he has nothing else to do, the aging Hongrong sits on a little wooden chair, smoking and staring at the river—gazing at the ducks, or perhaps watching to make sure the kids don't fall in. When the day comes that he's no longer around, there'll be no trace of his family in Shen Village.

Cao Xie'er and Hongrong's family line has been in Shen Village for three hundred years.

IN THE FALL of 1923, Locust's one-year-old son died. Tormented by grief, Locust asked the carpenter to make a small, sturdy coffin of the very best wood. He placed his son's body in it and buried it in front of a mausoleum to the west of Shen Village. A feng shui master told him this was a good location that would bring prosperity to the family.

The mausoleum was over ninety meters long and seven or eight meters high. It was the Caos ancestral resting place and dated back to the Qing dynasty Kangxi Emperor's reign.

One of Cao Xie'er's ancestors had been a member of the faction seeking to overturn the Qing and restore the Ming dynasty. In order to escape rampaging Qing troops, he fled to a relative's home in Shen Village, bought some land, and settled here. This ancestor was likely a leader in the volunteer army, well-versed in military matters, and probably brought a good amount of money with him. He bought more than twenty mu of land in the wilderness to the west of the village and dug streams all around it to cut it off from its surroundings. Poplar and willow trees were planted on either side of these streams. The only connection to the outside world was a stone bridge he built leading toward Shen Village. More than a thousand meters east of that bridge was my home.

The Cao family lived on this knoll outside the village. It was on higher ground, in the middle of the wilderness, and apart from nearby Shen Village, every other dwelling in sight on the far horizon. No one could approach without being seen at a distance. When the first generation of these ancestors began passing away, the family built a mausoleum by the river. People for dozens of li around knew there was a Cao Family Tomb near Shen Village. The purpose of this structure wasn't to show off their wealth, but rather to provide an observation post. From the roof of the mausoleum, you could see all around, including the whole of the village.

When I was a child, Shen Village formed a citizen's army. These soldiers frequently carried out drills near the mausoleum. They dug some rudimentary bunkers some distance away and crouched in them firing at the targets stuck into the ground outside the tomb. There was a trench beneath each target, with someone crouched in it. After each round of gunfire, they'd raise up a sign on a long bamboo pole, and wave it around to indicate how many hits that rifleman had scored.

From the roof of the mausoleum, a red flag flapped in the wind. It went up to indicate that a drill was in progress, and everyone should stay far away. When it came down, that meant the drill was over, and the area was safe once more.

NOT LONG AFTER Locust buried his son, Cao Xie'er's father summoned Shen Village's yin yang master. He spent two days surveying the area, scribbling down words and diagrams, and finally produced a piece of paper that read, "The small grave to the southwest is inauspicious for the Cao family. At best, it will cause a fire, and at worst, death. Two ways to break this curse: move the grave, or move the house."

Locust had deep pockets and was prone to flashing his wealth around. He completely ignored the Caos' request to move the grave, and so the two families ended up in court.

This was the most famous court case ever to take place in Shen Village. It lasted from 1923 to 1925, and the Caos sold virtually all their possessions in order to bribe everyone at the local courthouse. Locust disbursed generous gifts too, but his family had quite the business empire, and this was no skin off his nose. Because of this case, the Caos liquidated all but five or six mu of their land, and the knoll was no longer their property alone. After the case had dragged on for two years, the Caos had run out of bribes, and the court issued a ruling: the grave could stay where it was, but Locust would turn it to face another direction.

This muddled verdict was essentially a loss for the Cao family. Cao Xie'er's father was exhausted, body and soul, and within a month he was lying ill in bed. He called for his son. "Remember who was responsible for destroying more than two centuries of Cao success. If we are not avenged, I won't be able to rest easy in the underworld. Get married quickly, while I still have breath in me, so at least one of my worries can be assuaged."

Twenty-year-old Xie'er did as his father asked, and married the girl he'd been betrothed to as a child, a Miss Dai. Half a month after she entered their household, Xie'er's father died, aged fifty-one.

Xie'er sold a mu of land to pay his father's funeral expenses. Not many people showed up, and the ceremony was rather slipshod. It rained heavily the day of the burial, so the family hurriedly deposited the coffin at the cemetery and fled. Only Xie'er remained kneeling by his father's grave until dark.

Their few remaining mu of land were not enough to sustain them. Xie'er had no choice but to leave for town, where he became apprenticed to the black-smith Tian Er.

Xie'er was a tall, burly man, and although he'd joined the profession late, he turned out to be a capable blacksmith. After only a year of training, he'd learned all the skills he needed. Back in Shen Village, he set up his smithy by the entrance of the Cao compound, and business wasn't bad at all.

In the summer of 1944, after the wheat had been harvested, the fields irrigated and the new seedlings planted, there was some free time for the blacksmith Cao Xie'er to light his forge and begin making farm equipment. In the distance, he noticed Xi Wang the village head crossing the bridge and walking slowly in his direction.

The blacksmith was shirtless and had a tattered black leather apron around his waist. As the forge blazed, he pulled red-hot metal from it with a pair of long tongs and placed it on the anvil. With his other arm, he brought down the hammer. The *clang clang clang* was unhurried, but full of heft.

The blacksmith never used to have time for Xi Wang. He'd been even poorer than the blacksmith, practically a beggar. But that was before. Since becoming the village head, he'd risen up in the world. Nowadays he was forever going in and out of people's houses, collecting the grain tax or recruiting stretcher bearers. Whenever there was a dispute, he'd be invited to resolve it, and of course would get wined and dined along the way. The blacksmith was jealous of him.

The local magistrate had ordered Xi Wang to find an assistant, but he'd had his position for over two months now and still hadn't managed to do this. He'd approached a few people, but they'd all declined. If he wasn't completely desperate, he'd never have sought out the blacksmith, a bothersome man with a strident voice who fretted needlessly and could be ruthless on occasion. Making him a village cadre might be asking for trouble. But with the local magistrate pressing him more and more urgently, Xi Wang had no choice but to brace himself and head for the Cao family knoll.

When Xi Wang explained why he'd come, the blacksmith briskly plunged the metal, which he'd just beaten into a blade, in the water. It hissed and a plume of steam rose above it. Tossing aside his tools, he straightened up and said briskly, "Since you've come all the way here to ask me, how could I say no? Besides, this could be a good thing. Someone has to do what needs doing in the village, and I'm not afraid to step forward." With that, he asked his wife to pour a cup of tea and offered it to Xi Wang himself. Next, he offered his pipe. This was one of the blacksmith's treasures, and normally no one got to touch it but him. Only very special guests were allowed to take a puff or two. The stem was made from best-quality mottled bamboo, and he'd made the bowl himself out of a river snail shell. The tobacco was his family's crop. This simple pipe never left his side, but hung from his belt at all times.

The blacksmith spent the next five days in a froth of exhilaration and anxiety, until Xing Wang finally invited him to a meeting. The blacksmith and Xing Wang arrived at the ancestral hall to find the local magistrate, Yu Fei, and several other important cadres already there. These were the first Communist Party members in the vicinity of Shen Village. Several years later, when the

New Fourth Army retreated to the north, every one of them would be slaughtered by the Nationalists.

Yu Fei invited the blacksmith to take a seat and said, "All of you know Blacksmith Cao. We've vetted him, and he fulfills our entry requirements. We would like to invite him to join the Party today. Do any of you object?"

The group said they had no objections.

"Then let's swear him in." Yu Fei stood and raised his right fist in the air. The blacksmith did the same and repeated the words after him. The others came over and shook his hand. The blacksmith would only experience handshakes twice in his life. This was the first occasion. He felt very moved. Yu Fei told him that he couldn't tell a single soul about any Party business, not even that he'd joined—absolutely no one, whether up (his parents), down (his children), or within (his wife). This was an iron-clad rule. The blacksmith nodded again and again. "I know, I know." Yu Fei looked him in the eye and said icily, "Breathe a single word, and you'll be shot dead." The blacksmith was so scared, he felt his throat seize up, and he didn't dare to move.

The magistrate allocated the blacksmith the role of fanshen leader. Yu Fei said, "Your job is to assist Xi Wang in organizing the poor to rise up and seize the property of landlords and wealthy farmers. Only when we've divided the land between them will they come with us, donate food, labor for us, and join our army." The blacksmith could only nod. He had not expected this glorious business to carry the risk of getting shot dead. This made him feel uneasy, and even a little regretful. Nonetheless, at this point, changing his mind was no longer an option.

The day after the meeting, the blacksmith visited Wei Jing, a wealthy man who lived in the north of the village.

The blacksmith got straight to the point. "Sir, now the Communists are here, our days will be more stable. You have a broadsword just sitting there. As you don't have much use for it, why not lend it to me?"

The blacksmith had forged Wei Jing's broadsword, and he was prouder of it than anything else he'd ever made. But Wei Jing had provided the steel and paid in advance, so he hadn't been able to keep it for himself. The blade was truly beautiful, and the blacksmith often thought longingly about it. He'd tried making a couple of others in the same style, but either because the quality of the metal was different, or because he hadn't been able to get the forge as hot, the results hadn't been as good.

Wei Jing's face sank. "I spent quite a few silver dollars on this sword, and I need it to defend myself against burglars and bandits. How could I lend it to anyone?"

"I'll tell you the truth, sir," said the blacksmith. "I'm the fanshen leader now, which is to say it's my responsibility to overthrow local tyrants and share out their land. If you want to hold on to that sword, it's nothing to me. I'll go now."

Taken completely aback, Wei Jing reached out to prevent the blacksmith from leaving and yelled into the house for his wife to rustle up some meat and eggs. "You've just gotten a big promotion, brother, I ought to congratulate you. Don't go yet."

With that, he went into the house, took the sword off the wall, and handed it to the blacksmith. "Now that you're an official, I don't need to keep this sword around, do I? When you said you were overthrowing tyrants, I wonder who you were talking about? People like us who do good works—will anything happen to us?"

The blacksmith took the sword and wiped it so it gleamed. Tucking it into his belt, he said, "Sir, you have nothing to worry about. Ours is a friendship between influential people. As long as I'm around, I'll make sure you don't lose out."

Wei Jing kept nodding as he poured the wine and respectfully invited the blacksmith to come inside, so they could continue their conversation over a meal.

This was the first time Wei Jing had ever invited the blacksmith to eat with him, and even gave him the seat of honor. The blacksmith ate and drank his fill, and as he left Wei Jing's home, he couldn't help humming a little ditty.

The following day, Xing Wang summoned the blacksmith to another meeting at the ancestral hall. The blacksmith changed into trousers and a tunic of dark cloth, and set off with the broadsword in his hand. He chose a circuitous route that took him through half of Shen Village, so he could smile and call a greeting to everyone he met. The villagers had no idea what kind of cadre he had become, but they were speaking to him much more politely all of a sudden.

· · ·

HE MAY HAVE become the fanshen leader, but his household finances weren't any better than before. The position didn't actually come with a salary. After this meeting, he returned to a scolding from his wife. "You're never home— you're out all day helping people with this, that and the other. We're going to run out of food tomorrow. The children and I will starve to death while you're out gallivanting and having a good time." Annoyed, the blacksmith turned around and went straight back to the village. He wasn't paying attention to where he was going, and somehow ended up back at Wei Jing's front door. Flustered by the blacksmith's return, Wei Jing hastily greeted him. "Brother, come in, have a seat."

The blacksmith didn't refuse, but went inside and drank a cup of tea in silence. Wei Jing said, "You don't look too good. Is something causing you trouble?"

The blacksmith sighed. "I've been running around all day long, busy with affairs of state, and I've neglected my own family. Now we're about to run out of food, and I'm in a panic about it."

Wei Jing said, "You're a cadre, you shouldn't be worrying about petty things like household provisions. If it's convenient, I can give you some rice and flour now, and that should tide you over. How about that?"

The blacksmith was overjoyed to hear this. He jumped to his feet and blurted out his thanks over and over. Wei Jing sent his son to fetch a sack of rice and a sack of flour. The blacksmith didn't attempt to turn down this gift, but tied the sacks together and hefted them over his shoulder. He carried them home, beaming the whole way, and plopped them down in front of his wife. "You've been nagging away, but tell me this: if I hadn't become a cadre, where would this food have come from?" This sight of these provisions silenced his wife, and she stood there letting him scold her.

AFTER THE BLACKSMITH became the fanshen leader, there were indeed big changes in Shen Village. His strident voice was heard almost every day. From time to time, he struck a gong and relayed a variety of notifications from the higher-ups. Now he was gathering all the young and middle-aged people for mass calisthenics, now he was organizing a stretcher relay, now he was distributing public rations. The atmosphere in Shen Village grew frenetic and tense, which was completely in keeping with the chaos of that era. From his lips, the villagers picked up information, true or not, about the changing situation in the outside world. They weren't particularly concerned about most of these events, though, apart from the Japanese surrender.

Blacksmith Cao only heard that the Japanese had given in two days after it actually happened. He still got very worked up and immediately banged the gong to pass on this important and joyous news to the rest of Shen Village. When they heard that the Japanese devils had surrendered, they ran back home to dig out whatever firecrackers they had left over from the New Year and set them off. Shen Village felt festive that day, as if they were celebrating some special holiday. This was the only time the blacksmith brought happiness to the people of Shen Village.

Around this time, Locust's son Tongyue became the resource manager of Shen Village, which meant he was in charge of the money and rations that the New Fourth Army stored here. Tongyue was originally a tailor and was indeed skilled with a needle and thread. Because he'd had a few years of schooling and was a handsome man from a rich family, he looked down on the blacksmith from a great height, despite their being colleagues. If they happened to bump into each other, Tongyue would turn his face aside rather than meet the blacksmith's eyes. The blacksmith naturally responded with equal froideur, given the grudge between their families, which would eventually lead to a great tragedy.

After the Japanese surrendered, the Communists launched a county-wide rectification movement. The local magistrate held a meeting of local Party members, whose numbers were formidable by this point. This was purely for appearances—all the talk of "criticism and self-criticism" and "mutual surveillance" was just talk, nothing more. Even so, the blacksmith sensed an opportunity.

Actually, a few months before this, the blacksmith had got wind of the tailor skimming from army provisions and sometimes replacing best-quality flour and rice with second-rate stuff. Back then, it hadn't seemed like the right moment to strike. Then this rectification movement came along. Overjoyed, the blacksmith immediately got someone to write an accusatory letter. The magistrate was surprised to receive this tip-off about the tailor the day after the rectification meeting. There was no other option, so without hesitation, he had the tailor arrested.

The truth came out very quickly. During his time as the resource manager, the tailor had indeed misappropriated more than a hundred pounds of provisions. The magistrate knew that the tailor liked getting little advantages and thought a lot of himself, but these were hardly major issues. Not wanting to make a big thing out of this, he said, "Tell him to replace the food he stole, and pay a small fine. Go find some people to bail him out."

And so the tailor was released. The following day, he was once again swaggering around the village, as arrogant as ever, claiming he would get revenge on whoever had reported him. Everyone in Shen Village knew this was the blacksmith—he hadn't exactly been discreet about it. This was worrying. The tailor had money, and one of his relatives was a Nationalist deputy captain in Kou'an Town. If things went south, the blacksmith might be the one getting a bite taken out of him. He gritted his teeth. So this would be a fight to the death. He set about searching for more evidence, then got someone who was good with words to help him write another accusation, this one much more grave.

This time round, the blacksmith not only charged the tailor with corruptly purloining army provisions, but also with "attempted collusion with reactionary Nationalist elements to retaliate against the Communist Party."

Once again, the tailor was seized and locked up in Dongyue temple. My grandfather the carpenter was well aware of how serious this situation was. He went to the tailor's home several times, begging his mother to intervene. Unfortunately, she assumed nothing serious was going to happen and wanted to teach her son a lesson. Besides, she wasn't willing to put up the huge amount of money it would have taken to get the charges lifted. And so she turned a deaf ear to his pleas.

A little over two months later, the local magistrate held a public trial in front of Dongyue temple, at the end of which the tailor was taken to face the firing squad.

Now that the tailor was finally dead, the blacksmith could let out a sigh of relief.

The tailor was twenty-six at the time of his death. His wife was twenty-two, and his son just thirteen months.

The morning of the execution, the blacksmith banged the gong and summoned the entire village to attend the trial. After he'd delivered this announcement, he headed there himself. Standing in the crowd, he didn't see the look of the tailor's face right at the end, nor did he want to. Only after the tailor had been shot did he follow everyone else to see the corpse, slumped on the ground covered in blood. After a quick glance, he shoved his way out of the gawking throng and headed home.

Skipping dinner, he went straight to bed and slept till dusk. Then he went and knelt at his father's grave and said to his father's spirit, "Dad, I've taken revenge." Then he sat leaning against the tombstone, got out his pipe, and drew on it again and again. It had been a whole twenty years since they'd lost in court to the tailor's family. The tailor had only been six back then.

After the tailor's death, no one in Shen Village wanted anything to do with the blacksmith. Everyone stayed well away from him. When he walked past, they would jump to their feet, point at his back, and yell curses after him. Never mind that none of them had liked the tailor either.

THE SITUATION CHANGED so fast that no one was prepared for it. Not long after the tailor's death, the civil war between the Nationalists and Communists began. In the winter of 1946, despite Commander Su Yu's seven victories against the Nationalists in central Jiangsu, the unstoppable tide of the Nationalist army kept approaching. Most of the New Fourth Army retreated to the north, taking some of the cadres with them. With the troops gone, the deposed landlords returned with their own militia, to take control of Shen Village. Of the seven people who were present at the blacksmith's induction into the Party, Xi Wang fled to Jiangyan city, where he turned himself in to the Nationalist district office, while the other six were captured and shot to death. The blacksmith hid in the Cao family home on the knoll outside the village, scared out of his wits.

When the militia showed up, the blacksmith jumped into a ditch and escaped along the back roads. They took all his livestock and destroyed every item of furniture. They would have burned the house down too, but someone suggested, "No, he'll never come back if we do that. Leave the house, and we can catch him when he returns." Before departing, they knocked a huge hole in the back wall of the house, allowing the wintry wind to howl in.

Every few days after that, the militia showed up again, mostly because it was on their way. They were patrolling Shen Village, and while they were at it they'd grab a few chickens and ducks, or some pigs and sheep, then they'd swing by the Cao hillock to have a look.

The blacksmith's son Hongxi sat on the roof of the Cao mausoleum every day, looking in all directions. Each time he saw strangers approaching, he'd blow on a willow leaf whistle, sounding the alert for the whole family. This went on for the next two months. The blacksmith knew that if he didn't leave, they'd catch him sooner or later.

And so he went to Jiangyan, where he turned himself in.

The blacksmith had never held any beliefs. He didn't even know much about the Communist Party. He'd only joined because he thought he would look good and stand out from the crowd. He'd never have thought it would land him in such a dangerous position. Now he regretted it bitterly. As he headed to the county town to surrender himself, his repentance was completely sincere.

The blacksmith was illiterate, so at the Nationalist district office, he verbally told them the names of all the Party members he knew of. Neither the Communists nor the Nationalists cared much about lowly figures like the blacksmith. His betrayal didn't cause any damage either. He gave them eight names. Six of them had already been shot by the militia, Xi Wang had surrendered, and the tailor—thanks to his accusation—had been executed by the Communists. After telling them all he knew, the blacksmith put his thumbprint on the paper and walked out into the streets of Jiangyan feeling like a weight had been taken off his shoulders. A kind soul warned him not to leave town. Only in Jiangyan did people know he'd turned against the Communists. If he left and the militias got hold of him, he'd be shot dead at once.

The blacksmith looked around for a way to support himself. Far too many people had fled to Jiangyan, though, and there weren't enough jobs for them all. Besides, once anyone found out he was a surrendered Communist, whether rich or poor, they'd refuse to take him in.

A few days after that, the blacksmith stumbled upon Xi Wang under a bridge. He'd been panhandling in Jiangyan for a while now. Fortunately, this was what he'd been doing before he became village head, and he knew the ropes well enough that he certainly wouldn't starve to death.

The blacksmith got hold of a chipped begging bowl and a bamboo walking stick and walked the streets behind Xi Wang. Unfortunately, he still had an imposing physique, and when he raised his eyes from time to time, a ferocious gleam lingered in them. Never mind tossing him a coin, every passer-by quickened their footsteps when they saw him approach, staying as far away as possible.

Xi Wang said, "This isn't going to work. Let me find you a good spot at the marketplace, and just sit there—pretend you can't walk." The blacksmith did as he said, plopped himself cross-legged on a couple of straw bundles at a street corner, waiting silently for alms.

After two years faking a handicap in Jiangyan, the strapping blacksmith had shriveled to a defeated, scrawny little runt. In 1948, the Communists surged back and forced the Nationalists to retreat. The blacksmith's son Hongxi came to town and found his father after half a month's search. By this point, poverty and illness had assaulted the blacksmith so badly, he didn't even have the strength to travel back home. Hongxi could only return haplessly to the village, where he asked my grandfather the carpenter and someone named Si to come to Jiangyan with him. They brought along a wheelbarrow, which they used to carry the blacksmith back to Shen Village.

BETWEEN THE SHOCK and the fear, the blacksmith's wife had been sobbing day and night, until she'd cried her eyes blind. After the militia put a hole in the back wall of their home, the family patched it up with sorghum stalks, but the north wind of winter still whistled through the gaps. The blacksmith's sixteen-year-old daughter Hongbao caught a chill which led to bronchitis, and now she couldn't stop coughing. Despite that, she still had to help her blind mother take care of the chores, as well as raising her two-year-old brother Honghua. Hongrong, the fourteen-year-old second son, was too small to take on heavy labor, so he followed Hongxi around doing casual jobs. The blacksmith lay in bed, quietly weeping to himself. He wasn't complaining that his own life was hard, but felt terribly guilty at the way he'd dragged his whole family down with him. After half a month, he finally managed to get back on his feet. He went straight to the magistrate, in the hopes that the government could arrange another job for him. Alas, the higher-ups had given strict orders that any cadres who'd surrendered to the Nationalists would not be given a position.

When the blacksmith's wife realized he could never be a cadre again, she cheered up. "Good, now you can settle down and be a regular person. Forget all that other stuff."

The blacksmith had no choice. He borrowed a bit of money, got his tools back in order, and went back into his old line of work.

Hongxi was now twenty-one. As a child, he'd been betrothed to Miss Dai from the south of the village. The blacksmith went to see Mr. Dai, who said only that the Caos were far too poor to give their daughter, an only child, the life she was accustomed to. He suggested that Hongxi come to live in the Dai household instead. When the Cao family fortunes changed, the couple could return to their rightful place. The blacksmith agreed to this proposal right away.

Hongxi was open and direct by nature, had an eloquent tongue in his mouth, and was tall and well-built too. In the countryside, that made him quite a catch. He moved into his in-laws' home, put up with any amount of hardship, and treated everyone with friendliness. It wasn't just his father-in-law and the rest of his wife's family, but even the neighbors couldn't stop praising him. A year later, his wife had a son, and then another year after that, a daughter. Both the Caos and the Dais were over the moon. Hongxi often came back to Shen Village with his wife to see his parents, bringing gifts of food and clothing. When the blacksmith found himself a little short of cash, Hongxi would give him whatever he asked for. In this way, the blacksmith managed to pass a few happy years after his return from exile. He began stockpiling a few hundred pounds of grain and a dozen good pieces of lumber. Soon, he thought, he would add an extension to the house, so his second son Hongrong could bring home a wife.

IN 1952, ON the last day of the lunar year, the blacksmith's family was cheerfully steaming buns in bamboo baskets. This was a Shen Village custom: you had to steam dozens of pounds worth of flour into buns just before the New Year, which you would then eat over the course of the first month. This was a big annual event, and even the poorest families would borrow flour to make buns.

The eldest daughter, Hongbao, was the first to notice the fire. The whole family desperately tried to put it out, but the strong wind kept fanning the flames. They'd once had two large water tanks built by their ancestors, but the Nationalist militia had smashed them, and the small one they now had didn't hold nearly enough to extinguish such a blaze. The villagers saw the fire from far away and hurried over to help, but in just four hours, everything the family owned was burned. They hadn't even managed to save a single piece of furniture.

After the villagers departed, the blacksmith's family sat among the ruins weeping and howling. Hongrong and six-year-old Honghua went around scavenging steamed buns, but every one they picked up had fallen into the mud and was no longer fit to be eaten. The last day of the year was a time for family gatherings, but the Caos could only wipe away their tears and sit in the wilderness as the north wind assaulted them. They didn't even have a blanket, but had to huddle under heaps of straw for warmth. The adults gradually quieted down, and soon only Honghua could be heard crying out that he was cold and hungry. The blacksmith unbuttoned his own shirt, scooped up his son, pressed him to his chest, and swaddled him in his clothes. Honghua kept babbling, "I want steamed buns, I want steamed buns," then his voice trailed off, and he fell asleep.

This was like a repeat of what happened to my family in 1911, except that was a case of arson, whereas this was an accidental fire. Nonetheless, the torment they suffered was the same. It was the custom in Shen Village that any family whose house burned down wasn't allowed to take shelter with anyone else for three days, in case they brought the fire spirits with them. So the Caos had nowhere to go. But how were they supposed to get through this bitterly cold winter night?

A short while later, they saw a stream of people coming from Shen Village with torches. Some had brought fish and meat and tofu, others steamed buns and cakes, and someone even showed up with a table. Grandpa gave them the quilt from his own bed.

The blacksmith clasped his hands and bowed, thanking them over and over.

The next day, New Year, Party Secretary Tianning dropped by. He walked around the ruins of the Cao family home and told the blacksmith, "Go to the village and we'll issue you thirty pounds of rice and thirty pounds of flour. You can have a bit of money too, to build a new house." The blacksmith bobbed his head in gratitude, and walked the secretary all the way to the village gate.

This was the first day of 1953, and many people from Shen Village came to help out. In a single day, they put up a simple thatched hut, so at least the Caos wouldn't have to spend another night in the open. Hongxi, the eldest son, had been sent by the government to work on a river-dredging project in Yangzhou. When the Dais heard the news, they arrived with their daughter in tow. After offering their commiserations, the two families talked it over and decided to ask Hongxi to come home and take charge of the household.

Hongxi was twenty-six at the time, in his physical prime. He could put up with any amount of hardship and had a nimble brain. Everyone liked him— from friends and family to his coworkers on the river project. When Hongxi heard that his family home had burned down, it was like a knife through his heart. He asked his supervisor for some time off, and given the special circumstances, he was granted ten days of leave.

Hongxi hurried home through the night, a non-stop journey of eighteen hours on foot to get home. Their house, their beds, their tables and chairs, their grain, all burned black. The water they'd thrown the flames had created so much mud, anything that remained had sunk into the swamp, impossible to retrieve. The thatched hut that now stood by what had been their front door was no better than a pigsty, and while it shielded them from the wind, it was no protection against the cold. Hongxi and his father discussed what to do next and decided the priority was to rebuild the house. Every able-bodied man in the village had been sent to Yangzhou, leaving no one behind to do the work—so father and son decided to do it themselves. Grandpa, a well-known carpenter, was needed in the village to repair grain stores and farm tools, so they'd excused him from the river dredging. The Party secretary felt sorry for the blacksmith's family and gave Grandpa a few days off so he could go help out. He and the two Cao men set to work sawing up trees and putting up walls, and in a week or so, they'd built a dirt-walled hut with two rooms that could just about accommodate the family. Now that construction was complete, and Hongxi's period of leave was running out, he hurried back to Yangzhou.

After almost twenty hours of walking, he got back to the work site with his feet covered in blood blisters. The supervisor kept urging him, so Hongxi only rested for one day, and the next morning he stumbled to the river, hauling earth with everyone else. They'd dug the riverbed quite deep by this point, and the channel was steep. When you were at the bottom, you had to crane your neck to see the top. It took three people to haul up soil from down there. Because his feet still hurt, his coworkers kindly allowed him to remain on the lowest level, which required the least energy. It took four or five days for his blisters to heal. After a day of work, he lay in bed at night breathing with difficulty. He'd been nineteen when his father fled to Jiangyan, and the whole family had lived on what he could earn doing odd jobs. After getting married and starting a family of his own, his life was finally settling down when another tragedy had befallen his family. Who knew how many years it would take to recover from this blow? And here he was, slogging away with these other men like a swarm of ants. What prospects did he have in life? He couldn't see any. Sometimes, in the middle of the night, he'd bury his head in his blanket and sob.

Hongxi was getting thinner by the day and finding it harder to haul earth. He couldn't ask for more time off, though—the cadres might accuse him of malingering. Sneaking off back home wasn't an option either. They'd drag him back, string him up, and beat him. So he said nothing, just gritted his teeth and soldiered on.

He'd been back a little over a month when, one morning, he felt a stab of pain in his stomach after hauling several loads of earth. Dropping his carrying pole, he squatted down, arms around his belly. His coworkers rushed over. Hongxi's face was the color of steel, and beads of sweat the size of soybeans were oozing from his forehead, dripping down his face. The cadre in charge ordered a couple of men to carry him to the medical office.

The young doctor examined him with a stethoscope, prescribed some painkillers, and told him to rest. Hongxi returned to his quarters and lay in bed moaning, not even getting up for dinner. His coworkers stopped by briefly to see how he was doing and poured him some water, but they were too exhausted to do much more before climbing into bed themselves.

The next morning, they called out to see how Hongxi was feeling, but he didn't answer. When they reached out to touch him, his body was ice cold.

Hongxi was twenty-six at the time of his death, the same age as the tailor at his execution.

Hongxi's passing sent shockwaves through the entire work site. Cadres hurried there from the company, the battalion and even the regiment headquarters. Now that he was dead, a coffin had to be bought for the corpse, and a delegation sent to escort it back to Shen Village.

A squad leader and eight conscripted laborers lifted the coffin onto a truck, then clambered on board and traveled with it. The truck could only take them as far as Jianghuang Road, more than ten li from Shen Village, and they would have to carry it the rest of the way. The squad leader sprinted ahead to bring the news to the Cao family.

When the blacksmith and his wife heard that Hongxi was dead, they collapsed weeping. News spread, and the villagers came in droves. The women comforted the family, and the men set up a tent for the body. The coffin arrived before they were done. The blacksmith, his wife, little sister Hongbao, and little brother Hongrong flung themselves across it, howling. The blacksmith smacked it again and again, unable to say a word. The villagers eventually managed to drag them away, just in time for Hongxi's in-laws to arrive with his wife and children. When Hongxi's wife saw the coffin, she dropped the one-year-old son in her arms, screamed, "Oh, Hongxi!" and crumpled to the ground before it. They hastily pressed her philtrum to revive her. She screamed and clawed at the earth, writhing on the ground like a lunatic.

NOW THAT HONGXI was dead, his wife married again. Occasionally, she brought the children to see their grandfather, but only once or twice a year. Hongxi's mother was blind, and her daughter Hongbao had to lead her everywhere. Spending days in the open air after the fire had exacerbated Hongbao's bronchitis, which the shock of her brother's sudden death worsened into lung disease that made her cough all day long. She fed seven-year-old Honghua, dressed him, and slept in the same bed as him. As a result, he caught her cough. Hongrong, the second son, was now nineteen years old, but lifelong undernourishment had left him no bigger than a child of twelve or thirteen, and he could only do light work.

The blacksmith didn't have time for sorrow—he was working as hard as he could. He was the only person keeping this storm-tossed family afloat. No matter how hard he pushed himself, there was only so much he could earn. He decided to raise chickens. When they were grown, they would lay eggs or be sold—that could be a way out.

He bought thirty little chicks. They were easy to raise—they didn't eat much, and given that the family lived on a hillock surrounded by farmland, they could easily grub for food. First thing each morning, the blacksmith opened the coop door and let them roam free. In the evening, he'd cup his hands around his mouth and call, "Ahoy, ahoy," and the chicks would scurry back from all directions.

As they grew, they required more food, and the bugs they could find for themselves were no longer enough. Hongrong was given the task of feeding them. But how was he supposed to do that? In the end, he pilfered a few ears of corn from here and there in the fields.

All the land had been returned to the state by now and was communally owned. Therefore the crops were communal too. People frequently snuck in to steal corn, and some fields were bare even before the harvest. The Party secretary was furious about this, and set Shoehead to guard the corn crop.

Shoehead was our neighbor to the west. He got his nickname because when he was born, they put a shoe out for him to slide out onto. Apparently, this was supposed to make a child easier to raise. They gave him the name "Shoe," which became Shoehead. Then he grew up, and everyone started calling him Shoe Daddy.

So Shoe Daddy was watching the cornfields, a job he took very seriously. If any more corn went missing, he would be severely punished, but if he managed to keep the crop intact, he'd be rewarded with extra provisions.

One evening, Hongrong had grabbed five or six ears, and was slipping out from the field when he bumped into Shoe Daddy, who'd been keeping an eye on him for some time now. Shoe Daddy hauled him straight to the secretary's house. The secretary opened his front door to see Hongrong, still holding the corn. Without another word, he had Shoe Daddy tie Hongrong to the locust tree in the yard.

The secretary brought out a chair and sat in front of him. "How much corn have you stolen?"

Hongrong said, "Five or six ears."

"Bullshit. How many?"

"More than ten."

The secretary smacked him across the face. "Stop lying! How many?"

"More than twenty."

Each time the secretary threatened him, Hongrong said a larger number. The villagers got wind of what was happening and came running over, as did the blacksmith and Hongbao. With so many people watching, the secretary decided he had to make an example of the boy. He kept pressing him, and Hongrong kept confessing to more. Losing patience, he said to Shoe Daddy, "Give him a good beating, and we'll see if that improves his memory. I bet he won't dare to steal again." Shoe Daddy came over and slapped Hongrong three times.

Hongbao couldn't stand it any longer. She ran forward and yelled, "You monsters! Do you have to hit him so hard? Are you even human?" Even as she screamed at them, she was trying to untie her brother. The secretary flew into a rage and whacked her twice, knocking her to the ground. The blacksmith charged over and picked up his daughter, shouting, "How can this be? We're in Chairman Mao's new society, and you're still trying to torture confessions out of people?" No sooner had the words left his mouth when the secretary cried, "String him up!" The leader of the conscripted laborers, the production brigade accountant and Shoe Daddy ran over to tie a rope around the blacksmith's hands, tying the other end to a branch. The secretary said, "Leave him out here all night, and send him to the township tomorrow."

The blacksmith's family watched this happen, mouths agape with horror. Hongrong and Hongbao wept, but didn't dare to say another word. The villagers jabbered away vigorously, accusing the blacksmith's family of stealing crops, but also grumbling that the Party secretary had gone too far. Someone else called out that he should say he was wrong and ask for another chance. Another voice said if he went to the township, even if he survived, they'd take a layer of skin off him. Suspended in mid-air, completely helpless, the blacksmith raised his head with some effort and said, "Secretary, I was wrong to say what I did. We shouldn't have taken corn that belongs to the People. It will never happen again."

The secretary nodded, and his anger ebbed away. He told Shoe Daddy to untie the blacksmith.

"The blacksmith will be fined fifty pounds of grain, and the same thing will happen to anyone else who dares to pilfer from the communal crops." With that, the secretary waved to dismiss the crowd. The blacksmith went back home with his son and daughter and cried till dawn.

After the shock they'd suffered, both the blacksmith and Hongbao lay ill in bed. Hongrong had no choice but to slaughter the chickens to feed them as they recuperated. By the time the blacksmith was well again, all thirty chickens had been eaten. Meanwhile, Hongbao's condition was worsening by the day.

Hongbao had been betrothed long ago to Guojun, who lived thirty li away. Guojun was extremely small in stature, so everyone called him Shorty Guojun. He often came to the blacksmith's house to help out with work. Hongbao wasn't getting any younger, but because she had to take care of her blind mother and sickly little brother, she'd kept delaying the wedding. She and Guojun were finally supposed to get married this year, until she was struck down by illness.

Hongbao died in the summer of 1958, after a year bedridden. The corn was ripening once more, and Hongrong made her a bowl of maize porridge. When he brought it to her, she shook her head. "Shoehead has a rotten conscience. When other people stole crops, he didn't dare to stop them—it was only our family that he bullied. I fell ill because of him. If I die, I'm not going to let him off." She was too scared to go after the Party secretary, so she put all the blame on Shoe Daddy.

"Hongrong, don't forget how he smacked you in the face. You mustn't forget."

Then Hongbao took her mother's hand and said, "Mom, I'm going to die."

Her mother said, "Bao, after you die, come back and see me often. I'm blind, I can't see what's around me. I need you to watch over this family for me."

Hongbao nodded and sat up in bed. She dressed herself in the clothes that had been prepared for her wedding, then lay back down. Her mother sat by her bedside and held her cooling hand.

The rest of Shen Village heard the news and came to see Hongbao. She was still lying in bed, looking like she was asleep. Shorty Guojun, who would never be her husband now, sat on a stool by her side, waving a palm-leaf fan to keep the flies off her.

NO ONE SEEMED much affected by Hongbao's death. No sobbing was heard from the Cao household. Even Shorty Guojun's face remained blank, without any sign of grief. Perhaps because she'd been ill for so long her death was expected, or perhaps their hearts were numb. The blacksmith got a broken old closet, stuffed Hongbao into it, and buried her like that. The next day, he was back at work.

Soon after this, the village was engulfed by collectivization. This meant everyone had to hand over all their food stockpiles and smash their cooking pots—they were only allowed to eat at the communal cafeteria. The black-smith's home was some distance from Shen Village, which made it inconvenient to get to the cafeteria, and also difficult to keep tabs on them. The village con-fiscated their home and built a two-room thatched house by the East Shan River, to the east of our house. The blacksmith's family moved in, permanently leaving the piece of land their clan had inhabited for three hundred years. The blacksmith didn't mind going. Life had been rough for him for many years now. Perhaps a change of location would also change his luck.

After they'd moved, the cafeteria closed down, and everyone had to fend for themselves again. The villagers were now going through an extremely dif-ficult time. Not a single person had a full belly. The blacksmith's blind wife lay in bed all day, groaning from hunger. There was no way she could work, so she gave her food rations to her husband and son. She couldn't keep this up, though, and eventually the blacksmith had no choice but to resume his old profession: begging. If someone gave him a bite to eat, he'd ask for a little more and bring it home to his wife. The blacksmith was a proud man, though. When he'd had to beg to survive in Jiangyan, due to the special circumstances, he hadn't found that shameful. Having to do it again more than a decade later left him so mortified, he couldn't bring himself to reach out his hand. Only when he'd gone a long distance from Shen Village did he pull out his begging bowl to ask for food. If he caught sight of anyone he knew, he'd immediately tuck it away again and pretend he was out for a stroll. Gradually, though, news found its way back to Shen Village. People began looking at him differently. When he sensed this, he stopped right away.

The blacksmith's wife was now so weak from hunger, she wasn't able to get out of bed. He hardened his heart and, in the middle of the night, crept into the next village's cornfield. He'd only taken four or five ears when he got caught. They strung him up from a tree by the threshing ground and hit him with bamboo poles and lashed him with ropes until they were good and tired. Then they untied him and tossed him to the side of the road.

The blacksmith returned home and stayed inside for several days, not daring to venture out. He didn't want anyone to see him like this, all bruised and swollen. His wife was mostly silent now, apart from an occasional quiet whimper. Hongrong didn't know what else to do, so he went to his uncle for help. The uncle arrived with a couple of flatbreads and five pounds of rice. It was all he had.

Hongrong's uncle brought one of the flatbreads to his sister's mouth, but she gently pushed it away. "I don't need this anymore. Give it to them."

The blind woman died in the fall of 1960. The village found some old pieces of wood for her coffin and offered the family a few dozen pounds of grain in condolence. The blacksmith buried her next to her daughter Hongbao, so they could accompany and take care of each other.

In 1966, the Cultural Revolution began. Life in Shen Village had taken a turn for the better by then. The blacksmith was much happier too. He was sixty-one and kept himself busy all day long. He had more energy now than just a few years ago.

The leadership of the rebel faction wanted to lift up a few "representatives from the association of impoverished rural people." My father Qingshan knew the blacksmith had always been one of the poorest people around and recommended him as the best representative they had.

That evening, Qingshan presented the blacksmith with a red armband on which were printed the words "Red Guard of Mao Zedong Thought," and invited him to be a representative of the rural poor. The blacksmith responded with enthusiasm, "If you want to talk about suffering, no one has endured more than me. I'm passionate about revolution too. When I was the fanshen leader, weren't all the landlords and wealthy farmers afraid of me?" Qingshan was happy to hear this. "We're going to have a struggle session soon. You'll be onstage, denouncing the bad guys. Be bold, and make your voice heard." The blacksmith said, "Don't worry, I'm an old hand at this. Listen, twenty years ago—"

When Qingshan sent up the list of recommendations, though, the Party secretary jumped at the blacksmith's name. "Representative of the poor? He's a big traitor. As soon as the reactionaries showed up, he sold out quite a few comrades. At tomorrow's struggle session, he's the one who ought to be onstage getting denounced."

Taken aback, Qingshan hurried back to see the blacksmith. "What's going on, Uncle? They're saying you're a traitor."

"Me? A traitor? I didn't betray anyone. I'm illiterate. I didn't write that confession."

"No need to say any more," said Qingshan. "Tomorrow morning, come to Huozhuang High School, and prepare to be denounced."

"If I don't show up at the production brigade, will I still get my work points?"

"Yes, yes, you will. The struggle session counts."

"As long as I get my points."

The next morning, without waiting to be summoned, the blacksmith showed up at Huozhuang High. He sat among the crowd, though he had no idea what a struggle session was. When everyone else held up their fists and shouted, "Tear down the counter-revolutionary so-and-so," he did the same. Then the loudspeaker blared: "Bring up the traitor Blacksmith Cao." Two people came over and hauled him up onto the stage. There were five of them up there, and he was the last in line. The others had placards hanging from their necks, but he didn't because he'd been added in at the last minute.

Copying the others, the blacksmith kept his head lowered and shouted out whatever they did. At noon, they were led offstage and brought to a classroom where they could continue reflecting on their actions.

The blacksmith took a seat and looked around at the others. None of them were young, and they were all neatly dressed and scholarly-looking. An older gentleman poured him a cup of water and offered him a cigarette. "Who are you all, sirs?" asked the blacksmith.

"We're teachers at this school. I've taught here for more than two decades," said the man, smiling warmly.

After a short while, someone called out the blacksmith's name. He was given a lecture, then allowed to return home.

Qingshan was worried about the blacksmith and went to see him that evening. "How did it go today, Uncle?"

"Oh, I was sent into a room. They poured me tea and gave me a good cigarette. Really, not a bad cigarette at all."

"When they asked you to explain yourself, what did you say?"

"I have nothing to explain. They said I sold out my comrades, but I sold no one out. I didn't take a cent for myself. They told me to mind my words and actions. Am I supposed to not move or say anything? It's not like I'm dead."

Qingshan had to laugh at that. He left feeling relieved.

The rebels didn't see any point denouncing someone like the blacksmith, so they didn't give him any more trouble. After that, he led a fairly uneventful existence.

THE BLACKSMITH'S SECOND son Hongrong missed his chance to get married due to poverty and remained a bachelor all his life. The third son, Honghua, found a wife in his twenties through a matchmaker. His lifelong cough meant he couldn't be too choosy. The woman he married had fallen into a well when she was a little girl and hadn't gotten any taller after that. Though she was very short and squat, at least her brain remained sharp.

The blacksmith turned eighty in 1985. One day, he was holding his granddaughter and chatting with my grandfather. Former Production Brigade Leader Si's son had dropped by for a visit too. As they talked, the brigade leader's son brought up a funny story from more than a year ago. Back then, many people from Shen Village had been sent to Jiangdu district to widen the Phoenix River. There wasn't much to do on the first day of work, and some people went for a stroll. Whenever they saw a tall building, they walked right in. A short distance away, they came upon a structure with a high chimney. They decided to go have a look, but at the doorway, they had to spit a full mouthful of saliva. This was a highly inauspicious place: a crematorium. They started work in earnest the next day. That evening, Hongrong abruptly complained of stomach pain. This alarmed everyone, because his big brother Hongxi had died while digging this very river, more than thirty years ago. And besides, they'd all picked up some bad luck by going near that crematorium the day before. Everyone got very worked up. When Hongrong heard what they had to say, he was so terrified that he curled up on his straw mat and howled. Someone sent for the doctor, who examined Hongrong and said, "It's fine, a bit of medicine and he'll be right as rain." Hongrong took the medicine and sure enough, his stomach stopped hurting, and he was able to get back to work. The others remained nervous, though, and made sure to check up on him every day. Only when the project came to an end three months later did they finally stop worrying.

The blacksmith didn't find this story funny at all. He picked up his granddaughter and grumpily headed home. That night, he had a bad dream about someone strangling him. The next day, at lunch, he choked on a clump of rice. Hongrong and Honghua brought their father to the hospital, where he was found to have advanced esophageal cancer.

One evening four months later, on the sixteenth day of the seventh lunar month, the blacksmith passed away. That very night, Hongrong and Honghua buried him in their backyard.

They hadn't expected the village cadres to discover this three days later. The cadres ran off to make a report to the rural residents' bureau and asked Bureau Leader Ma to come sort out the issue.

Bureau Leader Ma arrived at the Cao house right after a storm. Their roof leaked, and the interior was a giant mud puddle—there wasn't anywhere to stand. When he asked, "Where are your provisions?" Hongrong pointed at a metal bucket in the yard. Bureau Leader Ma started to wonder what he was doing there, but seeing as he *was* there, he spent some time enumerating the virtues of cremation to Hongrong, who nodded vigorously. Then he said, "How about this, you can pay a bit of a fine and screen a film about the importance of cremation, and we'll call it a day? Or we can skip the fine, but then you'll have to dig up the body and burn it."

Hongrong kept nodding, but said he didn't have a cent to his name. Bureau Leader Ma sighed and said to the village head, "Do as you see fit." With that, he walked away.

No one in Shen Village was willing to dig up the blacksmith after he'd spent three days in the ground. The village cadres had to get two people from outside. When the blacksmith surfaced, the stench permeated every corner of the village. Every household burned wormwood leaves to mask the smell. The body had started to rot. The two hired hands put on gloves, wrapped the corpse in a plastic sheet, and lifted it onto a tractor.

Finally, the blacksmith was cremated. No one paid for this, so after they'd been in the crematorium for a while, his ashes were tossed out.

Having their father's body get dug up was a heavy blow to Hongrong and Honghua. For a long time, whenever they ran into anyone in the village, they hung their heads in shame rather than saying hello. They felt they'd been useless and unfilial. Honghua had already been in poor health, and now he utterly collapsed. Half a year after his father's death, Honghua departed the world too, aged forty. He couldn't stop vomiting blood, and his eyes remained wide open when he passed. He refused to shut them.

After he died, Honghua's wife took her daughter back to her parents' house and stayed there, leaving Hongrong all alone in the dilapidated little hut.

Timid, loyal Hongrong is now in his eighties. He still pedals his trishaw around the village every day, calling out to collect empty glass bottles. For the last seven or eight years, I've run into him on every visit home. As I walk by the river, he'll be standing in front of his house, and as soon as he can make out that it's me, he walks over, accepts the cigarette I offer him, and stays for a chat. Whether he's speaking or not, he always has a delighted smile, and I've never seen a shred of worry on his face.

THE JACK-OF-ALL-TRADES

M Y UNCLE WAS KNOWN AS the jack-of-all-trades because he acquired all kinds of skills, but never mastered a single one of them. He meandered through his whole life. Apart from carpentry, which Grandpa made him learn, all the skills he picked up were things he enjoyed doing. He did whatever he wanted, which made him happy. Even when Grandpa said he was a useless good-for-nothing, that didn't anger him.

ONE SUMMER, RETURNING home from Nanjing, I saw the ginkgo tree by our front door in the distance.

The tree stands by South Gully, and a path leads from its trunk to the river.

My aunt was standing on the "water horse," staring in my direction.

"Auntie!" I called out.

"Oh my goodness, it's our Fishy back for a visit! Look at me, blind as a bat. I was wondering who that could be coming this way."

A "water horse" is a sort of rudimentary jetty made of a few floating planks nailed together. You crouch here to wash your clothes or vegetables in the water. When I was seven or eight, Grandpa taught me to swim from this water horse.

Now my aunt was squatting on the water horse, washing a basket full of crockery. She was expecting a lot of guests that day. My uncle was gone by then—he'd passed away the year before. When I came back for the funeral, my aunt kept telling me, "That night I cooked him a couple of dishes. He grumbled that he didn't like them. I said, don't fuss, old man, I'll make you some noodles instead. So I brought in the noodles, but he was still cursing away, saying they weren't good either. I plastered on a smile and told him to just say what the hell he wanted and I'd cook it. He said porridge, so I made him some barley gruel, and that actually went down quite well. He had two bowls. Afterward, Auntie Zhen from next door came by to borrow our bicycle, and he joked that she didn't need a bicycle, because he could carry her on his back. She laughed and called him an old rascal. The way he was grinning, who'd have thought he'd drop dead the next day?" On and on she talked.

Uncle started learning carpentry from Grandpa, but after a couple of years, it was clear that he was terrible at it. Grandpa stopped teaching him—he was an embarrassment. Even so, when a carpenter was needed in Shen Village, people would sometimes send for Uncle, and Grandpa would grumble, "Incompetent half-wit."

So if carpentry was out, what could he do? Next, he tried "grabbing yellow cats." And what did that mean? Basically, catching weasels. I witnessed this once; it was quite a production. First you found a huge haystack and surrounded it on all sides with nets. You needed four or five people for this, plus five or six dogs. The humans poked the straw energetically from all directions with long bamboo poles. The dogs scampered around howling. All the while, a leader would wave a sword around the empty air, as if he were casting a spell. You know what? It really did work—in a couple of hours a weasel squirmed out from the straw, straight into the net. They didn't beat it to death, but tossed it into a bamboo basket and clapped on the lid. Then, like a victorious army, they swaggered away with their captive. Uncle was the deputy leader. This wasn't really any kind of career—the money they got from selling the weasel didn't even pay for their beer afterward. I think Uncle only took part because it was fun. He was very playful and feared nothing.

Soon enough, he gave up grabbing yellow cats and turned to fishing. This took equipment, which he acquired one item at a time: he knotted his own net and chopped down some bamboo that he asked the bamboo-weaver to turn into a basket. That left only the leatheralls, which apparently he traded weasel skins for. I don't know what kind of skin they were made of, but they were basically coveralls, dark and watertight, that left only his head, hands, and feet exposed. Before going into the water, he'd tie the leatheralls tightly at his neck, wrists, and ankles to keep the water out.

Uncle was naturally good in the water and could stay under for the length of time it took an incense stick to burn. He sawed a hole in the ice, dove in, and emerged a while later with a fish in his hands. Fishing wasn't seen as a respectable profession in Shen Village, however, because the river belonged to the whole community, and you couldn't just help yourself from its bounty. He had to do this under cover of night, and his catch couldn't be sold, so the family ate it.

His next venture was raising silkworms. He ended up with too many to fit in his house and had to leave some of them with us. I was in elementary school at the time and found this all quite thrilling. I got hold of a little basket and headed to the woods to the east of our house every day to pick mulberry leaves. There were a lot of mulberry trees, none of them very tall, and I filled my basket easily. Uncle praised me for being so enthusiastic, and he promised that when the silkworms went uphill and spun themselves into cocoons that he could sell, he'd buy me a pair of sandals. I'd never had such a thing—I was either in cloth shoes or barefoot. I redoubled my efforts.

Finally, the silkworms went uphill. The "hills" in question were coarse ropes Uncle made by braiding wheat stalks. The silkworms, now transparent, climbed them and made cocoons.

He kept his word and came back from town after selling the silk cocoons with a pair of pillowy bubble sandals for me, the bright yellow of ducklings. I loved how they looked.

I don't know why, but, by the following year, Uncle had lost interest in silkworms and switched to catching toads instead.

This was done at night. You set out with an Eight Joints flashlight and a sliver of bamboo to scrape poisonous liquid off the toads' heads, drop by drop, into a jar. Apparently this substance could be turned into medicine.

Uncle didn't work alone. Five of them went out together. Most toads tended to congregate around remote rivers and ditches. You often had to travel quite a distance to reach them.

There was a cemetery seven or eight li to the northwest of Shen Village. Never mind at night—it was scary to walk by it even during the day. I always kept my distance, and went past as quickly as I could. The most frightening thing was a coffin that had been left in the open air, rather than getting buried. Inside was a young woman who'd fled from the north with her parents during the famine, and fallen ill here. Mr. He gave her several prescriptions, but none of them worked, and she died. The villagers pooled their money and asked Grandpa to make her a coffin, which they placed in this public cemetery. Because she was unmarried, they couldn't put her in the soil, but left her aboveground.

One night, the five toad-catchers walked by. From a distance, they could see a few flecks of ghost light drifting among the tombs.

"If anyone dares to sleep on that coffin tonight, I'll give him this whole jar of toad poison."

"How about it, Linhead? Do you dare?" Uncle's name was Qinglin, but people in Shen Village never used your whole name, it was always so-and-so-head. Qingtie became Tiehead, Qingguan was Guanhead, and my father Qingshan was universally known as Shanhead. Grandma was "Linhead's mom." Everyone knew Uncle loved to brag and hated looking bad. He was always going around saying how brave he was, so this bet was meant to show him up and take him down a peg or two.

"Hey, Linhead, spend the night here, and the four of us will give you a jar of poison each."

"That's right, full jars." They all laughed, egging him on.

A jar of toad poison was worth quite a bit of money; four would fetch an astronomical sum.

"Can I have a flashlight?" asked Uncle.

"No."

"Can I sing?"

"No. You'll lie there and sleep, that's all. Until daybreak."

"Fine," said Uncle.

He didn't come home that night. He took the lid off the coffin, flipped it over, put it back in place, and lay on top of it.

When they asked him about it afterward, he answered honestly that he'd lain there with his eyes wide open all night long and didn't get a wink of sleep. Just before dawn, bricks came hurtling toward him, which was actually reassuring. It was his companions who'd been lurking nearby. Disappointed by his lack of fear, they'd decided to toss some projectiles to scare him.

Uncle was so pleased with his winnings, he kept treating his friends to food and drink, especially the four colleagues who'd had to hand over their toad poison. Only when he'd exhausted this pot of money did things quiet down again.

A few months after the bet, the toad-catching was still going on. One moonless night, Uncle had walked a long way by himself when he realized the path had come to a dead end. He turned on his flashlight and found himself surrounded by brambles. Turning back, he'd only gone a short way, when there was another bramble patch. I'm in trouble, he thought, this must be ghosts walling me in. He knew how to fight this: pissing on the brambles. When he was done, he tried to find a way out, but a few hundred meters away, he got stuck again—more brambles. So he'd go around them. He got flustered and started running around in a panic. His clothes got shredded, but he didn't care.

At cockcrow, when the sky lightened, Uncle could see he was in a little forest. He clambered his way out and recognized the settlement ahead of him: Wild Village. His aunt's husband lived there. It was a few dozen li from Shen Village.

Uncle's aunt's husband welcomed him in. Uncle wasn't able to eat anything, so he just had a cup of ginger tea with brown sugar, wrapped himself in a blanket, and went to sleep. Before that, he asked someone to deliver a note to Grandpa in Shen Village.

The next day, Uncle was still a little dazed, but had recovered his strength. Uncle's uncle gave him a lift back to Shen Village on the back of his bicycle, a bumpy ride.

I'd heard about Uncle's ghostly encounter and was both scared and curious. Uncle's family lived in a thatched hut in the southwest corner of the village, more than a li from our house. His wife grumbled away as she cooked a pot of congee and ladled a bowl out for Uncle with a spoonful of brown sugar. There was a roomful of people at Uncle's house, all of them with mysterious expressions on their faces. Uncle needed to rest, so my father invited Uncle's uncle to our place.

I'd always been a little scared of Granduncle, because of the gruesome scars on his neck. Grandpa said he'd been stabbed thirteen times, though I never counted. In the winter of 1946, Granduncle got caught by one of the Nationalist militias who accused him of being a Communist cadre, because he happened to be nicely dressed. They tied him up and stabbed him in a ditch under cover of dark. Luckily his life force was strong, and he survived.

Granduncle said, "I've been ghostwalled too, but not this seriously—not dozens of li off track. Linhead must have run into a really vicious spirit. You can't swagger around being all full of yourself. If you're too bold, that's going to annoy people as well as ghosts—how could that do? A little ghost might give way to you, but you might just as easily anger a big ghost. Don't show all your strength—you don't want to get into a pissing contest with a ghost, do you? It would be better if he stopped walking around at night, especially alone."

Uncle spent the next week in bed, then the barber Ma Haiwan brought him to the Temple of the Thousand Buddhas. The barber had worked at the temple as a young man and was still friendly with the people here. The abbot gave Uncle a string of Buddhist beads and a set of scriptures. When he got back from the temple, Uncle gave up meat for a while and ate vegetarian for the next six months.

Uncle was born in 1937 and died in 2010. Auntie didn't shed a tear at his funeral, but carried on with her life, calmly accepting the fact of his death. It was as if she thought that's just how life was. But then, a month later, she suddenly fell ill and spent the next half year in bed.

"How's your health, Auntie?" I now said, taking the bamboo basket of dishes from her as we walked toward her house.

"What health? It's all because of your uncle."

"How could this be Uncle's fault? Anyway, it can't be easy living all by yourself, why don't you move in with Fishnet?" Fishnet was her son—he owned a snack bar in the city. He got his nickname because they caught him in a fishnet when he was born.

"No, no, I'm staying here. Do you know how I got ill? I understand now—it's because I offended your uncle. I was wondering: how could a perfectly healthy person sicken just like that? So I went to see a medium." There was a lady thirty-odd li northeast of the village who could invite spirits to possess her, so people in our world and the next could converse through her.

"She cast a spell and your uncle took over her body. He said to me, I've just died, but you're not at home, where have you gone this time? I said, I'm at Fishnet's place. He said, oh, very nice for you, staying with your son, plenty to eat and drink, not a care for me, I suppose I'll just go hungry. I said, I'm still making offerings to you at our son's place, aren't I? He said, it's so far away, how am I supposed to find my way there? You have to make the offerings in front of my tablet, or I won't get a taste. I'm so hungry, my stomach is sticking to my spine. If your head didn't ache, you'd never come home.

"And that's how I knew it was that awful man giving me a hard time." Auntie chuckled.

Before Uncle died, I went to see him at the hospital in Taizhou. He refused to stay at the hospital, but insisted on returning home. He was in good spirits, only a little thin. He was dressed in a traditional Chinese outfit and black cloth shoes, and his voice still boomed. He said, "If I'm going to die, I want to die at home. What do you think will happen if I die outside? I'll end up as a wandering spirit. Even if you burn offerings for me, I won't receive them—the local ghosts will grab them first."

Now he'd lost his temper, his son Fishnet had no choice but to give in and bring him home from the hospital. His spirits improved once he was back. When my father went to see him, he said, "You see? Now I'm here, everything's okay." Dad said, "The big mulberry tree in your yard is dead. We'll have to dig it up." Uncle said, "In a while. I'm not doing great—let's talk about it when I'm better."

Uncle never got better, and two months later he was gone. He'd been spewing up blood, but when Fishnet said, "Dad, let's get you to the hospital, as quick as we can," he kept a death grip on his bed. "No, I'm not going any-where, I want to die here." He was very insistent on dying at home.

Uncle was buried to the west of his house. His dog, who'd proudly fol-lowed him around, now sat near his grave, day after day, miserable at not having anyone to take care of it. The dog had a patch of white fur on the tip of its tail, and now the villagers said this was like a funeral patch, which meant bad luck for its owner. My father also claimed the death of the mulberry tree was a bad omen. This always happened when anyone died; afterward the whole village would retroactively see all kinds of signs and portents.

Uncle's pigeons, which he'd loved as much as his life, had completely van-ished a short while after his departure. When he was around, if anyone stole one of his birds, or even a single egg, he'd grab his club and head over to their house to whack them. The most important thing he did each day was to take the pigeons out. It was because of these pigeons that I understood the special love he had for my daughter, and also for me.

When my daughter was one, I brought her to Shen Village for the first time. She hadn't spoken yet, but when we reached the village and she saw all the rapeseed growing, she said the first word of her life, "Flower."

She couldn't say "Granduncle," but she smiled at him. He grinned back and popped home, returning a moment later with a bowl in one hand and a pigeon in the other. "This bowl of eggs is for the little girl, and you can turn this bird into soup for her." My father was stunned. He knew how much Uncle adored those birds. Even when he or his wife fell ill, he was unwilling to slaughter one of them. We insisted he take the pigeon back and only accepted the eggs.

That evening, we played a fortune-telling game: you set a tray of assorted items in front of a small child, and the first thing they grabbed would deter-mine their future path. My father laid out a fountain pen, a pencil, a calligraphy brush, a book, a ruler, and so forth, all kinds of implements related to scholar-ship. Clearly he wanted a studious grandchild. In order to make his bias less obvious, he placed a hard-boiled pigeon egg among these objects, as a sort of garnish. When we started the game, my daughter reached out without hesita-tion and grabbed the egg. We all burst out laughing, while her grandfather shook his head. Displeased, he said, "You still have one hand empty, my darling. Choose something else. Come on." My daughter ignored him and cupped the egg in both her hands, before bringing it to her mouth.

Uncle was present at this fortune-telling, and he laughed more heartily than anyone else.

Now, when I leave the village to head back to the city, I pass by his grave. He lies amid canola plants, and thick grass grows above him. More than twenty years ago, the first time I left home to work in the city, I walked past here too. The first glimmers of dawn light were just touching the sky, but Uncle and Auntie were already hard at work here, on the very piece of land where he's now buried. As I passed, he looked up and said, "Where are you off to, Fishy?" I pointed into the distance and said, "I'm leaving." I didn't know where I was going either. I walked quite a distance, then turned back to look. Uncle was still standing there, gazing after me. It would be a decade before I returned to the village after that. And today, each time I walk by this place, I see the spot where Uncle was standing, only now it's his grave.

THE TAILOR

A RIVER CALLED SOUTH GULLY FLOWS in front of our house, and on the other side is a small house of grayish brick, with a tiled roof. The river is so narrow the elm, locust, and plum trees on either bank almost touch branches. A thick willow tree slants to one side, reaching for the opposite shore and dipping its long branches into the water. As a teenager, coming home from school in the summer, I enjoyed perching on the willow trunk. I'd have a willow leaf in my mouth, whistling tunelessly, kicking at the river below. As I did this, the back door of the house across the river would open, and an old person would come out to stand by the tree and say in a quiet voice, "Be careful you don't fall in!"

She was only in her sixties, but her hair was already completely white, and her face was creased with wrinkles. She was soft-spoken, but because she'd lost her teeth, air whistled between her gums and made her voice sound odd. No one would have guessed that four decades ago, she was the most renowned belle of Shen Village.

· · ·

IT CAUSED QUITE a stir when she married into Shen Village. Not only because of her beauty, but also because she was becoming the second wife of Hele, the local tailor. Or rather, the local clothsmith, which is what we said in our village instead of "tailor."

The tailor was twenty-six when he died, and she was twenty-two. Because she came from Xu Village, people started calling her "the former Miss Xu" or "her from Xu Village." Later on, she was known as "Mrs. Clothsmith."

HELE'S FATHER LOCUST was a big cheese in Shen Village. He was middle-aged when he had his son. Given their comfortable circumstances, Hele was able to spend quite a few years at the village schoolhouse. At the age of four-teen, Locust sent him to the town to learn tailoring. He came back after two years of training, and his hands really had become skilled. He could cut and sew any style of clothing. All of a sudden, he became tremendously popular in Shen Village. Wherever he went, he had a gray cloth pouch under one arm, containing scissors, thread and buttons, and a long wooden ruler in his other hand. His hair was combed until it gleamed, and he hummed a little tune as he walked along. He sewed his own clothes out of superior fabric, with exquisite craftsmanship. Given his lithe figure and dashing manner, he was truly a living advertisement for his work.

At the age of eighteen, the tailor followed his parents' orders and, with extreme reluctance, married the daughter of his aunt, a Miss Chen.

Miss Chen was intelligent, upstanding, capable, and skilled in all kinds of housework. The only thing was, she'd had smallpox when she was seven or eight, which left her with a face full of pockmarks. To the tailor, who fancied himself a bit of a Casanova, this was completely unacceptable. He tried telling his father a few times he wanted to break off the engagement, but each time his father just yelled at him. And so, after they were married, he never once showed Miss Chen any kindness, but only snarled and bellowed at her.

After five years of marriage, Miss Chen still hadn't produced a child. This gave the tailor an excuse to tell his father he wanted a second wife. Locust was actually more anxious than the tailor about this. "There are three sins against your parents, and the worst one is leaving no issue," as the saying goes. If the tailor didn't have a son, who would take over their huge family business? And so, as soon as the tailor brought it up, Locust immediately sent a matchmaker scouring the district for a suitable candidate.

In less than a month, the matchmaker reported that Xu Village, to the north of Shen Village, had a maiden of nineteen who was attractive and virtuous. As her family was poor, she was willing to be a second wife. The following day, Locust and the tailor accompanied the matchmaker to Xu Village.

This was in the spring of 1943. The road from Shen to Xu Village was surrounded by yellow rapeseed flowers as far as the eye could see. Filled with a sort of antsy excitement, the tailor trotted along briskly. Even before they reached the house, the matchmaker spotted a figure doing laundry beneath the peach tree in their front yard, and cried out with a rapturous expression, "Clothsmith, look, that's her. What a woman!"

The peach blossoms were in full bloom, and the young woman sat beneath them with her arms in a long wooden tub of fragrant suds. When she noticed visitors approaching, she smiled at them, brushed her hands on her apron, went back inside the house, and refused to come out again. The tailor had only caught a glimpse, but that was enough to leave him besotted. He could hardly believe this was the woman the matchmaker had in mind. She had just turned nineteen, with delicate features and skin creamy as snow. Even the coarse dress she wore couldn't conceal her enchanting figure. The tailor spent four hours at the Xu house and the whole time kept his eyes peeled for the young lady, who didn't show herself again. His father spoke to her parents, but the tailor didn't take in a single word. Even when they left and headed home, his heart continued to thump violently.

The matchmaking went without a hitch. A month later, the tailor brought Miss Xu back to Shen Village. In order to demonstrate the depth of his love for her, he had some pigs and goats slaughtered and threw a huge banquet. The festivities lasted three days.

The tailor and his new bride were inseparable, leaving the first wife out in the cold. Xu respectfully addressed Chen as "big sister," and Chen was polite in return. Xu urged her new husband to be less cold to her big sister, but he refused. He didn't want to even look at his pockmarked first wife. Xu could only accept her husband's love, sweet and sticky as honey.

The honey-sweet days didn't last long. Just three years. Following which, the former Miss Xu spent nearly sixty years in lonely desolation. During these six decades, how long would she cling to the memory of this short-lived love? She dug into her heart, until it became a deep, dry well. For sixty years, she barely mentioned the name of the man who loved her and then bestowed upon her a lifetime of bitterness.

SIX MONTHS AFTER the wedding, Xu discovered she was pregnant. The tailor swaggered around with pride, feeling as if he were walking on clouds, humming all day long. Although the tailor was rather full of himself, the villagers didn't really dislike him. After all, his skills were first-rate. No matter how shabby the fabric you brought him, it could become rather splendid in his hands. His garments were neither dowdy nor so fashionable you wouldn't dare to wear them. Dressed in his creations, you looked extremely respectable. Young people especially, when they were ready to get married, would come to him for new outfits. After his second marriage, the tailor started behaving himself. Although he still teased the maidens and matrons outrageously, he now kept his hands to himself. This kind of flirtation was very welcome to the young people of Shen Village.

When Chen saw that Xu was pregnant, she realized her hopes of remaining in the Shen family were completely at an end. She packed her clothes and returned to her parents' home. A few days after this, her mother came and said to Locust, since your family doesn't want her, why not let her marry someone else? Locust talked it over with his son, who was all too eager to rid himself of her, and agreed right away. Two days later, Chen sent a servant with a wheelbarrow to pick up the rest of her dowry. After this, the two families had nothing to do with each other. The former Miss Chen didn't disappear, though. Many years later, she would return in an all-too-common manner to create all sorts of fearful scenes for the family. She wanted her revenge, even though the person who ought to have been her real target, the tailor himself, had now been dead for many years.

In 1944, the tailor's life was at its happiest, and yet he still wasn't content. He could write and paint thanks to his years at the Shen Village schoolhouse, and he was highly skilled—you could definitely call him accomplished. Despite this, he was often harassed by a couple of poor men.

These two had once been completely penniless and used to bow and scrape whenever they saw him. Then they became cadres and grew bold, losing respect for the tailor and starting to order him around. The tailor thought how unfair this world was, to leave a man as talented as him so powerless, while these low-lifes got to lord it over him. He would show them.

The Nationalists didn't really reach Shen Village. The only Nationalist in the whole place was, apparently, Wan Bao's son, who spent most of the year in Nanjing and rarely returned home. Even when he did, he only nodded and offered a cigarette when he bumped into anyone, but spoke so little that no one knew what he was up to in Nanjing. As far as the villagers were concerned, the Nationalists were an unfamiliar group who had nothing to do with them. China had become a republic by now, but life in Shen Village continued exactly the same as it had for centuries. Only when the Japanese army arrived was there a bit of a panic. Even then, they were only passing through, and didn't linger. Long before the Japanese devils showed up, people came running from neighboring villages to sound the alarm, and everyone in Shen Village cleared out. They waited for the devils to get well away before returning to their homes.

What really changed Shen Village was the Communist Party. According to our family records, the Shen clan settled in Shen Village more than six hundred years ago. For six centuries, the villagers rose with the sun and retired at dusk, and nothing much changed in their lives. Shen Village had always been like a torpid farmer who knew nothing of the outside world, but after 1940, it abruptly livened up.

In August 1940, two months before the Battle of Huangqiao, the Communists arrived in Shen Village once again. This was different from 1927, when only a couple of them showed up to quietly complete their business before vanishing again. This group looked like they were here for the long haul. With the firepower of the New Fourth Army backing them up, they no longer had to skulk around, but could openly recruit for the Party and appoint their own people as the head of each village they came to. Because of what happened to Kerong, though, most people in Shen Village politely declined, afraid they would get into trouble too. Kerong was the first Communist in Shen Village. In 1927, he returned from abroad to start a revolution, and also to open a teahouse in Xinjiezhen. After only two years of this, he was murdered. His body was never found.

The local magistrate came several times to see my grandfather, Tongshou the carpenter. "Carpenter, you've shared meals with a hundred families, you know everyone and you've seen everything, and you get on well with people. Why don't we make you the village head? Everyone respects you, and you'll find the job easy." Again and again, Grandpa turned him down. Finally, the magistrate lost his temper. Whipping the Mauser pistol out of his belt, he smacked it down on the table. "Why are you causing me so much trouble, Carpenter? Think about it: why not take this on as an honor, rather than a punishment? If you keep saying no, that will make you a counter-revolutionary, and I won't be so nice to you."

Alarmed by this, Grandpa went to ask Mrs. Fifth Life for help—the local magistrate was her nephew. She said, "Don't worry, carpenter. If they come for you, just hide yourself and send for me."

Two or three days after that, Grandpa got up before dawn, grabbed his plane and saw, and was about to set off for a client's house when he saw the magistrate and a couple of heavies approaching along the southern road. Flustered, he said to his wife, "Mother, go fetch Mrs. Fifth Life quick." With that, he climbed the ladder and hid behind the "household head," a couple of wooden boards, half-human height, nailed together in a T-shape. One end was fixed to the rafter, and the other to the wall. This provided a shelf for ancestral tablets and a Buddha statue, with enough room for a person to crouch behind it. Grandma got rid of the ladder and opened the door to the magistrate.

"Where's the carpenter?"

"He's gone out to work. He just left," said Grandma.

The magistrate waved, and his two heavies came in to search. The house was small, just three thatched rooms, and it was clear at a glance that no one else was here. The magistrate said, "Go fetch the carpenter right away. We'll wait here. If he doesn't show up, we'll hogtie him ourselves."

"All right, all right, I'm going," said Grandma. She hurried off to Mrs. Fifth Life's house.

And so it wasn't Grandma who returned, but Mrs. Fifth Life.

Fifth Life was the scale-operator's second son. As a child, he was betrothed to a girl who would later become a great beauty. This was Mrs. Fifth Life.

When she appeared, the magistrate jumped to his feet. "What are you doing here, Auntie?"

"Why are you men sitting around here? Come home with me, I'll fix you something to eat. If there's a problem, we can take our time to talk it over."

She brought them home and sent someone out to buy some fish and meat. After the meal, she said, "The carpenter is a good man, but he won't make a good cadre. He has too many burdens at home. Four or five children, and a sickly wife, all dependent on him. Where is he supposed to get the energy to do the Party's work? You'll have to think of something else. There must be another suitable candidate. I'll help you come up with ideas too."

It took some persuasion, but the magistrate eventually agreed. Decades later, Grandpa was still talking about how Mrs. Fifth Life saved him.

No one could be found to serve as village head, and the magistrate was growing increasingly agitated. He went to see Mrs. Fifth Life a few times, urging her to make more of an effort. Just as she was at her wits' end, she happened to see Xi Wang passing by her door one day, on his way back from panhandling in another village.

"Wait up, Xi Wang. Come in for a visit." When he realized it was Mrs. Fifth Life calling him, Xi Wang doubled back, set his dog-beating club against a wall, and set down the patched cloth bundle from his shoulder. Before he could put down his begging bowl, Mrs. Fifth Life pulled him indoors. "Come on in, we've just finished cooking." She heaped his bowl with rice, added a few chopstickfuls from the other dishes on top, pulled out a stool from under the table, and invited him to sit.

Xi Wang lived in the wilderness to the northwest of the village. His family didn't own any farmland, and there were a lot of them, so there wasn't much they could do except roam around and beg. They never did that in Shen Village, though, but went as far as they could, ideally to places where they knew no one, so they wouldn't be recognized. Even so, everyone in Shen Village knew what they did, but no one would ever say so—that would make things awkward.

"You can't go on like this, Xi Wang. The magistrate is looking for someone to be the village head. If you become a cadre, you'd be able to feed your family."

Xi Wang said nothing as he bent over his meal. He finished every bite, licked the chopsticks, and put down his bowl. When Mrs. Fifth Life went to give him more, he said, "I've had enough, thanks. You know, a couple of days ago, I heard that the magistrate came to see the carpenter, but he refused. He's a skilled worker, he's got food on his table and money in his wallet, he's not going to want to put his head on the chopping block."

Mrs. Fifth Life said, "Things are different now that the New Fourth Army is here. We're not asking you to go off and be a soldier. You just need to sort things out here in the village—it's not as bad as you're making it sound."

"I know you mean well," said Xi Wang. "To be honest, I'm not scared of becoming the village head. The thing is, I'm a beggar. Making me the head-man might make the Communist Party look bad."

"That's no way to talk! So, if you're willing, I'll have a word with the magistrate."

"I'm willing," said Xi Wang. "Anything's better than begging."

Mrs. Fifth Life got Xi Wang's begging sack from the doorway and half-filled it with uncooked rice. He thanked her a thousand times, and set off happily for home.

The magistrate went to see Xi Wang the next day, and was so delighted to find him loyal and honest, he appointed him on the spot. "The Communist Party is the party of poor people. You're a member now. Go find yourself a blade—you'll carry it with you at all times, firstly for protection, secondly so people will know who you are. You'll also have to find someone else in Shen Village to be your deputy. You'll need a helper."

Xi Wang went into the village and sought out Cao Xie'er, the blacksmith. In contrast to Xi Wang's steadiness, the blacksmith was a layabout who loved stirring up trouble. When he heard that having an official position meant you could get fed without having to work in the fields, he happily agreed on the spot.

So Xi Wang was the village head, and the blacksmith was the fanshen leader. The two men would get up first thing in the morning and wander round the village with gleaming swords hanging from their belts, looking for people to have meetings with, or soliciting donations of money or grain from the masses. "The New Fourth Army has arrived—they'll defeat the Japanese devils and their collaborators. Give what you have, whether that's cash or food or the sweat of your brow."

By 1944, Shen Village had become a transport hub for supplies. Food, ammunition, and clothing would arrive in bags and get heaped up into little mountains. The higher-ups wanted to appoint someone in the village who could keep track of it all. The only people who knew how to write or keep accounts were the rich folk, and most of them had fled. The only one still around was the tailor. The magistrate went to tell him he was needed as the village's resource manager, which meant he would be in charge of the supplies passing through on their way to the front line. The tailor agreed right away. He was already annoyed at being bossed around by the arrogant, penniless pair.

Which meant Shen Village now had three Communist Party cadres.

The tailor had two main tasks, keeping track of provisions and maintaining order, both of which he enjoyed. Managing resources meant he had plenty to eat and drink, and anyone coming to get supplies had to go through him, which meant he could order them around. As for maintaining order, that was a prominent position, and allowed him to cut a very dashing figure.

One time, the village head sent a stretcher team to the front line. Before setting out, they had to see the tailor to collect their rations. According to the regulations, this had to be done on the first day, but some people only arrived on the second day, and the tailor fined each of them three pounds of rice. A few came the day after that, and he refused to issue them anything at all— they'd missed the deadline. These unfortunates went to their fanshen leader, the blacksmith, and said they weren't going if they didn't get their rations.

The blacksmith went to see the tailor, who was too busy canoodling with his new bride to even meet the blacksmith's eye. Head tilted to one side, he said, "I'm just following the rules. Look, I've kept accounts of all the surplus rations, and they've been handed back. Nothing left over at all. Here's my ledger, you can see for yourself." But how was the blacksmith supposed to do that? He was illiterate. All he could do was leave in a rage, borrow some grain from a wealthy household, and send the stretcher-bearers on their way. This was just one of the many grievances between the blacksmith and the tailor. There was a vast gulf between the thinking and behavior of these two men, one rich and one poor. They resented each other and often brought their quarrels to the magistrate to resolve. The magistrate had far more important matters on his mind than their petty squabbles, so he usually shouted at them both and sent them on their way.

At night, the tailor would stroll around the village with a lantern. Other people saw patrolling as a hardship, but not him. He took it as an opportunity to swagger. On this occasion, it was around midnight when he walked behind a house to the east of the village, and saw two figures: a man and a woman. As the light flashed across them, they darted into the nearby bamboo grove. The tailor shouted, "Who's there?" No response. "If you don't come out, I'm sending for the militia." The bamboo stalks swayed, and out came Political Commissar Xiao from the local district office. "Oh, it's you, Clothsmith. What are you shouting about?" When the tailor saw who it was, his face blanched and he scurried away.

This time round, the tailor kept his mouth firmly shut. He told his family what had happened, but absolutely no one else. Although he'd had a shock, he didn't really take it to heart. Rather, he felt this incident had brought him a tiny bit closer to the political commissar. And so, the next time he saw Xiao, he behaved much more chummily. It wasn't till the moment before his death, a year later, that he would realize this encounter had actually been a fatal one.

The tailor's father, Locust, was a man of the world. When he saw how the tailor was constantly causing trouble all around him, he summoned his son and yelled at him, jabbing a finger at his nose, insisting that he had to give up his resource manager position right away and stay home. "You have everything you need here, there's no need to go charging around outside raising hell. You might feel good about yourself now, but be careful you don't put yourself in the line of fire. You're not leaving this house again. If I see you running around after this, I'll break your legs."

But of course, the tailor was hardly going to listen to that. He kept himself as busy as ever, strutting around arrogantly.

In the fall of 1944, the tailor's son was born, and he grew even more dissipated and frivolous. All day long, he wafted around proclaiming, "I have everything I need." This unwarranted smugness attracted quite a lot of dislike, which he was blissfully unaware of. He continued using his petty authority to order people around, got into a power struggle with the blacksmith, and stirred up all kinds of trouble.

Locust was burning with worry that some misfortune would befall the tailor. When repeated scolding didn't work, he turned to soft words and pleas. "You've just had a child. Shouldn't you be spending more time at home taking care of your wife and child? What good does it do going around raising a ruckus like that? Do you know what people are saying behind your back?" But the tailor ignored him and continued doing exactly as he pleased. When he wasn't calling meetings, he was running around chasing debts. Locust couldn't stand it any longer. One day, when the tailor was having a meeting, he grabbed a club and charged in. The tailor snatched the club from him and tossed it outside. The magistrate, who was chairing the meeting, roared, "You old recalcitrant, are you really trying to be a counter-revolutionary? If you keep interfering with the Revolution, we'll string you up from a tree."

Locust returned home in such a fury that he fell ill. His wife, old Mrs. Zhou, came to see the tailor. "Hele, my son, you see how sick you've made your dad? Stop doing this. Just stay home." The tailor ignored her too. Luckily he adored Xu, and though he continued busying himself all day, he returned to her each night. Locust lingered for a few more months, but eventually died from his illness on the eighteenth day of the second lunar month in 1945. Now that there was no one to restrain the tailor, he grew even cockier, combing his hair into a pompadour and swanking around the village with his baby son in his arms.

On August 15, 1945, the Japanese surrendered, and the New Fourth Army decided to liberate Huangqiao Town and Taixing County City, which had been Japanese-occupied. The Shen Village cadres were very busy now. The tailor handed the child to Xu to look after and stayed out all day. He had to organize stretcher teams, recruit volunteer soldiers, distribute money and rations—and the more exhausted he got, the happier he was, because this hardship and tiredness was the best way to demonstrate his importance and make him look good. On August 29, they recovered Huangqiao after the Japanese pulled out. On September 12, they entered Taixing, which had been taken over by the Nationalists, and captured the Nationalist county leader.

Now that they'd claimed Taixing back, the county was temporarily at peace. Then the higher-ups sent a notice that the cadres would have to undergo a rectification exercise.

The rectification meeting was chaired by the local district's Political Commissar Xiao, who said, "If any of you present has done anything wrong, it would be best if you confessed it yourself. If someone else says it, that won't go well for you. And if you know of anyone else's misdeeds, they mustn't be concealed. You must report your findings, regardless of personal relationships. Anyone who holds back will also be punished."

The tailor wasn't interested in this so-called rectification. He thought it had nothing to do with him and treated it as just another meeting, speaking with his usual carelessness. "Rectifi-what? We're working hard all day long, and we don't get a cent. What's there to investigate?"

The day after the meeting, the magistrate received an accusation against the tailor for appropriating army rations. That evening, he was arrested and brought to the township. Soon, the truth came out: during his time as the resource manager, he'd purloined over a hundred pounds of rice. The magistrate said, "What a mess! Tell him to replace the food he stole, and pay a small fine. Go find some people to bail him out."

When Locust was still alive, he'd gotten on well with the carpenter. Now the carpenter heard that the tailor could be bailed out and hurried over to discuss this with the tailor's mother. Old Mrs. Zhou said, "I'll have to rely on your help. Where could I possibly find bondsmen?" She shook her head helplessly. This was indeed the truth—no one really cared much for the tailor. His high-handed attitude had turned almost everyone away. Now that he was in trouble, they were happy to look on and laugh at him.

Finally, thanks to the carpenter's efforts, ten people got together to bail out the tailor. Old Mrs. Zhou bought meat and liquor to thank them. After they'd eaten and drunk, the carpenter brought them, along with money for the fine and rice to pay back what the tailor had stolen, to the township. The tailor was released after the ten of them had inked their fingerprints on a "letter of forfeiture," meaning if the person who'd been bailed out were to re-offend, everyone who'd placed their fingerprint on the document would have all their property confiscated.

The day after the tailor was released, he put on a brand-new outfit, oiled his hair, and resumed strutting through the village.

"Hey, Clothsmith, you're back!"

"Yes, I'm back."

"How did it go at the township?"

"Very well. I had a meal with the township cadres and we all hung out. No big deal."

Someone asked, "How come they arrested you?"

"Well! Someone tried to make mischief. I know all about it. But that's nothing. I'm me, aren't I? What could he do to me? When someone sends me trouble, I'll return it with interest."

Another person asked, probably with bad intentions, "Tailor, isn't your aunt's husband a deputy captain in the Nationalist Army at Kou'an Town?"

The tailor said, "Yes, that's right. I've had a chat with him. The person who tried to harm me is going to have so much trouble on his plate, he'll have to get a doggy bag."

Despite the tailor's vehemence, he didn't actually know who had accused him and wasn't capable of taking such revenge in any case. Nonetheless, his words quickly spread through the village.

A couple of days later, the tailor was arrested again. This time, along with corruption, he was accused of "attempted collusion with reactionary Nationalist elements to retaliate against the Communist Party."

Again, the magistrate was in charge of interrogating him. The tailor said, "When my uncle heard I'd become a Communist cadre, he threatened to kill me. How would I dare ask him for anything? I was only talking nonsense."

He was locked up for seven or eight days, but they couldn't find any evidence of collusion. The township knew he was prone to talking recklessly and decided to give him a scare. They announced, "This time, we want a hundred forfeiture bondsmen and a much bigger fine before we'll release him. If not, he'll face the firing squad."

The carpenter was in the middle of a job when he got wind of this. He flung down his ax and hurried to the tailor's house, where he said to Old Mrs. Zhou, "This is bad. We need to think of something quick, otherwise you may never see him again."

Old Mrs. Zhou said, "Where would I find a hundred people? Anyway, I haven't got any more money for the fine. Let them cut him or kill him as they like. He'll get reincarnated, and twenty years from now he'll be just as fine a figure of a man."

The carpenter and some friends visited again and again, trying to impress upon Old Mrs. Zhou just how serious this was. She continued ignoring them. Perhaps she was still angry about how the tailor had driven Locust into such a rage that he died and wanted to teach her son a lesson. Perhaps she wasn't willing to part with such a large sum. Or perhaps she knew the tailor hadn't actually done anything wrong and thought this was some sort of extortion scheme.

The township waited a couple of weeks, but there was no response from the tailor's family, and they'd all heard about Old Mrs. Zhou's repudiation. Someone else said, "We can't let him go. If we do, he'll return with the Nationalists and take revenge." The magistrate lost his temper. "This clothsmith is a born troublemaker. Just get rid of him." And so he wrote a report to the District. Commissar Xiao read it, and when he realized it was the person who'd barged in on him at the bamboo grove, he gave the order, "Punish him severely!"

The date of the tailor's execution was set for the sixteenth day of the tenth lunar month in 1946. When the carpenter heard this, he rushed to see Old Mrs. Zhou in a panic, but she remained unmoved. Xu sobbed and pleaded, but all she said was, "Everyone has their own destiny. If he's not meant to die, then he won't. But if his fate is at an end, nothing we do will make a difference. We can't interfere."

The tailor sent many messages asking his mother to save him, but got no reply. Only now did he understand how big a grudge she bore him, and regretted what he'd done. Still, wasn't he her son? How could she stand by and let him die? When he found out they'd fixed a time for the firing squad, he completely gave up hope and said, "I don't hate anyone, except for my hard-hearted mother." He got the guard to pass his wife a message. He wanted to see his son one last time.

The night before the execution, Xu came with liquor, food, and their one-year-old child, to the room in Dongyue Temple where the tailor was being held. He was sitting on the ground, both arms tied to a pillar. When he saw Xu holding the baby and weeping, he burst into tears too. The guard untied him, so he could eat and drink. Instead, the tailor hugged his wife and son, and sobbed, "I've let you down. All I ask is that you raise this child." They tied him up again before he could take a single bite. Xu went home with their son, crying all the way.

When Old Mrs. Zhou heard Xu's account, she finally went to the carpenter's house and asked him what she should do. "You're asking this now?" roared the carpenter. "He'll be shot dead tomorrow. What do you think you should do? Go home and get ready to receive his corpse."

Without another word, Old Mrs. Zhou went back home. Only now, when confronted with the tailor's imminent execution, was she starting to feel some remorse. She had no idea, though, what horrifying consequences the tailor's death would bring to her household, her grandson, and the remaining twenty-eight years of her life.

ON THE MORNING of the sixteenth, Shen Village's fanshen leader, the blacksmith, banged his gong and shouted, "Listen up, there'll be a meeting in front of Dongyue Temple after breakfast. One representative from every household."

Everyone's hearts went into their throats. The dashing, cocky tailor would soon be dead.

And the whole village knew it was the blacksmith who had denounced him.

Some cursed, "That son of a bitch. He's hurting everyone, including himself. He'll come to a gruesome end."

Others sighed, "The tailor's an arrogant loudmouth, but he doesn't deserve the firing squad!"

The blacksmith didn't care what people were saying about him. He had guts of steel. In all of Shen Village, he might have been the only person who was happy about the tailor's death. This was the greatest thing he'd accomplished in all his life. Not long after this, his fate would take a sudden turn. The most glorious period of his life was already over, even though he was only in his thirties, in his prime. He would live on into his eighties, but what would the remaining fifty-odd years contain? While he was still around, I never had any idea that he'd had anything to do with the tailor's death. His family lived to the east of mine. From our front door, you walked along the river a couple of minutes, and you'd be at his place. Grandpa often brought me there for a visit. I loved it there—this kind, interesting old man would tell me all kinds of weird stories. I didn't know that all those years ago, there'd been a day when everyone in Shen Village was cussing at him and despising him. He ignored them all, charged around with a gleaming knife under his arm, exuberantly urging everyone to go see the tailor get shot.

People came from all around, and soon Dongyue Temple was thronged.

The trial took place on a threshing field next to the temple. They'd set out four eight-immortals tables, which three township cadres stood atop. At noon, the magistrate declared proceedings open. "Bring in the accused." Two volunteer soldiers with rifles slung across their backs led the tailor from the temple, bound hand and foot. They hoisted him onto the central table and forced him to kneel before the crowd. The mass of people were utterly silent. The tailor kept his head bowed and said nothing. The magistrate held up a paper and proclaimed the verdict. "Clothsmith, you have corruptly stolen army provisions, and attempted to collude with counter-revolutionaries against the Communist Party. I am authorized to sentence you to death by firing squad, to take place immediately." He gestured, and the soldiers dragged the tailor off the table by his collar. Each holding one of his arms, they hauled him to the graveyard southeast.

The crowd cautiously followed behind.

The soldiers shoved him against a large tomb and forced him to kneel. One of them retreated a dozen paces, and the other pressed his pistol to the back of the tailor's head. A flash, a bang, and the tailor pitched forward. He arched his back, his head began spurting blood, and his legs twitched a few times. Then he was still. The shooter kicked him a couple of times, then bent to remove his shoes, and flung them away to the southeast. Then he swiftly untied the tailor, stripped off the new clothes Xu had brought the night before, rinsed them in a nearby stream, and walked off with them over his arm.

With the soldiers gone, the crowd swarmed over. The tailor was flat out on the ground, blood all around him. When the first round of people moved aside, another round replaced them. Small kids were darting back and forth. It was more than an hour before the onlookers finally dispersed. The tailor's uncle, the carpenter, and a few others wiped the blood off the tailor with cotton wool, wrapped him in a thin blanket, and pushed him away in a wheelbarrow.

At the tailor's house, Old Mrs. Zhou and Xu were howling. After this had gone on awhile, the carpenter yelled at Old Mrs. Zhou, "What are you crying about? You could have done something about this!" Then he sent someone to buy some wood, and stayed up all night making the tailor's coffin.

Because the tailor had been killed by the government, the coffin could only remain in the house for a day, and they weren't able to have a funeral when they buried him. The tailor was just twenty-six at the time of his death, Xu was twenty-two, and their son Mingjiu was thirteen months old.

THE SCHOOLTEACHER

ALTHOUGH SHEN VILLAGE WAS RIFE with rumors about Grandpa and Mingjiu's mom, that didn't stop our families from being close. Mingjiu and my father were the same age, and the two boys were the best of friends. I've met Mingjiu, but he didn't leave much of an impression on me. He taught at a school some distance from Shen Village, which kept him away most of the time. I remember him as a scrawny young man with a very neat haircut—unlike most of the men in Shen Village, who kept their balding heads shaved. I'd just started elementary school, so knowing he was a teacher meant I had a huge amount of respect for him.

Mingjiu died when I was eight years old.

We were eating dinner that evening when an earth-shattering howl came from across the river. Dad dropped his bowl and dashed out, calling as he went, "Oh no, Mingjiu's dead." I followed him to the doorway, and saw villagers arriving from all directions, all running toward Mingjiu's home.

Mom pulled me back inside. "This isn't for little kids. Finish your food and go to bed."

I woke up in the middle of the night, but Dad still wasn't home. I could hear sobbing from the opposite bank. It filled me with fear. I shut my eyes, but didn't dare to fall asleep again.

THE DAY THE tailor was executed, Xu also wept all night long. Mingjiu was only thirteen months old then and had no idea his father had died. More than thirty years later, he too would leave this world. Like Hele's, his coffin would rest on two benches in the middle of the hall. His son had just started elementary school and knelt to one side in his mourning clothes, uncertain what to do. Only when he saw his mother faint did he panic and start sobbing too.

At this year's Tomb Sweeping Festival, I went home to tend to Grandpa's grave. On the way back to the Shen Village from the cemetery, I ran into Mingjiu's son. He eyed me for a long moment before smiling in recognition. "Fishy! You've come back too!"

We hadn't seen each other in over two decades. After graduating from middle school, he left to work at a factory in Jiangnan. I finished high school, then went wandering across southern China. The last time I saw him, he was still in his early teens, and now he was a middle-aged man of forty with a stubbly chin. It's a horrifying business, suddenly adding more than twenty years onto a person's body. I'm sure he felt the same shock, looking at me.

When I turned back to watch the middle-aged man walking away, a shovel over one shoulder, I thought of Mingjiu's and the tailor's deaths.

IN THE TENTH lunar month of 1945, the tailor was shot dead. After all the mourning rituals were complete, very few people from the village stepped into his house.

Everyone pitied the widow Xu and loathed Old Mrs. Zhou.

She was seen as a scourge, a plague.

There was no visible change in Old Mrs. Zhou's behavior—she ordered her two servants around just as much as ever. Xu locked herself in her room and wept, refusing to leave the house.

After the six-week mourning period was over, Old Mrs. Zhou went into Xu's room and told one of the servants to take Mingjiu out to play.

"You're still young, just twenty-two. If you want to remarry, I won't stop you. But let me make this clear: if you leave, you're not taking so much as one stalk of grass from this household with you. Mingjiu will stay here with me, and you won't ever see him again."

Sobbing, Xu said, "Don't worry, Mom, I'm not leaving. I promised Hele I would raise Mingjiu. I'll serve you for the rest of your life."

Old Mrs. Zhou said, "This family owns over thirty mu of land. We have plenty of money and grain. If you stay, all this property will belong to you. It will be your fate to live without a man."

Xu said, "My fate is bad, but I accept it."

As far back as I can remember, the widow Xu, resigned to her fate, was already an old woman. She no longer possessed the beauty of her youth, and her sorrow was gone too. She wore her grayish-white hair in a bun caught up in a black net, with a silver pin stuck through it, a plain, neat look. I often went into her yard to pick little red berries off a tree that grew there, which I used as pellets for my bamboo blowpipe. She would watch me, smiling warmly, unlike the other grown-ups who always looked ferocious. She never chased me away, only softly said, "Fishy, be careful not to aim your shooter at anyone. If you hit them in the eye, you could hurt them badly!" Now and then she'd emerge from the house with a metal container, from which she'd produce a piece of candy for me. I never once saw her lose her temper, cry or shout at anyone. She was always as placid as still water, and she lived to be seventy-nine, all alone in that house.

XU'S OLDER SISTER had married into a family in a small town not far from Jiangyan. Two months after the tailor's death, she came dozens of li on foot to see her little sister in Shen Village. When their elder brother heard, he hurried there from Xu Village to be with his sisters. The three siblings wept to be reunited. Old Mrs. Zhou sent her servants out to buy liquor and meat to welcome these visitors from afar. The elder sister saw that even though Xu and Old Mrs. Zhou were widows of two different generations, without a man to run their household, they still had a tile-roofed five-room home that stood out from the thatched cottages around them. A couple of bullocks stood in the cowshed in front of their home, and behind were three ginkgo trees that were nearly a century old. Two of the rooms in the house had been set aside for storage, and held five or six rush containers with peaked lids, each holding at least a thousand pounds of grain. Up to this point, Xu's sister had been worried that Xu might not have enough to live on. She'd wanted to bring money or provisions, but her family didn't have any to spare, so in the end she'd come with a couple of laying hens as a gesture of her affection. Seeing the wealth of her sister's household, she felt as if a rock had been lifted off her heart, but then immediately grew ashamed of her own straitened circumstances.

Fifteen-month-old Mingjiu was walking but still couldn't speak. He laughed as he ran jerkily around, grabbing whatever he could get his hands on to take a bite and drop it on the ground. He loved coughing like their caged mynah, who in turn was mimicking the late tailor. Xu's sister thought the little boy was adorable, but whenever she tried to hug him, Mingjiu would struggle away. His mother was the only person allowed to pick him up. Their brother laughed and said to the sister, "If you like him that much, why not betroth him to Xiaofen? They're already cousins, they could be husband and wife too." Xiaofen was the sister's only daughter, a year older than Mingjiu. Xu's sister said, "I'd love to! But we're so poor, I'm afraid Xu won't think we're good enough for her." Xu laughed. "What kind of way is that to talk? Xiaofen is so pretty, she's more than good enough for any family."

Xu's sister went home with her brother's words ringing in her ears. A few days later, she asked her brother to go back to Shen Village to formally ask Xu what she thought. In fact, as soon as her sister left, Xu had begun wheedling Old Mrs. Zhou for her consent—she didn't have the authority to make any decisions in this household. Unfortunately, Old Mrs. Zhou's answer was a frosty, "The child is still so young. Let's wait till he's a bit older, and we'll see." Xu knew the older woman wasn't going to agree, because her sister was poor.

Up to now, Xu had given way to Old Mrs. Zhou in everything. Even when she'd refused to rescue the tailor, Xu had wept in private, but didn't dare to say anything. This was partly because she was afraid of her mother-in-law, and partly because she thought the old woman must have some sort of plan— surely she wouldn't send her son to his death? Then the tailor was executed, and although Xu's behavior remained docile, she began forming ideas of her own. When Old Mrs. Zhou refused to agree to Mingjiu and Xiaofen's betrothal, Xu began a cold war. All day long, whether tending to her son or doing her chores, she kept her face completely blank and refused to say a word to her mother-in-law.

The way Xu saw it, she might have married into a rich family, but they lacked men to work in the fields. During the busiest times in the farming year, they were completely rushed off their feet. Her own family had plenty of people and not enough land, which meant surplus labor. If she and her sister betrothed their children to each other, her family would surely be even more eager to help out. If this marriage fell through, it would look like Xu only cared about money and sucking up to rich people, which would hurt her family's feelings so much they might even turn their backs on her, which would cut off her escape route.

Old Mrs. Zhou's heart had begun to soften after the tailor's death, and Xu's cold war further wore her down. Finally, she gave in and agreed to let Xu's son marry her sister's daughter.

Even today, more than sixty years later, it's hard to say whether Xu's persistence left Mingjiu better or worse off. In any case, this betrothal shaped his destiny. It was the origin of his joy and also his pain. Again and again, it gave him a shot in the arm when he was in dire straits, but also plunged him back into the abyss.

THE OFFICIAL ENGAGEMENT took place on the sixteenth day of the eighth lunar month in 1946, one day after Mid-Autumn. Mingjiu was two years old, and Qian Xiaofen was three. The matchmaker was Xu's cousin, Zhang Ruxue.

On the morning of the sixteenth, Old Mrs. Zhou asked the carpenter, Mrs. Fifth Life and others to come by and help. Mrs. Fifth Life would be the ladle-holder, meaning she was in charge of the cooking. This was considered a great honor in Shen Village; only the most upstanding, distinguished women were invited to take this position. As for the carpenter, he'd been the best friend of Locust, Old Mrs. Zhou's late husband, and she now went to him for all kinds of advice. At this point, he was part of the backbone of this family. She asked him to greet the guests as they arrived.

The festivities lasted two days. Finally, the guests began to depart. Only Xu's cousin Zhang Ruxue remained behind.

Zhang Ruxue was Xu's mother's sister's son. He was a short man with delicate features and a rather genteel manner. Although he was a barber, he looked more like a scholar who never saw the sun. At the age of twenty-three, he was still unmarried. He'd been fond of Xu, but because his family was so poor, he could only watch as she went off to be the tailor's second wife. After the tailor's death, Ruxue often came to Shen Village to work for Xu. He worked hard, had a sweet tongue, and came across as an honest guy. Everyone in the village loved him—at least to start with. As time went on, rumors slowly began to spread about the murky relationship between him and Xu.

Xu put the whole thing out of her mind, and steadfastly ignored the tittle-tattle. Old Mrs. Zhou was on full alert, but she didn't have the smallest scrap of evidence, so she couldn't actually do anything.

After Mingjiu's engagement came the peanut harvest. Zhang Ruxue stayed back to help. He dug up each plant with a shovel, and Xu plucked off the peanuts one by one. Ruxue kept his head down as he worked, and said, "Cousin, you're still young, and you have a very small child. If you go on like this, what will your life become?"

Xu hesitated for a long time, then she sighed. "You know how I feel, Cousin Ruxue, but it's not possible between us. Leaving this family would mean abandoning Mingjiu, and I can't do that. I wish we could bring you into this household, but Old Mrs. Zhou would never agree to that, and the clan wouldn't allow it anyway. This is my fate. I'll have to struggle on alone."

"Why are you doing this to yourself?" Ruxue looked up at her, his eyes full of worry and desolation. "I've waited so many years for you. I'd given up, but now you're widowed, I'm allowing myself to hope again. Life with me might be harder, but I'll work as hard as I can, and eventually things will get better."

"Ruxue, we see this differently, and there's no point saying any more. All of Shen Village is already murmuring because you come here so often to help out with chores. You should visit less often. Go home and work on establishing yourself in the world. That will be better for both of us."

Ruxue said nothing, but lowered his head and dug up more peanut plants. When they'd cleared the entire patch, he looked up again. "I understand what you're saying, Cousin. I'll go now."

That very evening, Ruxue gathered his barbering tools and left, never to return. Xu locked herself in her room and cried all night long.

Two days later, Xu took Mingjiu to visit her parents in Xu Village. Along the way, she made a detour to Ruxue's house.

It was noon when she got there. He lived in a stumpy two-room thatched cottage, its roof pitted and sunken, with many sparrow nests tucked into it—clearly, it had been many years since it had last been refurbished. Xu had visited as a child with her mom, but she hadn't expected to find it in just as dilapidated a state more than ten years later. Her aunt was delighted to see Xu and the child. She hurried over to her neighbor's place to borrow some flour to make flatbread. Her uncle came back from the fields, washed his hands, and went to the next village to fetch Ruxue from his barbering work.

Xu ate a few flatbreads and drank some tea as her aunt said, "Ruxue makes my heart ache. He's not as young as he used to be, but he refuses to let us find him a match. He stays out all day and never comes home. It's good that you're here. Maybe you can talk some sense into him."

Xu nodded and responded absently, playing with her child and waiting for Ruxue to get home.

After a couple of hours, Ruxue rushed in the door. He dropped his barbering tools by the entrance, scooped up Mingjiu, and planted a kiss on his cheek with a loud smack. Then the aunt took the little boy and went out with her husband, leaving Ruxue and Xu to talk alone.

Xu took ten silver dollars from her bundle and said, "Cousin Ruxue, this is the money I've managed to save over the last few years. If you still value our friendship, please accept it. You can fix up your house, buy some new clothes, and get married. When you've done that, you and your wife will be welcome to visit me anytime."

Ruxue couldn't find a way to say no and accepted the money.

He borrowed a neighbor's wheelbarrow and wheeled Xu and Mingjiu back to Xu Village.

That autumn, Ruxue gave the thatched cottage a makeover and married a short, skinny woman from the next village.

Even now that he'd married someone else, Ruxue's ardor for Xu hadn't dimmed. He was never able to forget her, nor did he ever truly leave her. When she was in trouble, he went to her and helped her. He would have done anything for her, but Xu refused to ask him for a single thing.

IN 1953, NINE-YEAR-OLD Mingjiu was in second grade and still breast-feeding. He only stopped because his classmates were making fun of him. Old Mrs. Zhou worried he wasn't getting enough nutrition and constantly bought him snacks.

My father was the same age as Mingjiu, and since their houses were close together, he often went over so they could walk to school together. Their school was four or five li away, in the run-down old ancestral hall.

Every time Dad dropped by, Mingjiu would be eating something delicious, a flatbread or dough fritter or sesame cake. It made Dad's mouth water. He asked Grandma, "How come Mingjiu has all that tasty food, and we have nothing at home?" Grandma replied, "You can't compare yourself to him! Their family has plenty of grain and money. Mingjiu's the only son and heir, he can have whatever he wants. The next time you go by to get him for school, don't go inside, just wait by the side of the road. It's awkward for everyone to have you standing there watching him eat." Dad nodded haplessly, and from then on, he would stand a long way from Mingjiu's front door when he called his name.

Dad passed his childhood remembrances on to us. When my little brother and I were kids, we would go round playing at all the neighbors' houses, but no matter how much fun we were having, as soon as a guest arrived, we would have to leave at once. Shen Village was still a poor place in the seventies and eighties. Only when you had a visitor would you cook maybe half a pound of pork. The aroma of stewed meat would waft across dozens of households, and there'd always be two or three children unable to resist the temptation. They'd invite themselves over to play and linger till the meal was served so the host would give them a bowl of rice with a sprinkle of gravy and one or two bits of meat. Dad told us that this was deeply embarrassing behavior. If we did anything like that, we'd grow up to be useless. He made eating a slice of pork sound like a matter of personal integrity that could affect your whole future. Thanks to him, I've ended up with an inflated sense of dignity. A single dismissive glance has the power to wound me deeply.

IN 1953, SHEN Village underwent land reform. Xu was a widow with a child to raise, so the villagers took pity on her and only appropriated part of her land. She was left with over twenty mu to support a small household, which made her much more well-off than most.

The old schoolhouse became a new school that taught classes such as language, math, drawing, and gym. Six grades, five teachers. Over a hundred students, aged between six and twenty-something. Often, an eldest child would show up with younger siblings in tow, and they'd all sit in the same classroom. Chinese classes consisted of the teacher writing characters with a calligraphy brush, which the older pupils would copy out and teach the younger ones. The older kids didn't take this very seriously, though, and didn't have the patience to pass on any knowledge. As a result, if the first graders could learn more than a hundred characters a year, they were doing very well.

Old Mrs. Zhou had asked a relative with a few years of schooling to come live with them, so he could teach Mingjiu to read and write. As a result, when Mingjiu started first grade, he knew more characters than anyone else in the class, which the teacher frequently praised him for. Mingjiu worked hard too and was always bent over a book rather than horsing around. Everyone liked him.

Mingjiu enjoyed making pictures, so Xu sent someone to the county town to buy some items the school lacked: paintbrushes, paint, and drawing books for children. The other students were very jealous, although Mingjiu was generous enough to share these items with anyone who wanted them. The others only played around—they were too shy to actually paint pictures, the way Mingjiu was doing. At his young age, Mingjiu was already getting a bit of a reputation in the school as an artist.

MINGJIU FINISHED ELEMENTARY school in 1958. Compared to other people his age in Shen Village, his life was comfortable and happy. Despite his wealthy background, he didn't swank around, but remained meek and impeccably polite. Unfortunately, these virtues weren't helpful at this moment in time. Graduating from elementary school was a turning point in his life. His placid life was gone, never to return, and he was plunged into the maelstrom of the era, aged just fourteen.

The meeting to launch the policy of collectivization was held on a threshing ground in the middle of the village. The only person to speak was the village secretary. It was September 1958, and the secretary stood on a large stone roller, waving his arms for silence. "Chairman Mao has proclaimed that the People's Commune is now official Communist policy."

Thus began the collectivization of Shen Village.

The first order of business was to dig up the so-called coarse cereals—sorghum, millet, and so on, even though the current crop had already grown waist-high—and replace them with sweet potatoes, a high-yield crop. Next, a vacant piece of land was enclosed and turned into a livestock yard, where the various pigs, cows, and sheep owned by the villagers were gathered to be reared together. Thirdly, everyone's provisions were confiscated. No one was allowed to cook at home anymore—all meals would be eaten communally at the cafeteria.

Because Xu's house was larger and nicer than most, with its gray brick walls and tiled roof, it got turned into the cafeteria. Xu, Old Mrs. Zhou, and Mingjiu were turfed out and had to live in what had been their cowshed.

This took place just as Mingjiu finished elementary school. Many of his classmates with much worse grades were offered places in middle school, but he wasn't. The reason was his relatively wealthy background, as well as the fact that his late father had been a counter-revolutionary who'd been suppressed by the government.

Mingjiu came home sobbing. The next day, Xu brought him to see Mr. Wang Xiaofu, his former flute teacher. Mr. Wang was fond of Mingjiu and had often visited the family until a year ago, when he'd been denounced as a rightist and deported back to his hometown.

Holding Mingjiu by the hand, Xu walked more than forty li, asking directions all the way, until they reached Mr. Wang's home. He had a couple of thatched rooms containing a rickety old bed, a table, two chairs, and nothing else. His wife had been mending a shirt, but when she saw they had guests, she hastily dropped her sewing and offered them her chair. She wore a simple cotton tunic and patched gray trousers, and though she was only in her thirties, she looked like an old woman. A girl of seven or eight sat on a little stool, and she neither moved nor said a word as they came in.

Xu had brought a packet of cookies, which she placed on the table in front of the little girl. The girl looked at her mother, and then at the cookies, but remained still. Only when her mother nodded did she take one and put it in her mouth.

They'd only been sitting a short while when Mr. Wang came in holding a shit shovel, with a basket of manure on his back. He was pleasantly surprised to see Xu and Mingjiu and urged his wife to hurry up and cook some food.

Looking at the way Mr. Wang was living, Xu stammered, uncertain how to begin. In the end, it was Mingjiu who blurted out why they'd come. Mr. Wang sighed and pointed at the three tile-roofed buildings behind the hut. "That's my home. They shared it out to other people because of land reform, and the place we're living in now is the shed we used for rearing pigs and storage. I've been denounced as a rightist, so I'm just doing farmwork—" He paused a moment, then got a brush and paper. "I have a friend named Lu who teaches middle school in Gaozhuang. We get on well. Go see him, and say Mingjiu was my pupil. See if he can help."

Xu and Mingjiu's worry turned to happiness, and they thanked Mr. Wang over and over. As they talked, Mrs. Wang came back in with the food: a bowl each of nice, thick barley congee, not watery at all, served with stir-fried vegetables, extra salty to make up for the lack of oil. Xu and Mingjiu didn't try to refuse. After they'd eaten, they said goodbye.

The next day, Mingjiu went to Gaozhuang and found Mr. Lu. He was in his twenties, but because his family was well-off, he hadn't been given a place in college after high school. Instead, he was teaching Chinese at Gaozhuang Middle School. He was delighted to hear that Mingjiu had been Mr. Wang's pupil, and invited Mingjiu into his hostel room, where he poured him a glass of water and asked how Mr. Wang was doing. Mingjiu told him, and he sighed despondently. Then he told Mingjiu, "Come back in ten days. You'll have to take a test, and if you pass, you can join the class."

Mingjiu aced the test.

IN WHAT FELT like no time at all, Mingjiu had been studying at Gaozhuang Middle School for three years, and it was time for the final exam. When the results came out, Mingjiu thought he hadn't done badly, but he wasn't offered a place in high school. He didn't give up, but repeated his last year and took the exam again. Once more, he was unsuccessful.

There was nothing else he could do. He packed up his books and returned home.

It was 1962. Collectivization was over, the cafeteria had been closed down, and Xu had moved back into their old place with the rest of the household. Mingjiu wasn't content being a farmer and never went to the fields. Instead, he spent his days with his nose in a book. Often, in the middle of the night, he would pull the covers over his head and sob. He wanted to keep studying.

Xu said, "Mingjiu, I'm living this life for your sake. If I had to climb a mountain of knives or swim a sea of flames, I would—but I can't do anything about school. Why not visit your aunt's house again, and see if your uncle can help?"

Mingjiu's uncle, who was also his future father-in-law thanks to his betrothal aged two, had been an impoverished schoolhouse teacher for many years, but then became an educator at a state school, and was now the principal of a local high school. Mingjiu caught a couple of old hens, steeled himself, and walked the thirty-odd li to his uncle's home.

Once again, his aunt was delighted to see Mingjiu. As she ushered him into the house, she sent Xiaofen out to buy some pork. Xiaofen was now in high school and had grown into a slender young woman. They hadn't seen each other for quite a few years, but she wasn't bashful around Mingjiu at all—in fact, she cheerfully asked him to come to the shop with her. They chatted and laughed all the way there, feeling very close.

Mingjiu's uncle came home around noon. He heard what Mingjiu had to say, turned it over in his mind, and said, "I'll think of something. Go home and wait to hear from me."

Mingjiu waited for more than a month. The school year was starting soon, and still there'd only been silence from his uncle. Two days before term began, he couldn't stand it any longer and hiked the thirty-odd li again. As it turned out, his uncle was out at a county meeting. His aunt said she'd asked him several times, but nothing had turned up.

"It looks like this year won't be possible. When your uncle gets home, I'll nudge him to come up with something else."

After they'd eaten, Mingjiu's aunt asked him to stay the night, but he shook his head and headed back, weeping as he trudged the thirty li. Back home, he went straight to bed without dinner.

Mingjiu had a high fever that night and couldn't stop shaking. Xu was in a panic, and as soon as day broke, she went to ask the carpenter for help. He pushed Mingjiu to the hospital in a wheelbarrow, with my father and Xu following behind. Mingjiu was hospitalized for a couple of weeks. My father, his best friend, visited a couple of times. Mingjiu wasn't able to get out of bed and couldn't even piss or shit without help. Tears poured down Xu's face all day long. Sorrowfully, Mingjiu tried to comfort her. "I'm fine, Mom. Let me go home."

The run-down small town hospital couldn't do much about Mingjiu's illness, and Xu's money was soon gone. She had no choice but to ask for her son to be discharged.

Back home, Mingjiu was still unable to eat, and Xu had to spoon rice congee into his mouth. In the middle of the night, addled by fever, he would shout, "I want to go to school, Mom!" Xu would silently weep and reply, "Yes, all right, Mingjiu. When you're better, Mom will take you to school."

My father visited Mingjiu too. When he saw how seriously ill his best friend was, and how helpless the grown-ups seemed, he said to Xu, "Why not get Mr. He to take a look at him?"

These words snapped Xu out of her stupor, and she hurried out to find the village's old traditional medicine man. Mr. He lived alone in a three-room thatched cottage in the center of the village. He grew medicinal herbs by his front door, and next to them was a pond. "He" means "lotus," and perhaps that's why the water was full of lotus plants. He never harvested the lotus seeds or roots himself, though. When they came in season, anyone in the village was free to help themselves. If they offered him some of their bounty, he would smile and get some paper to wrap it in, murmuring, "This is too much, too much." When he treated the villagers' illnesses, the well-off could give him a bit of money, and those without the means could offer him some grain, or just a meal was fine. Because most villagers had switched to believing in Western medicine, his patients were largely the elderly and those who couldn't afford to go to the clinic in town. This meant Mr. He had a lot of free time, which he spent sitting in a rattan chair behind his desk, peering through his glasses at a book.

Mr. He followed Xu back and sat by Mingjiu's bedside to examine his eyelids and the coating on his tongue. Next, he shut his eyes as he took the boy's pulse, then glanced at his medical report from the hospital. He asked Mingjiu some questions, turned to Xu and nodded. "It's not serious. He just needs to take some medicine and have half a month's bed rest. You ought to see a turn for the better after that." As he spoke, he sat at the eight-immortals table and reached into his cloth bag for an inkstone, a half-used slab of ink, his brush, and some paper. My father quickly ground some ink for him, and he wrote out a prescription. "I don't have all the herbs I need to hand," he said to my father. "Go into town and help me get these from the medicinal shop across from the hospital." He reached into his bag again for his stamp, which he inked onto the bottom left corner of the paper. "You won't need to pay—I'll go and settle up in a few days. He'll give you the medicine if you show him my stamp."

Sure enough, Mr. He's medicine did the trick, and Mingjiu soon started feeling better. Xu continued watching by his bedside day and night, not even changing her clothes.

OUR HOUSE WAS just across the river from Mingjiu's, and Dad often popped by for a chat. Mingjiu was better now, but couldn't stop sighing. He wanted to be in school.

"Without school to go to, I feel like there's no point being alive," he said.

"Don't talk like that. You're not the only person who didn't get a place. There are plenty of people in Shen Village in the same boat. So we're not going to high school. Life goes on."

Dad was trying to comfort Mingjiu, but actually felt a twinge of his own. The truth was, not going to high school meant joining the rest of the villagers working in the fields each day, doing their share of the farming work—for the rest of their lives. Just like Mingjiu, my father found it hard to accept that this looming fate was what the future had in store for him.

He said to Mingjiu, "Destiny has no dead ends. There'll be a way."

Mingjiu shook his head in disbelief. Still, his body began to recover. After a month, he was able to get out of bed and move around. Xu and my father were both delighted. They helped him outdoors so he could take a few breaths of fresh air.

When the villagers came to visit, they almost didn't recognize Mingjiu. The tall, clean-cut youth was now scrawny as a bundle of sticks, with a waxen, sallow complexion. Shaking their heads, they sighed. "Such a promising child, and look at him now."

Mingjiu was clearly very different from his father—he had a somber personality, his manners were impeccable, and he always had a smile on his face. He'd worked hard at school and was an excellent son and grandson. When the villagers scolded their mischievous children, they would say, "Why can't you be more like Mingjiu?"

The young villagers who hadn't got into high school, including my father, all joined the production brigade. Mingjiu recovered just in time for the autumn harvest, so he and my father teamed up to reap the wheat and tie it into sheaves. For ten days in a row, they worked till midnight. When the team leader blew the whistle to say they were done for the day, the two boys would lie on a heap of wheat and gaze up at the starry sky as they chatted.

"Do you think I'll ever have a chance to keep studying?"

"You still want to?"

"Yes, for my mom, my grandma, and also myself. I want to bring honor to my family."

"Why don't you go see your uncle again?"

"I've asked him twice and that didn't do any good. I can't keep pestering him."

"He's your only way out. Your families are close, so it shouldn't be embarrassing to ask. Just man up and do it, otherwise you'll have to keep working on this production brigade every day."

After the autumn harvest, Mingjiu steeled himself to see his uncle. He couldn't abandon the idea of continuing his studies—the thought tormented him every single minute. He wouldn't be happy again until he was back in school. This was the only way he could see of changing his life. On the surface, he was no different to anyone else in Shen Village, but there was an enormous pressure inside him he couldn't resist. All he wanted was to escape as far as possible from this place.

Mingjiu's uncle had already heard how Mingjiu had gotten ill and almost died over not going to school. Even knowing this, he was still shocked to see how thin the boy had gotten. He said, "Go home and keep revising. I'll definitely help you think of a way. It's too late for this year, but wait to hear from me next year. You'll still have to pass the exam to get in, though."

Hearing his uncle's words, Mingjiu couldn't help being overjoyed.

Back in Shen Village, Mingjiu worked in the fields all day, then hit the books at night. Even during breaks in the farm work, while everyone else sat around chatting, he would pull out a book to study. Even this wasn't enough for him—he worried that he was slacking off, so he copied out some lines by famous people with his calligraphy brush and stuck them up for encouragement. Soon, all his walls were covered, and he saw inspirational quotes everywhere he looked.

The following summer, Mingjiu was so anxious about the exam that he stopped joining the production brigade altogether and stayed home to study. With only Xu working, the household's rations were much reduced. At this point, Old Mrs. Zhou's hair was completely white, her back was so hunched over that her chin pressed into her chest, and she could only walk with the help of a stick. She said to Xu, "I'm ancient now and won't last many more years. Give my portion to Mingjiu instead—don't let him go hungry." Xu didn't know what else to do, so without letting Mingjiu know, both women ate much less than they needed and gave him the lion's share.

In the summer of 1963, Mingjiu went to his uncle's house again. Looking relaxed, his uncle said, "One of my classmates has become the deputy principal at Jiangyan High School. I spoke to him, and he said it shouldn't be a problem, as long as you can pay a hundred yuan. Go home and get ready, and come back the day after tomorrow. You'll take the exam the next afternoon."

Mingjiu had a meal with them and then rushed home.

His family didn't have such a huge sum, though, and nowhere to borrow it from. Old Mrs. Zhou reached into the bottom of her chest and brought out a gold ring, which she gave to Xu. "This was part of my dowry. I don't need this anymore, sell it and see what you can get."

Mingjiu went back to his uncle's house with this money.

Because it was the summer vacation, Xiaofen was hanging out at home with nothing to do, so she decided to come along to Jiangyan too. Mingjiu was elated, of course. The three of them walked for more than an hour, laughing and chatting, until they reached Jiangyan High. Principal Zhang ushered them to the cafeteria for a meal.

"You don't need to worry too much about this exam," said the principal. "It's just a formality. There aren't too many people who can come up with a hundred yuan. As long as you aren't terrible, you should be fine."

More than sixty people sat for the exam, competing for fifty places. That afternoon's paper lasted two hours. Mingjiu emerged from the hall and saw Xiaofen standing a short distance away, craning her neck to look for him. She clapped her hands to see the smile on his face. "You must have done well?"

"I think I'll be okay!" Mingjiu had never felt so good.

"My dad's shooting the breeze with Principal Zhang. He said he'd see us in the cafeteria at dinner time. Let's go have a look around—it's not every day you get to visit Jiangyan."

Mingjiu had only brought a hundred yuan with him, his school fees. Now that he'd handed it over to his uncle, he didn't have a cent on him. As he walked around with Xiaofen chatting away, he didn't dare to linger in front of a single shop.

Then they came to a department store, and Xiaofen darted in before he could stop her. All he could do was follow.

"Do you have any flutes?" she asked. The sales clerk nodded at a display case in the corner.

Xiaofen bought a flute and a packet of membranes. Back outside, she presented them to Mingjiu. "I know you enjoy playing the flute, so here—my gift to you, for getting into high school."

"I can't accept this! Besides, I don't know if I've got a place yet."

"I've already bought it, so you can't refuse." She pretended to be upset, so he had to take it, heart filled with bliss.

It wasn't just in that moment he liked that flute, but for many years after, he kept it by his pillow at night. Without it there, he couldn't fall asleep.

MINGJIU'S DREAMS CAME true, and he got into high school. The work was a lot harder now, and although he did his utmost, his grades were only middling. By his sophomore year, they'd begun to slide. Despairing, he gave it some thought, and went to see Principal Zhang at the end of the semester. "Sir, the way things are going, there's no way I'll get into university—which means my fate won't change after all. I'd like to repeat a year."

Principal Zhang was fond of this patient, determined, hardworking pupil, and he nodded immediately. "Very well, then, you can repeat your sophomore year."

Sure enough, the second time round, Mingjiu had some of the highest grades, and by his final year, he was at the top of his class. Principal Zhang was thrilled. When he wrote to let Mingjiu's uncle know, he said, "This boy is definitely going to achieve great things!"

That's when the Cultural Revolution began.

All classes were canceled, and everyone joined in the Revolution. Mingjiu got swept up in the crowd, doing whatever everyone else did: chanting slogans, writing big-character posters, marching through the streets, neither in the front nor back of the pack, but squarely in the middle. He was aware of his own status, and thought it would be best not to attract any notice, as if he didn't exist at all.

The Red Guards of Jiangyan City were split into two: "Red Iron" and "August First." Mingjiu was in the former group. Both sides wrote big-character posters and had struggle sessions, and their conflict eventually erupted into open violence. When Mingjiu saw the way things were going, he asked the leader of the Red Iron Guards at his school for some time off, saying he was too ill to move. The leader asked two of Mingjiu's classmates to escort him back to Shen Village.

Three days after he arrived home, fighting broke out among the Jiangyan Red Guards, and it only stopped after the local political commissar had words with them. By this time, the hospital was full of casualties. When Mingjiu heard the news, he became even more fearful of returning to school.

One night a couple of weeks later, Mingjiu was woken from his sleep by someone shouting his name outside. He opened the door and saw his uncle, Xiaofen's father.

His uncle was still the principal of the high school in town. By this point, the Cultural Revolution had reached the elementary and high schools. The rebels had had a meeting that evening and decided to enact revolutionary tactics against him the next day. One of his students had secretly passed him a warning.

He knew what these "revolutionary tactics" consisted of, because he'd attended just such a struggle session. The principal of a school in the next town had been hauled up on a makeshift stage and made to wear a paper dunce hat, then to stand in a wooden tub of ice water. Next to him, the guidance counselor was kneeling with a bowl of water balanced on his head. All the other teachers had had half their heads shaved and were standing with large cards hung around their necks, on which were written their names crossed out thickly in black. Mingjiu's uncle was so scared of being tortured to death that he'd run thirty li through the night, all the way to Mingjiu's house.

Mingjiu reassured his uncle. "Don't worry, you can hide here—you'll be fine. My good friend Qingshan is the commander of our commune's rebel faction. I'll ask him to come see you. With him around, no one will dare do anything to you."

This alarmed his uncle. "No way, I'd be in trouble if the rebel faction heard I was here."

Mingjiu smiled. "You don't need to be scared, Uncle. Shen Village is different from other places. With Qingshan leading the rebel faction, there hasn't been any violence, and we've even secretly protected people. Many of the principals and teachers from Jiangyan are hiding out in our commune. Some of the village landlords are taking shelter in Qingshan's house, where no one will dare to seize them. You can relax."

Although his heart was still at sixes and sevens, his uncle managed to get an uneasy night's sleep sharing Mingjiu's bed. The next morning, Mingjiu took him to see Qingshan.

Qingshan happened to be my father. After graduating from middle school, he wasn't content to work in the fields, so instead he set up Shen Village's first elementary school. There were only two teachers, him and one of his former classmates. The school was in a two-room thatched cottage; they knocked out the center wall to make it one big room. There were only twenty-odd students. I suppose you could say my father was a private tutor, though he didn't take a wage. The village, which was now a production brigade, had him on its workers manifest, and he could accumulate points to be exchanged for provisions. Because he was so articulate, he was chosen as the rebel faction commander of the commune when the Cultural Revolution started. The revolution hit the Xinjie Commune much later than the neighboring ones. By then, people had heard that its targets were landlords, wealthy farmers, counter-revolutionaries, negative influences, and rightists. Many old cadres were seized, strung up, and beaten half to death. When my father came home from the commune and proudly proclaimed that he was leading the rebel faction, my usually mild-mannered, gentle grandmother flew into a rage and began whacking him with a broomstick. "Get out! This family doesn't need a troublemaker like you. If you want to be a rebel whatever leader, you can forget about ever setting foot in this house again!"

My father was very respectful of his elders and didn't dare talk back to my grandmother. He went out and paced around the yard. Grandma kept him locked out all night long.

The next day, he said to her, "Mom, the way things are now, I don't have any choice. If I don't accept the position, they'll turn on me instead, and maybe I'll even get tortured to death. But I promise you, once I'm a commander, I won't do a single bad thing, and I won't torture anyone."

Grandma said, "Listen well. If I hear a single person tell me you've done something you shouldn't have, you'll no longer be my son."

And so my father became a person with two faces. Onstage, he was as impassioned as any other revolutionary, more fired up than anyone else. And yet he refused to denounce anyone. When he really had no alternative, he would just go through the motions: put a dunce cap on the person, and do a bit of playacting onstage. When the meeting was over, that would be the end of that. He proclaimed, "The situation here is getting even better with each passing day. Our main duties are to grasp hold of revolution, increase productivity, promote work, and push readiness for war." As the Cultural Revolution progressed, every single person was in peril, and no one knew if they would be the next to be denounced. At this point, people began to condone or even praise my father's strategy of inaction. The Xinjie Commune, particularly Shen Village, became a little safe harbor within the storm of the Cultural Revolution. Old revolutionaries and intellectuals in the neighboring counties to the north and south would take shelter here if they had the slightest connection to anyone in the village, and the villagers received each of them warmly.

MINGJIU'S UNCLE HAD been in Shen Village for more than two months when his wife asked him to come back. Things had settled down at the school, she said, and he could resume work. He lingered a few more days, to make sure the storm really was over, before he returned.

Two days after his uncle's departure, Mingjiu's classmates from the county town came to Shen Village with some Cultural Revolution propaganda—more than thirty of them, boys and girls. That evening, the village blazed with lights as everyone, old and young, brought their stools to the threshing ground in the center of the village to see the students perform. The villagers didn't really understand what the students were doing, but they nonetheless applauded and cheered vigorously. This was the first time they were seeing a modern play, and also their first time seeing Mingjiu onstage. Perhaps because they were in Mingjiu's hometown, the propaganda team had insisted that Mingjiu perform. He didn't know how to act, so they asked him to play the flute instead. Mingjiu played two tunes for his fellow villagers: "The East Is Red," and one that everyone in the village knew, "Pluck a Reed Flower." They all joined in the chorus, which brought the evening to a high point. Who would have thought this would be the most dazzling appearance of Mingjiu's life! After his passing, the way people in Shen Village remembered him was as a spirited young man playing the flute. He stood center stage with the lanterns illuminating his handsome, smiling face. The pretty female students from the county town danced around him, and the audience sang rousingly along with the flute. After the show, all the villagers agreed that Mingjiu was a real talent and should surely become a prominent figure who achieved great things. In the days after that, many of them came calling at his house, to congratulate Xu for having such a fine son. This was the pinnacle of Xu's happiness. Old Mrs. Zhou was completely deaf, and her vision was blurry, but she still managed to understand Mingjiu's glory. Smiling broadly at the visitors, she assumed everyone was speaking to her and praising her grandson. She luxuriated in this time of joy longer than anyone else.

Still, Mingjiu was most concerned about his studies—he hadn't graduated from high school yet. He returned with the propaganda team, but didn't follow them on their tour—he just stayed at the school. The building looked completely different. The main gates had been smashed, and not a single classroom window was intact. The principal and guidance counselor were being detained at the police station. Most of the teachers had been sent off to farming villages for reform through labor, and the few that remained had nothing to do, so they stayed at home, apart from the four who'd been appointed advisors to the two rebel factions and were expected to devise strategies for them. The person nominally in charge of the work was Deputy Principal Zhang. He was a veteran revolutionary, and as he was a centrist with no political leanings, both factions tolerated him. All he could do was patrol the campus each day, watching big-character posters fill the walls.

Mingjiu lived alone in the dorm—his five roommates had either gone home, or were in Beijing for the Great Networking. He took out his textbooks and placed them next to his compendium of Chairman Mao's quotes, feeling dazed. He didn't know what he ought to do. He didn't dare to take part in either faction's activities. He was aware that he was the sort of person who deserved to be denounced. All he could do was wait.

One evening, there was an unexpected knock on his door. It was Deputy Principal Zhang.

"The August First Faction summoned me to a meeting, and I had to go. When the Red Iron Faction found out about that, they said I'd betrayed them, and they're going to lock me up tonight so I can be dragged out and denounced tomorrow. You're in the Red Iron Faction. If I hide in your room, they might not think of looking for me here. Is that okay?"

After a flustered moment, Mingjiu calmed down enough to say, "Don't worry, Principal Zhang. You can sleep here tonight, and I'll go next door. I'll lock the room from the outside, so no one will be able to tell there's anyone in here. Tomorrow morning, I'll bring you some food. You can just stay in here, and I'll deal with them."

Sure enough, the Red Iron Faction had people searching everywhere that night. Mingjiu joined in too. They focused on the other faction's dorm rooms. After a bit of argument, the other faction let them in—after all, they weren't actually hiding anyone. Red Iron found nothing, of course.

The next morning, Mingjiu bought a dozen steamed buns and gave them to Principal Zhang to eat with hot water. He didn't dare buy two full meals, as the others would notice.

Principal Zhang spent more than three weeks hiding in Mingjiu's dorm room. He asked, "Aren't you scared to protect me?" Mingjiu replied, "If you hadn't given me a place at this school, I'd be working in the fields now. Even if I get caught, at worst they'll shave half my head and send me back to the countryside. That's nothing to be scared of."

Principal Zhang thought a moment. "Are you willing to deliver a message to August First?"

Mingjiu said, "Sure."

He was aware of the danger. If his own faction found out he'd betrayed them, he might end up getting tortured to death.

Mingjiu passed the August First Faction a letter from Principal Zhang, and they sent people that very night to spirit the principal away to their headquarters in the county town.

Now that Principal Zhang was gone, Mingjiu returned to his dorm and let out a sigh of relief. He fell into bed without undressing and slept for a full day and night. He was afraid of being found out, afraid of being sent back to Shen Village. He no longer feared having to do farm work, but didn't want to face his mother and grandmother so ignominiously. They wouldn't be able to accept it.

When Principal Zhang took Mingjiu into his school, he couldn't have imagined that this pupil would, at the most difficult moment of the principal's life, end up turning around and taking him in. Without realizing it, he'd planted the seed of his future escape from a tricky situation. And Mingjiu had no idea that his protection of Principal Zhang was a foreshadowing of what lay in store for him. That's how life is, a series of interlocking circles.

Mingjiu remained at the school, with nothing to occupy him, until the end of August 1967, when he finally got his diploma. Now he could pack his bags and return to Shen Village. The day after that, he was carrying two buckets of night soil, working alongside the other members of the Commune.

After a year back home laboring, Mingjiu was already twenty-three and, at his mother's urging, went to see his uncle's home to talk about his marriage to Xiaofen.

When he told his aunt why he'd come, she sighed and said, "To be honest, I can't make any decisions about this marriage. You'll need to ask Xiaofen and her father. Why don't you stay the night? It's Sunday tomorrow, and Xiaofen will be back from school."

Xiaofen had finished her teacher's training and had recently been deployed to an elementary school in Jiangyan.

The next day, Xiaofen got home and seemed pleased to see Mingjiu. She asked how he'd been doing and told him what was going on in the county town. She was very content with her new job. The two of them chatted as Mingjiu's aunt bustled in and out, not saying a word. After lunch, when Mingjiu would soon have to take his leave, he had no choice but to ask Xiaofen directly what her thoughts were about their marriage.

Xiaofen said, "I have no thoughts, I'll do whatever my father tells me to."

Instead of going home, Mingjiu went straight to his uncle's school. This high school was quite a distance from the house, and as its principal, he was so busy he often spent the night there.

Mingjiu's uncle was very surprised to see him there. He led him to his dorm, poured him some water, and they sat down. Mingjiu explained why he'd come, and his uncle said, "I don't think this is a good time to talk about marriage—Xiaofen's only just started her job. Let's wait a year and see."

Mingjiu returned unhappily to Shen Village. When Xu heard what had happened, she was shocked. Old Mrs. Zhou immediately started complaining. "What did I say right at the beginning? But oh no, you wouldn't listen. Now you see, they're going back on their word, and you've turned the boy into a laughing stock. We sent them so much money over the years, and for what? This is humiliating."

Xu had nothing to say. A couple of months later, she packed a bundle and went to see her sister, who again would only say this wasn't her decision, it was her husband who called the shots.

A year passed quickly. Mingjiu came to see my father. "He said I should wait a year, Qingshan, and it's been a year. Whether he's allowing the match or not, he'll have to give me an answer. The thing is, I don't feel brave enough to go alone. Do you think you could come with me?"

And so Qingshan went with Mingjiu to his uncle's school.

The uncle said, "Look at your family's position, and your current status. Even if I gave my consent, do you think Xiaofen would agree? She has a good teaching job in the county town. How could she give that up to marry into your village? The way I see it, taking the long view, it would be better if you looked elsewhere."

Qingshan said, "Uncle, Mingjiu's a talented man and a good scholar. He wasn't born into the right family, that's all. The river flows eastward for thirty years, then westward for the next thirty. Who's to say he might not rise up again in a few years? Why don't you think about it a little more?"

The uncle said nothing, but looked down and took a sip of water. Qingshan went on, "Forget that your two families have been close for decades, just look at Mingjiu. He's a very determined person, and sure to make something of himself in the future. Haven't you always thought well of him?"

The uncle looked up and said, "Don't say the word 'marriage' again."

Mingjiu stood up. "We'll go now, Uncle." He walked out and didn't look back.

Back home, he told his mother everything. They buried their faces in their hands and wept bitterly.

Mingjiu was from a well-off family, and his father was a counter-revolutionary who'd been executed. Never mind a city woman like Xiaofen, even the village girls would hesitate to jump into this pit of fire.

When Old Mrs. Zhou heard that the marriage was off, she fell ill and took to her bed. Even her son's death hadn't made her collapse like this, but her grandson's misfortune was a death blow. A little more than a month after this, she left this world. Her coffin was already prepared—she'd asked the carpenter to make it for her more than two decades ago. There was no funeral. Mingjiu hired a few people to carry the coffin to the cemetery, while he and his mother followed behind. When it was buried, they kowtowed three times in front of the grove, then returned home in silence.

MINGJIU WORKED MORE industriously than anyone else, but never managed to get into the good graces of the production brigade leader. His very birth made him worthy of being denounced and despised. Mingjiu himself was well aware of this fact. He never got into any fights, no matter how much he was mortified and insulted. At times, he would sit on the bank across the river from our house, playing his flute, or just holding it and staring into space. In 1970, his twenty-seventh year, it was three years since he'd left the school. By now, he had nothing but despair for his future. Xu, too, had accepted that his fate was to be a farm worker all his life. However, many people his age had already married, but he had no one to call his own, and this was like a knife through her heart.

Zhang Ruxue, the cousin who'd once loved Xu so deeply, hadn't been to Shen Village for many years now. When he heard about Mingjiu's broken betrothal, though, he showed up again.

He said to Xu, "If Mingjiu doesn't think this is beneath him, he's welcome to marry my daughter Guibao."

Xu wept. At the most desolate moment of her life, Ruxue was reaching out a helping hand. Memories surged into her mind, and she felt a multitude of conflicting emotions, leaving her speechless. She and Ruxue stared at each other in silence, completely forgetting to tell Mingjiu the good news.

Mingjiu accepted this arrangement without complaint, but also not seeming particularly happy about it. He hadn't been as anxious as his mother about facing a lifetime of bachelorhood. The thing causing a dull ache in his heart wasn't the lack of a wife, but the absence of Xiaofen.

The wedding was fixed for the day after the Double Ninth Festival.

The evening before the wedding, Mingjiu sat on the riverbank playing his flute. This was the last time his music would be heard in Shen Village. After his death, Guibao treasured the flute and treated it as the most important thing he'd left her. She knew it was more precious to him than anything else, and that it had been a gift from Xiaofen.

After lunch on the tenth, Mingjiu asked two of his older neighbors to serve as matchmakers, and Qingshan to be his groomsman. The four of them set off for Zhang Village to fetch the bride. Ruxue had laid out food for the reception: a bowl of meat, a plate of fish, a plate of fried eggs, and a bowl of vegetables. Guibao was dressed in khaki. After they'd eaten, she and two bridesmaids followed Mingjiu back to Shen Village on foot. No wedding gifts, no dowry. When they arrived, Xu hung a small string of firecrackers from a bamboo pole, and lit them so the neighbors could hear the festivities.

The wedding party ushered Mingjiu and Guibao into the bridal chamber. This was actually just his bedroom, with a red "happiness" character stuck to the door—nothing else about it had changed.

The next day, the two bridesmaids returned to Zhang Village, and the bride changed into work clothes, picked up her hoe, and followed Mingjiu to the fields. Although Guibao wasn't beautiful, she was healthy and strong, always cheerful, and eager to take on any work both in and out of the house. When it came to Mingjiu, she was utterly protective of him. If she could have, she would have stopped him from so much as touching a blade of grass. She wished he could be at his books all day long, never mind that studying was meaningless given the future that lay ahead of them. She just liked the idea of Mingjiu being an educated person.

Everyone said that Mingjiu had married a good woman. But then, not long after this, the good woman began to experience mental issues.

Their son arrived in 1972. Long before the birth, Mingjiu had come up with a name. "If it's a boy, we'll call him Jianqiang. 'Jian' for good health, and 'qiang' for strength, because a gentleman is always striving to become stronger." Three days after Jianqiang was born, Guibao had a high fever that made her thrash around, feeling as if her head was splitting apart. When Mingjiu asked her what would make her feel better, she crawled out of bed, stood against the wall, and got him to press his forehead to hers. Mingjiu was too tall to do this comfortably, so he asked his mother to step in, and the two of them took turns doing this all night long. At dawn, Mingjiu truly couldn't take any more of this, so he bundled Guibao back into bed. No sooner had she lain down when she jumped up again, screaming and howling, smashing random objects and ripping the clothes she was wearing. "I'm a poor farmer," she shrieked. "I don't want to marry a rich man. You're a punching bag, and I don't want to get punched. I'm leaving." Then, turning to her husband, "Mingjiu, you're such a good person, you're good-looking, you're educated, you ought to become a cadre." The neighbors came over to see what was happening, and they all said that Guibao had lost her mind.

Mingjiu brought Guibao to the hospital. The doctor tied her to the bed, brought down her fever with ice cubes, and gave her a saline drip. Mingjiu didn't leave her side the whole time.

Guibao was in the hospital for more than ten days before showing some improvement. Mingjiu brought their newborn son Jianqiang to the hospital so she could feed him. As soon as she was discharged, she had another episode. Xu borrowed money from as many people as she could, but still couldn't get enough together to pay the medical bills. In the end, she had to ask around for someone to buy the three century-old ginkgo trees in their yard. As the buyer sawed down the trees, many villagers gathered around to sigh, "With those trees gone, Locust's family is truly finished." Locust, Mingjiu's late grandfather, had once been a wealthy man and prominent figure in Shen Village.

Xu and Mingjiu were discussing whether to sell their ancestral home, when Guibao's mind suddenly seemed to clear. "You can't sell the house," she said. "Where will my baby sleep, if you do?" She climbed to her feet and took Jianqiang from Mingjiu's arms. "Let's go home."

Xu was certain that Guibao's condition was the result of spirit possession, and wanted to get a witch to carry out an exorcism. Mingjiu didn't believe this, but couldn't talk his mother out of it, so he let her go ahead. The witch drew a charm and chanted some spells. As the ritual went on, Guibao abruptly said something terrifying.

"You, Xu, what a cruel creature you are." She pointed at her mother-in-law. "You're beautiful, and you can have children, so you stole my man from me. Haven't you done nicely for yourself now, with your son and grandson? And me, I have two men pulling me this way and that, without a moment of peace. If I have to suffer, then you will too."

Xu was scared out of her wits. After the witch left, she made some inquiries and found out that the tailor's first wife, the pockmarked Chen, had died a few years ago, around the same time as her husband. Could it be her spirit that had

taken over Guibao's body? Xu kept kowtowing and bowing to Guibao, pleading for forgiveness. Guibao didn't understand what was going on, but kept
babbling.

One evening a little over a month later, Guibao dropped by the home of
their neighbor to the right, Big Tiger. Big Tiger's wife brought their three
daughters and two-and-a-half-year-old son out to play in the yard. Guibao
leaned against the mulberry tree by their front door and said casually, "Oh my,
you have quite a few children, don't you? How many are there?"

Big Tiger's wife said, "Can't you count?"

Guibao pointed at them in turn. "One, two, three, four. My goodness,
four children, that's a lot. Can you raise them all?"

Big Tiger's wife rolled her eyes at this nonsense. "That's none of your
concern."

After dinner, Big Tiger's wife gave her son a bath, then set him down on
the bed. He was crawling around, then abruptly he stopped moving. The
woman shrieked, and Big Tiger came running. When he held his finger up to
the boy's nose, he couldn't feel any breath. By the time Dr. He had hurried
over, the child's tiny body was cold and stiff.

Mingjiu rushed around buying yellow and red paper, which he asked the
paper craftsman to turn into clothes and ingots, to be burned for the child.
After a night's sleep, Guibao was suddenly back to normal the next day, and
went off to work with her hoe.

Not long after Guibao's recovery, the schools reopened. Mingjiu heard
that Deputy Principal Zhang was now the head of the Jiangyan County Education Bureau. Mingjiu decided to go ask him for help. He didn't want the rest
of his life to continue in this way and was still hoping for a way out.

When Bureau Head Zhang saw how piteous and scrawny Mingjiu had
become, he immediately wrote a letter and told Mingjiu to go see his uncle.
Mingjiu begged, "Does it have to be him? Couldn't I go somewhere else?"
Bureau Head Zhang said, "There are no vacancies anywhere else. I know this
is hard on you, but there really is no other way. Go see him, and he's sure to
help—if not for your sake, then for mine."

Mingjiu went home and stayed in bed for two days. His wife and mother
cajoled him until he felt he had no choice but to get out of bed and, without so

much as a mouthful of food, set off once again on the thirty-li journey to his uncle's house.

His aunt was shocked to see him. She was about to rush off to buy some meat for their meal when Mingjiu stopped her. "This is a letter for uncle from Bureau Head Zhang. Please pass it to him. If there's any hope, he can write back to me. I'll be waiting at home."

His uncle didn't respond for several days. His aunt wept and said to her husband, "Mingjiu wouldn't have come to us if he had any other choice. You ought to help, if only to make up for what we did to him."

The uncle sighed and brought the letter to his school, where he talked the matter over with the head of education. Seeing as Mingjiu had a recommendation from the bureau head and was a relative of the principal, the head said, "Okay, I'll tell that pregnant teacher to start her maternity leave tomorrow."

Mingjiu's uncle let him know that he could come and be a substitute teacher for a year, teaching first-year Chinese. After that year, they would see where they were at. He would get twenty-four yuan a month. When she heard the news, Xu couldn't even muster a smile.

When he was teaching, Mingjiu seemed to come alive all at once, as if he'd forgotten reality. He dazzled and was full of passion. Mingjiu at the lectern was a completely different person from in real life. All of a sudden, he was breezy and humorous, bursting with talent. From time to time, laughter could be heard from his classroom. As soon as he stepped out, though, he reverted to his glum, unsmiling self. The students enjoyed his classes, respected him, and were happy to do whatever he asked them to. He lavished all the care he had on them. Whenever he had any time to spare, he would spend it with his students. He wanted to be a part of their group, even though they were only freshmen. He was humble and polite with his colleagues, but hardly ever interacted with them. He did his best to avoid his uncle, and his uncle tried to stay far from him too.

When the year was up, all Mingjiu's students and colleagues asked him to stay on. His uncle had observed him through the year and was also very satisfied with his teaching. And so Mingjiu continued as a sub. He would never be able to get a full-time position and would spend each summer waiting anxiously to hear from the school. No matter how dedicated and dutiful he was, he would only ever be stepping in. Each time someone else got promoted to full-time, he would lock himself in his hostel room, too afraid to join in the celebrations in case he ended up crying in public.

In 1977, college entrance exams resumed. Mingjiu was overjoyed at this news. Finally, his fate had changed. He went back home and got out his textbooks, which he'd kept tied up in a bundle hanging from a rafter. It had been almost a decade since he'd cracked these open. He studied them day and night, spending virtually all his time outside of teaching buried in them. His obsession began to affect his teaching, but everyone understood, and no one blamed him.

The exam took place on July sixth. Guibao got up very early to wrap and steam some dumplings for good luck, because the word for "dumplings" sounded like the one for "pass." After the first paper, though, Mingjiu was completely deflated. It might as well have been written in a foreign language—there were many questions he hadn't even understood. He got through it somehow, went home, and crashed into bed. After that day, he never said the words "college entrance exam" again.

Term started, and he went back to school. A colleague had gotten a place in an agricultural college in Nanjing, and everyone was sending him off. Mingjiu didn't normally touch alcohol, but this time he had a few glasses. Back at the dorm, he slept for a full day and night.

Seeing how dazed and distracted Mingjiu had become, his uncle worried about him. He didn't feel he could say anything, though, as they'd barely spoken in all the years Mingjiu was teaching at the school. He decided to get his wife to give him a pep talk, to soothe him and make sure he would carry on with his substitute teaching job. And so, after school one day, he went up to him and said, "Mingjiu, your aunt would like you to drop by for a visit."

It had been several years since Mingjiu had been to their house. He was afraid of running into Xiaofen.

That Sunday, Mingjiu put on some clean clothes and went off to his aunt's house. As he approached, Xiaofen was sitting by the doorway. He steeled himself and walked on. Xiaofen stood. "Oh, Mingjiu, you're here!" He nodded. She was pregnant—her belly was huge, swollen in front of her. His aunt heard and hurried out to warmly welcome him. "Xiaofen, talk to Mingjiu while I cook."

Mingjiu brought a stool over and sat next to Xiaofen. She was silent, and he couldn't think of anything to say either, so he kept his head down and his mouth shut. The atmosphere felt stiff and awkward.

Finally, Mingjiu said, "Have you . . . Have you been well?"

Xiaofen said, "There's no such thing as well or not well. We're born to get through each day, that's all. Just one day after another."

Mingjiu was startled. Looking closely, he could see that her skin was sallow and mottled, and her eyes had lost their shine. In just a few years, a lively young girl had become a middle-aged matron. Mingjiu had thought she would be living in comfort and happiness and wouldn't have guessed she would talk like this.

"You have to look on the bright side." People were always trying to cheer Mingjiu up with these words, and now for once he was using them on someone else. "You ought to smile. You're not like me. You have happiness. Your life should be happy." He was babbling.

"Everyone has a different understanding of happiness. If you have regret in your heart, and you can't forget it, then you'll never be happy." She stood up. "Let's go for a walk."

Mingjiu stood too, and they walked in silence through the fields, each absorbed in their own thoughts. By the time they got back, his aunt had finished cooking. As they ate, his aunt tried to comfort Mingjiu, but Xiaofen kept cutting her off. After the meal, Mingjiu said goodbye. He had to get back to the school. Xiaofen stood at the doorway to see him off. He'd gone quite a few steps when she called out, "Mingjiu!" He turned back, but she didn't say anything else. There were tears in her eyes. He forced a smile, waved, and left.

What Xiaofen saw was a desolate old man walking away from her. He was only in his thirties, but it felt as if he'd already lived his whole life. Already he was exhausted and despairing. Although he'd kept smiling at Xiaofen, working hard to seem cheerful and friendly, there was something bitter and withered behind that smile. This was Xiaofen's last sight of Mingjiu. A man slowly moving farther and farther from her, soon to disappear forever.

A COUPLE OF months later, two more teachers got permanent positions, and once again there was a riotous celebration at which Mingjiu had a few drinks.

He still felt a little dizzy the next day, but he had a class to get to, so he struggled out of bed and headed off to teach.

Mingjiu stood at the lectern and opened his textbook, but before he could speak, his body went limp and he crashed to the ground. The other teachers came running. They loaded him onto a trolley and wheeled him to Jiangyan Hospital.

The diagnosis was swift: late-stage liver cancer.

After a few days in the hospital, Mingjiu was sent home. Guibao stayed by his side every minute of the day. She cleaned him, fed him, sang to him.

At the end of the year, Mingjiu's uncle came to Shen Village to see him, bringing a hundred yuan and ration coupons for a hundred pounds of grain. He said to Mingjiu, "I've gotten approval to give you a permanent position. As soon as you're well again, I'll sort out the paperwork."

"I don't need it anymore, Uncle," said Mingjiu. "Give it to someone else."

His uncle was silent for a while. Before leaving, he said, "Xiaofen had a daughter. She asked me to bring you this letter. Get well soon."

Mingjiu nodded. His uncle said goodbye, and Guibao walked him out. Mingjiu raised his hand to wipe away his tears.

One evening in 1978, Mingjiu breathed his last in Guibao's arms. She lay next to her husband's body, hugging him and kissing his icy temples from time to time. She refused to let him go, even when the coffin arrived. She insisted he wasn't dead, just sleeping, and he would wake up in a while. It took four men to drag her away so Mingjiu could be placed in the coffin. They put on the lid, and hammered in the nails with the back of an ax. Guibao flung herself at them and snatched the ax so she could smash the coffin open. "I want to be with Mingjiu," she sobbed. "I want to be with Mingjiu."

Once again, Guibao had lost her mind.

THE SCALE-OPERATOR

F OR THE LAST FEW YEARS, I've been going back to Shen Village for the New Year. On the first day, as soon as I get up, I'll wish everyone in my family good morning, then head out to visit every household in the village. New Year's visits are very simple—as you come to each house, you shout through the open front door, "Happy New Year, Grandpa!" or "Uncle" as the case might be, at which they come out and cheerfully reply, "Happy New Year!" Then you'll be asked to come in and sit and get offered the steamed buns and brown sugar date tea the hosts would have prepared. You mustn't actually consume any, but say, "Keep it for yourself." After offering your host a good cigarette, you then go on your way. You need to visit dozens of households on that first morning, and you'll never make it if you linger. Saying "Keep it for yourself" is another way of wishing plenty upon the families you visit. As for whether steamed buns or stewed red dates can actually keep, it's best not to think too much about that.

I left the village when I was eighteen and didn't return for more than ten years. When I finally went back, the people a couple of generations older than me had mostly passed away, including my grandpa. As for the generation below, some were already in their teens, and as far as they were concerned, I was a complete stranger. When they ran into me in the fields, or when I stopped by their houses, they looked at me with surprise, until their parents told them to greet me, at which they'd force out an "Uncle." Only when I made the round of New Year visits did I feel a deep connection to this place again. Fortunately, I was only away for a little over ten years. Everyone in my and my parents' generations were still as close to me as ever. I was still a part of Shen Village.

HEADING HOME AFTER these visits, I usually catch sight of Fifth Head as I pass by East Shan River. He doesn't have a real name, but being the fifth child in his family, he's known as Fifth Head. He's in his forties, and is developmentally disabled. Wearing a new padded jacket and holding an unlit cigarette, he'll smile and say, "Heh heh, New Year," and I'll nod in response. Then he'll gleefully traipse after me, hands clasped behind his back.

All year round, Fifth Head walks around the village with his hands behind his back, stopping by each house. There was a time, just after I started elementary school, when my little brother and I became fascinated with a mini-tractor. We scampered across the fields following it. The tractor went back and forth, plowing the soil, and we ran back and forth too. This strange behavior aroused Fifth Head's interest, and he joined in the procession. He fled when we chased him away or pelted him with earth clods, but as soon as we turned our attention back to the tractor, he'd show up again. For fear of becoming the laughing-stock of the village, we abandoned the tractor. After that, though, whenever the tractor was in action, Fifth Head would run behind it from one end of the field to the other, over and over until the sky darkened. He remained the tractor's biggest fan until it short-circuited and died.

It's hard to believe, but a full hundred years ago, a Taoist priest predicted that Shen Village would have someone like Fifth Head.

THE SCALE-OPERATOR HAD invited this Taoist priest to his home to predict his family's fate in the third year of Emperor Pu Yi's reign, 1911. My grandfather Tongshou was born that year, in the sixth lunar month. That autumn, the Xinhai Revolution took place. Then in the winter, my family's rice business was burned to the ground.

THIS WAS WHAT changed my entire family's fate. Late one night, a crackling outside awakened Grandpa's father. He jumped out of bed and saw flames roiling through the window. My grandfather was less than six months old at the time. There wasn't time to dress him, so his father wrapped him in a blanket and carried him out.

Grandpa had been born into a rich family, but the fire completely destroyed their wealth. Having only been able to attend a year of classes at the schoolhouse, he would later become a carpenter. The only piece of good fortune was that no one was hurt in this sudden fire. The family business was gone, though, leaving nothing but ashes.

More than thirty huge tubs of rice were reduced to cinders. For days afterward, no one was willing to help clear the terrifying aftermath, and the family could only sit by the burned-out ruins, weeping in despair.

When an investigation showed the fire was the result of arson, my family's feelings switched from grief to rage, and they stopped crying. The women marched through the village, cursing this unknown villain. The men gritted their teeth and told every well-wisher they were determined to get vengeance.

The person who'd been running the rice business, Grandpa's uncle, ignored the neighbors who came to visit and sat there looking ashen, writing a name with his calligraphy brush. Then he'd tear it up, write it again, tear it up again, on and on.

Grandpa's uncle was named Wanhao, a generous, open-hearted man of six foot three whom everyone called Big Hao. The whole village knew him as a stand-up guy. Grandpa's father, Wanli, was the second son, a strapping man. Each day, he got a handcart full of grain from Jiangyan and hawked it around the neighboring villages. The third son, Wanshan, had a feeble body and stayed home to look after the business.

The rice business had been gradually prospering over the last decade, but the fire wiped it out.

New Year 1912 was a desolate time. Three makeshift shelters were put up, one for each brother's family. The patriarch, Wenji, moved in with Wanshan.

On the first day of the New Year, the three families huddled in their shelters. They couldn't make any New Year visits after such a huge catastrophe, in case they passed on their bad luck. The villagers could come and see them, though, to express their concern. They brought steamed buns, fish, meat, tofu, and rice. The account books had gone up in the fire, but anyone with a tab paid roughly what they felt they owed. My family expressed their deep gratitude to each of these visitors.

RIGHT AFTER THE New Year, Wanhao summoned Stutter Yu Long, a sorcerer from Ni Village, which was to the south of Shen Village. He wanted him to cast a spell to find the arsonist.

Ever since the fire, Wanhao had been sleuthing. His biggest suspect was a worker he'd recently fired, Thin Pock, a scrawny man with a pockmarked face, a real slippery rascal.

Three months before this, the big Jiangyan rice firm that supplied Wanhao's business needed to send a boatload of rice to Shanghai, but they were short-handed. They asked if Wanhao could loan them someone to make up the crew, and he told Thin Pock to go with them.

The boat arrived in Shanghai and began unloading. The captain warned them not to go wandering, because there were revolutionaries about in the city. Thin Pock was a born rogue who'd never been to Shanghai—he was hardly going to follow instructions and stay on board. When no one was looking, he slipped off the boat and, grinning broadly, began exploring the city.

This was three years and nine months into Pu Yi's reign, November 1911. The Xinhai Revolution had taken place in Wuhan over a month ago. Thin Pock was ignorant of all this. He'd heard there were peep shows in Shanghai and wanted to have a look—something to brag about back in the village.

As he walked past an alleyway, someone suddenly grabbed hold of his head and, with a crisp snip, lopped off his long, thick queue with a pair of scissors. Thin Pock screamed, "My God!" Clapping his hands over his scalp, he sprinted back to the dock.

Thin Pock's encountering a revolutionary and getting his queue cut off was big news back in Shen Village. Everyone stopped by our rice shop to gawk at him. Thin Pock wore a hat, and if anyone dared to lift it, he'd jump to his feet and hurl a selection of swear words at them. The villagers had a good laugh about this and joked that there was now a revolutionary in the rice shop.

This made Wanhao very nervous. He wasn't sure exactly what a revolutionary was, but he knew it meant a rebel of some kind—perhaps like the "long hairs," as the fighters of the Taiping Heavenly Kingdom were known. Rebels got executed—this was no joke. Wanhao was getting new information from the big rice company in Jiangyan every day. Apparently there was a war going on in Nanjing, and the "queue soldiers" of the Qing were going at it hammer and tongs with the revolutionaries. In the face of such chaos, the best thing was not to do anything differently, to avoid getting sucked in.

And so he sent Thin Pock packing.

The newly shorn Thin Pock slunk away resentfully, his heart filling with anger.

The following night, Thin Pock snuck back into the rice shop. He tied the bottoms of a pair of pants and filled the legs with rice. Perhaps this was his way of getting back at Wanhao for his unjust treatment. Unfortunately, as he clambered back over the wall, he was caught by Wanli and Wanshan.

They dragged Thin Pock back inside and tied him to a pillar. Wanhao said, "Leave him here all night, we'll deal with him in the morning." Thin Pock lost his temper and roared, "I only got my queue cut off by those fake foreign devils because I was working for you. You think that's fair? Firing me after that happened? Fine, leave me tied up. I'm not married, I have nothing to lose. You'll have to let me go sooner or later, and when you do, I'll burn your house to the ground. I'm not afraid. I'll do it, you wait and see."

Wanhao's wife came in with Wanli's wife in tow, and told Wanshan, who'd been keeping watch, to leave. They walked up to Thin Pock. Without saying a word, Wanhao's wife held up a nail, the sort used for soling boots, and plunged it hard into his thigh. Thin Pock screeched as blood seeped through his trousers.

"Are you going to steal again?"

"Kill me if you dare, you vicious bitch. I'll burn down your house."

She stabbed him again, and he yelped, "Fuck!"

Wanhao's wife held up the nail once more, and his whole body slackened. "Please, Madam. I won't do it again."

"Are you going to burn down our house?"

"No! No!"

"Go ahead and try. If I see you again, I'll poke you full of holes." Wanhao's wife swept away, with Wanli's wife trailing after her, pale with fright.

A short while after that, a worker who was close to Thin Pock came in and untied him. "Get out of here, quick. They said they're taking you to the police tomorrow."

Wanhao had sent the worker in to free Thin Pock. It's easy to catch a thief, but setting him free is harder. Now he'd been taught a lesson. Stealing a bit of rice was no big deal, really.

After the fire, Thin Pock was the first person Wanhao thought of. He made some inquiries. Thin Pock had said, "I'm all alone in this world, and that's a fact. To be honest, I came by several times intending to burn the place down, but whenever I got to the doorway, I remembered Wanhao's wife holding that nail in her hand, and my legs started to shake so hard, I couldn't walk another step. Such a nasty woman. I didn't set this fire. Good for whoever did it, but it wasn't me."

THE ONLY SOLUTION was to get Stutter Yu Long to work his magic.

His real name was Yu Long, but he stuttered, hence his nickname. He arrived in Shen Village with his sacred blade, sacred whip and two disciples, ready to cast a "circle of light" to catch the culprit.

On a vacant piece of land in front of the ruins of my family's business, he laid out four eight-immortals tables: one with incense and candles, one with offerings of food and liquor, one with a religious figurine, and one with an upended long bench, on which was a scroll of blank paper. Stutter Yu Long was dressed in Taoist robes with a paper hat on his head. He swirled around his sacred whip, which consisted of wooden blocks strung together, and chanted constantly. On a square of yellow paper, he scrawled a charm to be burned in front of the holy figure. He murmured, "I've invited the celestial general and his celestial troops. In a while they'll capture the soul of the person who set the fire and pin it to the white paper on this bench—watch and see."

The whole village had been summoned here, including Thin Pock. Once they arrived, no one dared to leave before the circle of light had concluded.

Stutter Yu Long's spell continued from morning to afternoon, and just as everyone was flagging from exhaustion, he shouted, "The person who set the fire is right here. The celestial beings have caught his soul, and in a short while he will fall to the ground."

With that, he took his sacred blade in one hand and his sacred whip in the other, and strode into the crowd, eyes blazing. One moment he was dashing up to someone and yelling, "Was it you?" Then the next he'd burst into a long peal of laughter, or start babbling nonsense.

The scale-operator stood beneath a locust tree, looking more and more uneasy as time went on, glancing around as if he might flee at any moment. His behavior had attracted Stutter Yu Long's attention for a while. After he'd made a round of the onlookers, Yu Long's eyes abruptly widened and he dashed over to the scale-operator, looking furious. Raising his knife in the air, he shouted, "You—" Before he could finish the sentence, the scale-operator tumbled backward and landed on his ass.

He was the culprit.

The crowd began yelling and cursing. Some raised their fists against the scale-operator, others lashed out with their feet. He lay on the ground unmoving. The clamor got louder until someone shouted, "Stop! She's dead!"

When the scale-operator's wife heard her husband had been caught, her immediate reaction was to grab her cleaver and slit her throat. The scale-operator hurried home with the rest of the crowd behind him, and found his wife lying perfectly still on the floor, covered in blood. Some of the village women were bandaging her, and their eldest son was sitting on the floor staring at the cleaver, which he'd snatched from her hand.

In the end, the old woman didn't die, although she was left too weak to do any work. Wanhao was too afraid of killing her to press charges again. In the end, he took the clan leader Wanbao's suggestion and accepted six bushels of sorghum from the scale-operator to put an end to the matter.

As for why the scale-operator set the fire, we need to go back to when Sun Yat-sen became the Republic of China's first president.

It took a few days for the news that the Republic of China had been established to reach Shen Village. A little over a month later, people came from the county to put up notices everywhere announcing that Sun Yat-sen was now the president, and the president had decreed that all the men should cut off their queues, and any girls or women with bound feet should unbind them. Apart from Thin Pock, who got all excited and kept taking off his hat to reveal his shorn head, the other villagers received this news with equanimity. No one complied. They all knew that the emperor was still around, and it would be rash to cut off their queues so impetuously. As for unbinding feet that had been bound for many years, they refused that too. "That would never do. Just imagine if someone was walking up to you, but their feet arrived before they did!"

Nonetheless, words like "revolution," "president," and "republic" entered the villagers' chat.

Wanhao was astute enough to know that talk of war meant the price of rice would soon go up and reckoned there would be a shortage. So he began building a stockpile, buying up all the land he could. If his family could increase their own crop, the business would be truly secure.

The scale-operator was purchasing land too. Nothing else was safe in the fog of war, neither money nor buildings, and owning land seemed like the safest thing—it couldn't be stolen or burned. If he had enough land, his family would be secure.

Land is the lifeblood of country folk, though, and no one sells it unless they absolutely have to—and even then, they only let it go one or two mu at a time.

After making many inquiries, the scale-operator finally heard that a family in the north of the village had eight mu they wanted to get off their hands. He showed up at their door right away.

The owner welcomed the scale-operator in and politely offered him a seat, some tea, and a puff on his water-pipe. As soon as he brought up the question of buying the land, though, the owner told him Wanhao had been there the day before, and they'd already agreed on the sale. This lit a fire in the scale-operator's heart. He was a stubborn man and found it hard to let go of anything he'd set his mind on. He said, "I'll pay more. You still haven't done the paperwork. Just say you've changed your mind, and sell it to me instead." The owner was an honorable man and said, "Wanhao has two brothers—there's a lot of them, and they don't have much land. Your family has more land and fewer people. Besides, I've already promised it to him, and I don't want to go back on my word."

The scale-operator ought to have been an even-handed, reasonable person. Each year, on the spring equinox, officials would check the accuracy of every measuring tool—apparently, this was due to an edict issued by the emperor himself. Spring equinox is when the day is exactly as long as the night, a symbol of equality. The artisan operating the scales began work on this day to show that they would be fair and upright. In ancient times, scale-operating was also known as "weighing-up," and indeed the scale-operator of Shen Village was someone who weighed up every matter to see what was in it for him. The only thing is, he went too far.

After failing to buy that piece of land, the scale-operator went home and brooded on it. He decided that Wanhao had surely done this on purpose, to get in his way—he must have heard that the scale-operator had his eye on the property and made sure to swoop in first.

This was around the end of the lunar year, and word got around that Emperor Pu Yi had abdicated. Wanhao spent more time outside the village than most and picked up the change in the air. He didn't cut off his queue, but his conversation was now peppered with words like "revolution" and "republic." The scale-operator was actually completely indifferent to the revolution, but now he became determined to oppose Wanhao in everything. Wanhao praised the revolution, so the scale-operator said it was better in the old days, when an emperor was on the throne. He and Wanhao got into several arguments over this. But the world had changed, and the scale-operator's anti-revolution rhetoric got him into trouble. One day, someone from the county town who was probably only passing through the village happened to hear that the scale-operator was against the revolution and knocked on his door to give him a warning. Terrified, the scale-operator offered the visitor a spread of good food and liquor, then cautiously sent him on his way. After this, he loathed Wanhao even more. Clearly, Wanhao must have tattled to this man and sent him after the scale-operator. You could say anything you liked in the village—how could his words have reached all the way to the government? Where was Wanhao's loyalty to his fellow villagers? The scale-operator couldn't swallow this injury.

And so, on a dark night when the wind was high, the scale-operator lit a flame and burned the rice business to the ground.

AFTER BEING REVEALED as the arsonist, the scale-operator was too ashamed to face anyone. All day long he sat on his doorstep on a little stool, hunched over with his head between his knees, thinking about god knows what. His wife spent a lot of time in bed, and their elder son still seemed traumatized by his mother's suicide attempt. The second son, Fifth Life, was becoming more disturbed as time went on. The scale-operator had had five sons, but the first three had died as children. That's why they named the youngest Fifth Life, meaning their fifth child should have more life. Unfortunately, Fifth Life's brain was gradually slowing down.

The scale-operator felt as if he were sitting on a bed of needles—everything in his life was going wrong. Finally, he summoned a famous Taoist priest from Dongtai, hoping to break free from his problems.

The priest spent some time walking back and forth, studying the area around the house, then he asked the scale-operator many detailed questions about the family's situation, and finally scrutinized his face. Shaking his head, the priest said, "You live on such a deserted piece of land, with no one around you—a lone boat on the vast ocean. That's very dangerous. And going by your face—" Here he made an extravagant show of studying the scale-operator's features, then shut his eyes and muttered some words before opening them sharply again. "You used to be the accountant in the court of the Malignant Star, until you became too covetous and were banished to the mortal realm. Having become human, you refused to turn over a new leaf, and continued to transgress—" The priest sighed long and deep and said to the scale-operator, who was gaping at him, "This is your fate: your family will produce three generations of imbeciles, and Fifth Life is the first of them."

The scale-operator panicked. Over and over, he asked the priest to save them. The priest put up some token resistance, then agreed to perform a ritual.

First thing the next morning, the Taoist priest swirled about waving colorful banners and chanting. He burned a lot of incense and many paper horses. Then he found a broken old millstone, carved "Mount Tai Spirit Tablet" on it, and placed it in front of the house. Next was a large chunk of limestone, on which he inscribed "Grand Lord Jiang Is Here," and placed it in the backyard. The ritual went on for three days. At the end, he said to the scale-operator, "From now on, you must accumulate as much merit as you can, to expiate your past sins." With that, he accepted three scoops of rice and three silver dollars as payment, then went on his merry way, metal rings clanging.

Now that the priest was gone, the scale-operator started feeling short of breath, and soon he was ill in bed. This dragged on for a year, and when his health still hadn't improved, he decided to marry off his second son Fifth Life, hoping for a wave of good fortune. Everyone knew that Fifth Life was developmentally disabled. When he was just a month old, he'd been betrothed to a baby girl in Yu Village, to the northeast of Shen Village. The scale-operator sent someone to Yu Village to fetch the bride. Fifth Life's fiancée was beautiful as flowers and bright as jade, clever and capable. She'd long heard what kind of man she would be marrying, and when the matchmaker showed up at her door, she felt her life was over and declared she would rather be dead. Her father said to the matchmaker, "The girl is still young, and her dowry isn't ready yet. Why don't we wait a bit and see?" Now that it seemed his youngest son's wedding might not happen, rage filled the scale-operator's heart, which worsened his condition. He called his elder son to his bedside and told him, "After I'm dead, make Fifth Life get married in mourning. If the Yu family doesn't agree, have my corpse carried to their house. Unless Fifth Life is married, I won't rest in peace."

The scale-operator left the world that very night. It was the sixth day of the fourth lunar month in the second year of the Republic, May 11, 1913.

THE WEAVER

F IFTH HEAD STANDS OUT IN my memories of childhood. He was the scale-operator's great-grandson, three or four years older than me. When the villagers realized he was developmentally disabled, they immediately thought of the Taoist priest's prediction from decades ago. At the time, the scale-operator had been shocked, but naively thought putting a broken old millstone at his front door would be enough to fix the situation.

When he was revealed as the person who'd burned down the rice business, the scale-operator's depravity was laid bare for everyone to see. He spent his days sitting outside his front door, hanging his head and listlessly sunning himself. His hatred for many of the people around him only increased as they despised him, avoided him, blamed him, ostracized him. He might as well have been invisible. No longer could he pass off as a loyal, honest man. He fell

Content note: in this chapter, the author depicts historical attitudes to developmental disability that were typical of that time and place—including the idea that disability is a punishment for the sins of one's ancestors, and that being married to a disabled person is a grievous harm.

into a fearsome isolation. Everyone said he was the villain of Shen Village. Unable to stand this, he soon fell ill and was bedridden.

When a person is about to depart this world, the custom of Shen Village is to forgive him, no matter what evil things he might have done. Wanhao, the owner of the rice firm, came to the scale-operator's house one evening, sat by his bedside, and said, "What's past is past. Let go of it." The scale-operator sighed. "I'm a dying man."

The scale-operator's elder son, Haihead, knelt by his father's bed to receive his final instructions. Ever since he'd witnessed his mother's attempted suicide, steady, dependable Haihead had grown distracted. He asked his wife to bring their newborn child, so his grandfather could see him for the last time. The scale-operator smiled with satisfaction. He had no way of knowing this baby, whom he'd pinned all his hopes on, would turn out to be developmentally disabled too.

ON THE NIGHT of May 11, 1913, the scale-operator grabbed his son Haihead's hand and repeatedly told him, "When I'm gone, make Fifth Life get married in mourning. If the Yu family refuses, dump my body at their front door. I won't rest in peace unless Fifth Life is married."

With that, he sighed long and hard and passed away amid this anxiety. He used his death as the final blow against the future in-laws of his son Fifth Life. Old Mr. Yu was forced by this assault to give up his daughter, Mei, after which he slowly faded away too.

On the morning of May 12, Fifth Life dressed in the mourning clothes that had been laid out for him, and went to Yu Village with a couple of matchmakers. This was his first and last visit there, and Mei's first sight of the man she was going to marry.

When they arrived, the matchmakers gave Fifth Life a vicious beating. This was on his mother's instructions, so he would be sobbing when he walked into the house. Still weeping, he kowtowed to his father-in-law, then departed without saying a word. This gave the impression that his father's death had affected him so badly, he couldn't even speak—which was the intended effect.

Mei was hiding to one side, peeping at her future husband. Her father had arranged the betrothal when she was just a month old. As an adult, she learned all at once that she'd been engaged as a baby and that her fiance was "slow." Time went on, and she began worrying more and more about her future. She cried countless times over this. Now, though, seeing this silent, grief-stricken Fifth Life, so different from the image in her mind, she began to have a little hope. Nonetheless, she continued shedding tears as she asked her father one last time to cancel the betrothal. Her father was crying too, but all he could say was, "The only way out of this is if one of you dies."

WHEN THE SCALE-OPERATOR threw a first-month party for his son Fifth Life, Chinless got completely blotto. Chinless was a professional matchmaker and got his nickname from the combination of his receding chin and amazingly glib tongue. He must have had a real name too, but no one knew what it was. Spewing boozy fumes, Chinless reached out to push the fire bucket Fifth Life was lying in. A "fire bucket" is a sort of wooden cradle with a pan of burning coals under it for warmth. Chinless looked up at the scale-operator and said, "Uncle, this child has a good-fortune face. Why not get him matchmade early?" The scale-operator said, "Is there anyone suitable?" "Yes, Yu Shuqing of Yu Village has just had a baby girl." The scale-operator's eyes lit up. "Excellent. If you can make this happen, there's five silver dollars in it for you."

Shuqing was the head of Yu Village. His family owned more than eighty mu of good land, and he was known as an upright man whose word was sturdy as a mountain. He was held in great respect by many nearby villages. Whenever there was a neighborly squabble in Yu Village, Shuqing only had to say a few words, and the dispute would be instantly resolved. Being able to marry into his family would be a great honor. The very next day, the scale-operator asked Chinless to go make the match.

Chinless moved heaven and earth to persuade Shuqing, who finally agreed to visit Shen Village.

The custom of child betrothals persisted in Shen Village right up to my childhood. The year I started elementary school, a mother even brought her daughter to our home for a matchmaking session. I hid in the kitchen and refused to come out. The girl, who was two years older than me, boldly walked into the kitchen to have a look at her future husband. She found me with a large pork bone in my hands, getting my lips all greasy as I gnawed at it. She gawked at me and giggled with her hand over her mouth, then ran out so fast I didn't even get a good look at her face, just the impression of two swaying pig-tails. More fruitless matchmaking followed. These meetings only stopped when I left home to roam through one city after another. To be honest, being sought out for a betrothal meant either that the boy's father had a certain repu-tation, or his family's circumstances were reasonably prosperous. I was in the former group, Fifth Life in the latter.

Shuqing found out that the scale-operator had more than sixty mu of good land, a large plow bullock, a full set of farming tools, and a decent-looking five-room tile-roofed house. Also, he had two sons. This meant the future Mrs. Fifth Life would lead a relatively comfortable existence. As for Fifth Life himself, lying squalling in the fire bucket, Yu Shuqing barely glanced at him before agreeing to the match.

THE BETROTHAL CEREMONY took place a couple of weeks later, on the sixteenth day of the second month, an auspicious date. Chinless and another matchmaker went to Shuqing's home in Yu Village. Shuqing was ready with Old Mr. Yao from the local schoolhouse, as well as some of the village's influ-ential figures and a good-fortune couple. This "good-fortune couple" was an elderly husband and wife of means, blessed with sons, daughters, and many grandchildren. After they'd had some tea, one of the matchmakers reached into his shirt and produced a red envelope containing six silver dollars. The crowd hummed its excitement and nodded its approval. The bride price was normally just a few dozen copper coins. Shuqing clasped his hands in thanks and accepted the silver. Right after that, Old Mr. Yao laid out an inkstone and some yellow paper, got the matchmakers to grind some ink, and picked up his brush to write out one-month-old Mei's year, month, and day of birth, the so-called "eight numbers of life." Down the right side, he wrote "As long-lived as Peng Zu," and on the left, "More wealth than Guo Ziyi." He folded the paper and wrapped it in another sheet of red. On this he wrote, with great solemnity, "Good fortune in all things." Then red and green threads were wrapped around the papers, to represent marriage being two people a thousand li apart, joined by a string. The good-fortune wife took the eight numbers of life and stuffed them into Mei's hand where she lay in her fire bucket. The little girl thought this was good fun and gurgled with laughter, unaware that her destiny had been sealed in that moment. She only held the papers for a moment before the good-fortune husband retrieved it and placed it before the Bodhisattva statue in the middle of the ancestral hall. Mei's mother scooped her up, knelt in front of the Bodhisattva, and kowtowed resoundingly three times. Shuqing then took this paper packet, which was called a "rough paper sheet," and passed it back to Chinless with both hands. With that gesture, he handed over his daughter's life.

Back in Shen Village, a crowd had gathered at the scale-operator's front door, and when they saw Chinless in the distance, they set off firecrackers. The scale-operator took the rough paper sheet and reverently placed it in front of the family's Bodhisattva figure. Fifth Life was scooped up by his mother and made to bow three times to the deity and paper.

The banquet had been laid out in readiness. Chinless and the other match-maker sat at the eight-immortals table, facing south. In Shen Village, making a successful match was a glorious business. Eighteen times now, they had been given the south-facing seat of honor amid the joy and festivity of a successful wedding. There was a whole ritual to this. Never mind the other dishes, it was obligatory for the table to have "pork six ways": pig head, pig heart, pig stom-ach, pig lung, pig kidney, pig intestine.

This would be the only celebratory event connected to Fifth Life's betrothal. Although the usual rituals of the engagement and the wedding were all enacted, the atmosphere had turned tragic by then.

Fifth Life was five when he finally said "Mom" for the first time. He started school at eight, but after half a year, still couldn't read a single word. He was often found sobbing after being beaten up, but when they asked who hit him, he wasn't able to say. Nothing could be done—he had to be sent home. His appearance, too, was getting more obviously slow—when you came up to him, all he did was smile foolishly. The scale-operator was afraid the Yu family would find out what his son was really like, so whenever anyone visited from Yu Village, he would keep Fifth Life indoors and not let him show his face. Flames can't be hidden by paper, though, and Shuqing got wind of this eventu-ally. He found an opportunity to see Fifth Life in person and saw that he was indeed slow.

Meanwhile, Mei was getting prettier by the day and showing herself to be a quick-minded girl. She knew she'd been betrothed as a child, but no one told her anything about the groom-to-be. She had no idea what sort of man she would be marrying and hadn't even laid eyes on him before. Shuqing cared a lot about his reputation—he was known as a man of his word. He knew he'd promised his daughter to the wrong man, but gritted his teeth and refused to go back on his promise. At the New Year and other holidays, the scale-operator would send money and gifts, cementing the connection between the two families.

By 1912, when Mei turned sixteen, she had blossomed into beauty. The scale-operator had been revealed as an arsonist at this point, and his health was declining. He was determined to get his son married off. Once again, he summoned Chinless and sent him to Yu Village, where he would exchange the rough paper sheet for a red paper sheet. With most families, getting the rough paper sheet was considered as good as marriage, and there was no need for the red. Shuqing understood what the scale-operator was doing. Yet he couldn't say the words that would annul the betrothal, and he knew very well that even if he did, the scale-operator would take him to court, which would end with Shuqing losing his case and his daughter being married off anyway. When your teeth have been kicked in, you might as well swallow them.

Shuqing tried his best to think of a way out and finally settled on a waiting game. If he could drag things out long enough, surely the scale-operator would give up and accept some money to go away? Unfortunately, the scale-operator was more stubborn than expected. The more Shuqing thought about it, the angrier he got. He decided to make some unreasonable demands. Sure, he said, they could exchange papers, but first he wanted sixty-six silver dollars, sixty-six pounds of fish and meat, six sets of silk clothes, six items of gold and silver jewelry. Six sixes, and not one less. There was no way the scale-operator could have afforded all this, and yet he agreed right away.

The scale-operator was determined to marry Fifth Life off so he could have descendants and didn't care what price he had to pay. Gritting his teeth, he sold off the land he valued as much as his own life, got all the items for this dowry, and fixed an auspicious date for the ceremony to exchange the rough paper sheet for a red one.

Chinless came to the scale-operator's house and, after his morning tea, asked Shen Village's schoolmaster to write Fifth Life's date of birth on the red paper, then to wrap it up again. This was placed next to Mei's rough paper sheet. In front of the Bodhisattva Guided by his mother, Fifth Life kowtowed three times to the Bodhisattva. Then the matchmakers took both papers and paid four porters thirty copper coins each to carry the presents to the Yus' front door.

Shuqing's face was like steel, and he didn't say a word. This was as much as custom allowed him to ask for, and there was nothing else he could do. With a wave of his hand, he allowed them to place the papers before the Bodhisattva. Mei was led out by her mother and made to kowtow. Sobbing and carrying on, she refused no matter what. After some struggle, they finally gave up and didn't complete the ritual. Chinless didn't particularly care. He got Old Mr. Yao to write Mei's date of birth once more on the red paper, then he returned to Shen Village with it.

The scale-operator let off more firecrackers and laid out a banquet of several tables for his friends and relatives to spend a day carousing in celebration. After this, the matchmakers showed up every few days to urge the marriage on, but Shuqing always hid away and refused to meet them. Whenever Mei saw Chinless approach, she would scream and howl. The scale-operator could tell they were stalling, and his rage and anxiety over Fifth Life's delayed wedding made his illness worse. He passed away in May 1913.

HAIHEAD FOLLOWED HIS father's dying instructions and sent Fifth Life to kowtow to Shuqing, after which he arranged for the scale-operator's coffin to be carried to Yu Village. When Shuqing heard this news, he knew there was nothing else he could do. With tears streaming down his face, he ordered his daughter to get married right away.

This time round, Shuqing only demanded thirty silver dollars and thirty pounds of meat, and no other dowry. Haihead swiftly arranged for these to be delivered. The next day, six burly men came to fetch the trousseau. This had lain in readiness for quite a while: two quilts, a mosquito net, three rounds (a bucket, a foot-washing basin, and a chamber pot), and three squares (a wardrobe, a dressing table, and a desk). Plus her clothes and jewelry—a substantial amount.

And in the afternoon, the sedan-carriers, the lantern-bearers, and the trumpeters created a festive ruckus all the way from Shen Village to Yu Village. Normally they would have spent some time expressing their good wishes and joking around, but given the unusual circumstances, no one said very much. Shuqing had made the arrangements. They ate a meal in silence, then he saw his daughter onto the sedan chair. Right away, Mei, her mother, and her aunts were all sobbing loudly. The trumpets sounded mournfully. Every family shed tears when their daughter left to be married, but not usually so bitterly or sorrowfully. The villagers who'd come to say goodbye also couldn't help crying.

Mei sat in the sedan chair, and as Shen Village drew closer and closer, the trumpets began to sound joyful, the sorrow in them fading away. She had thought of ending it all, but couldn't abandon her mother like that. If she died, her mother would soon follow, so much did she adore her daughter. Perhaps this was simply fate.

"Come see the bride! Come see the bride!" A burst of children's voices told her they'd arrived at the house. The sedan chair was carried right in. The good-fortune wife selected by the village pulled aside the curtain, and she saw a man in a formal hat and blue robe smiling foolishly at her. At the urging of the good-fortune wife, Mei and Fifth Life, who continued grinning vacuously, knelt to kowtow before the Bodhisattva First the couple bowed to honor the heavens and earth, then Mei's new mother-in-law, and finally each other.

After some fuss, Mei and Fifth Life were bundled into the bridal chamber. The good-fortune wife handed Fifth Life a little baton wrapped in red paper, with which he was supposed to lift the bride's red veil. Terrified, he backed away, until the good-fortune wife slapped him. Shaking, he raised the veil, and saw a woman glaring icily at him, perfectly motionless. This scared him out of his wits, and he ran out of the room as the good-fortune wife called out, "Come see the bride!"

The crowd swarmed in, cramming the tiny room completely full. Mei's beauty had them completely enraptured. They couldn't stop praising her. But given the man she was marrying, they weren't in the mood for the usual bridal chamber antics. After a quick look around, they dispersed to their own homes, sighing with pity.

Fifth Life's mother found him outside, shooed him back into the bridal chamber, and slammed the door shut. He huddled in a corner, sneaking glances at Mei, not daring to make a move. She shoved two boxes together and tossed him a quilt. Then she pulled a pair of scissors from the dressing table drawer and said, "You'll sleep here. If you touch me, I'll take these scissors and—" She gestured menacingly, and Fifth Life nodded frantically, mouth agape, almost weeping with fear. "No crying!" she screamed. Fifth Life hastily clamped his mouth shut, then crept onto the boxes and lay down, pulling the quilt over his head.

Mei lay on the bed with her eyes wide open till dawn.

There were more rituals to endure in the morning. The first one was "wealth sitting": the bride and groom sat next to each other on the edge of the bed, while the good-fortune wife sang them an auspicious tune. Grow old together, have a son soon, that sort of thing. At the end of the song, the couple were supposed to kiss, then the groom would fondle the bride's breasts. Fifth Life's mother had explained to him what he should do, but how could he possibly have dared? He just sat there as if he were made of wood. And so the first ritual couldn't be completed.

The second ritual was "on the pot." The bucket that came with the bride's trousseau was filled with dates, peanuts, ginkgo nuts, and various eating utensils. The good-fortune wife then retrieved these one by one, placing them onto the bibs that the couple had put on. With each item, she said something auspicious. This was meant to symbolize the beginning of married life. Mei continued to say nothing, just going along with it. Fifth Life looked around for his mother, but when he met her eye, she glared at him so fiercely that he lowered his head and was still.

The third ritual was "Bodhisattva worshipping." This was quite laborious, as you had to go around to several dozen households kowtowing and offering incense.

Everyone had tidied up their houses and yards in expectation of the couple's visit. The good-fortune wife took the bride around, instructing her how to greet and bow to each elder. Fifth Life had a fake queue trailing from his formal hat and wore a blue jacket and black trousers, with thousand-layer cloth shoes on his feet. He allowed himself to be led around by the good-fortune husband, forced to kowtow endlessly. This prolonged torture wiped the usual smile from his face and made him look much more somber.

Several irreverent children scampered behind them raising a ruckus. Some hollered, "The imbecile married a wife!" Others, "Cretin Fifth Life, is your bride pretty?" Or, "Hey, lady, your husband's a moron!" The good-fortune couple couldn't chase them away, so they just put up with it. These taunts were like knives through Mei's heart. She clenched her jaw.

Bodhisattva worshipping went on till noon. Back at the house, Mei took to the bed, refusing to see anyone. Dinner brought yet another ritual: "the happy-together meal." Four plates of food were placed on the bridal chamber's low table. The groom was supposed to serve the bride, then she would reciprocate, as a sign of their mutual affection. Mei ignored Fifth Life completely, picked up her own bowl, and started eating. Fifth Life waited till she'd finished and gone to bed before he shoveled some food into his mouth and lay back down on the crates to sleep with the quilt over his head.

The next day was the scale-operator's funeral. Mei left off her red dress and put on a plain outfit. The others held her arms and brought her to the scale-operator's altar, where she kowtowed to him. After this, the assembled mourners carried his bier to the graveyard to be interred. Back home, Mei shut herself in the room and went to sleep. The following morning, she packed a small bundle of her possessions and told Fifth Life, "Let your mom know I've gone home."

Back in Yu Village, Mei embraced her mother as they both wept.

Mei refused to return to Shen Village, and continued staying at her parents' home. Shuqing was so tormented by guilt, it wasn't long till he'd collapsed with illness. In late 1914, he summoned his eldest son and daughter-in-law to his bedside for his final instructions. "The house and the land will be evenly divided between my three sons. Mei and her mother will take turns staying with the three of you, and no one will send her back to Shen Village." With that, he shut his eyes and left this world.

Now that her father was gone, Mei understood the bitterness of depending on other people for a living. After a month of this, she packed her bundle and returned to Shen Village.

ON A SITE far from where they used to live, Mei had two thatched huts built. They were sparsely furnished, and far from any other human habitation. She took one, and made Fifth Life stay in the other. It may have been her fate to marry a man like this, but she wasn't going to accept it. She used silence to resist her destiny. She took care of him, keeping him clothed and fed, but otherwise paid no attention to him. Why bother, when his only response was that foolish grin? The only things he could say had been painstakingly taught to him, and he could only repeat them parrot-fashion. If anyone tried to make him work, he strapped a bamboo basket to his back, pretending to pick ragweed, but actually just wandered around aimlessly.

Mei could ignore him because during her time back home, she'd picked up the air of weaving. Now she got someone to make her a loom, which she set up in the middle of her living room. All day long, she locked herself away, nimbly flinging the shuttle back and forth. This allowed her mind to empty of thoughts. She kept herself entirely sequestered. More and more fabric piled up in her home. She was like a ghost. She never took part in any village gatherings, nor any weddings or funerals, nor even holidays. She never smiled and grew more fragile-looking by the day. No one in Shen Village blamed her—they only sighed that a woman so beautiful could be in this position, but there was no help for it. She would have to stay with her husband for the rest of her life.

Fifth Life's mother, her mother-in-law, the woman who'd failed to kill herself when the scale-operator was revealed to be an arsonist, was filled with hatred for Mei. She lived with her older son Haihead, but was much fonder of her younger child. She kept a close watch on Mei, afraid she would treat Fifth Life badly—but Mei didn't mistreat him, she simply pretended he didn't exist. This made the old lady uneasy. The scale-operator had forced this marriage no matter the cost, because he'd wanted to continue his line. Death and poverty meant nothing in Shen Village, the true catastrophe was if you left no descendants. The older Haihead's son got, the clearer it became that he too was developmentally disabled. There was nothing the old woman could do about that, and it tormented her. Most worryingly, Haihead had a lung disease that made him cough all day long. He had grown so frail and emaciated, it seemed he might expire at any moment.

Mei was the old lady's last hope. First she tried urging, then pleading, but Mei ignored her. Finally, the old lady bit the bullet and asked an influential good-fortune wife from the village to have a word. Mei didn't offer her a seat, so the good-fortune wife had to stand awkwardly on the front porch making her case, but before she'd finished, Mei had shut the door in her face and gone back to the loom. The old lady moved on to daily threats, scoldings and attacks. Mei paid her no heed, looking more withered all the while. Everyone sighed and shook their heads as they walked past. A fresh young flower like that, slowly getting squashed by her mother-in-law.

The old lady's wailing and carrying on didn't earn her a single person's sympathy, and Mei didn't pay her any attention either. All she could do was go to the scale-operator's grave and complain to his spirit, usually directing blame at the dead man himself. "Husband, this is all your fault. Our family line will soon come to an end. It's fine for you, you're dead and gone. You've washed your hands of the whole thing, and left me to cope with the consequences. But I can't cope, I just can't."

She wasn't going to take this lying down. Summoning Fifth Life, she gave him careful instructions. He always obeyed his mother. At dusk, the old lady led Fifth Life to Mei's hut, knocked on the door, and shoved her son inside. Fifth Life stood still for a moment gathering himself, and then lunged at Mei, pinning her to the ground. She managed to grab a bowl from the low table where she'd just eaten her dinner and smashed it hard over his head. Fifth Life shrieked and danced with pain as blood flowed from his forehead. The bright red terrified him, and he fled from the room, screaming for his mother.

The old woman walked through the darkened village howling like a wounded beast, but no one came to her aid. Everyone knew this was yet another ploy to torment her daughter-in-law. Still weeping, she got a piece of cloth and bound Fifth Life's wounds. By this time, Haihead was completely bedridden. He asked his wife, who was taking care of him, "What's the old lady doing?" His wife replied, "Just making trouble again. Ignore her." Haihead let out a long sigh and said nothing more.

At dawn the next morning, the old lady dragged Fifth Life around to every house in the village to display his wounds and claim that her daughter-in-law had tried to murder him. Fifth Life allowed himself to be led around by his mother, gritting his teeth and trying to frown, though a smile kept flitting across his face. Everyone cajoled her till she left, though their faces remained impassive. Unable to quell her rage, the old lady brought Fifth Life to see Wanzhang, the clan leader. Wanzhang stood at the entrance of the ancestral shrine, holding a red copper water pipe and giving instructions to his day laborers. The old lady stood by till he'd dismissed the workers, then said, "Wanzhang, sir, look how badly Fifth Life's wife attacked him. It's unspeakable. You have to do right by him."

Wanzhang glanced at her, then at Fifth Life, whose head was still bandaged. He took a pinch of tobacco from his pouch and placed it in the bowl of his water pipe. The stem, as long as an arm, was held between two of his fingers. Now he turned it around and took a puff, making the other end of the stem glow. With these embers, he lit the tobacco in the pipe and drew deeply from the twisty copper tube. The pipe gurgled. When he was done, he exhaled a long stream of smoke from his nostrils, and satisfaction appeared on his face. Then, holding the pipe in his left hand, he raised the copper tube with his right and blew hard into it, so the ashes jumped from the bowl and fell onto the ground.

"Haihead's Mom, it won't do you any good to go around causing trouble every day. Go ask Wanhao, Wanrong and those others to come to your house and sort things out this afternoon." The old lady nodded, not daring to say any more, and scurried off with Fifth Life.

Wanzhang the clan leader had more than a hundred mu of good land, and employed dozens of laborers—he was easily the wealthiest man in Shen Village. He was in his thirties and, at six foot two, had an imposing appearance. Despite his stature, he never bullied anyone, but treated those around him with kindness and courtesy and was scrupulously fair in all his dealings. He had the full respect of Shen Village. Whenever there was a dispute, one word from him could resolve the matter.

The old lady went home, bought some fish and meat, and asked her neighbors to come help her cook. When she heard the clan leader and other prominent figures were coming to Fifth Life's home to mediate, Mei began to get a little concerned. She didn't get up, but shut her door and stayed in bed. She had no idea what kind of consequences hitting Fifth Life would bring her.

Before lunch, Wanzhang, Wanrong, Wanhao, and some others began to arrive, one after another. Wanhao's property had been destroyed in the fire set by the scale-operator, but his generosity in dealing with this loss had raised him even higher in the eyes of the village. And so, whenever anyone asked the clan leader to deal with a situation, Wanhao would also be invited.

Everyone knew the circumstances that had led to Fifth Life's thrashing. On the surface, it might have seemed like a small matter, but the truth was much more complicated. Wanzhang, Wanhao, and the others discussed it for a long time. Finally, they asked the old lady and Mei to come in and got Haihead's wife to help him in. Fifth Life wouldn't have been able to follow what was happening, so they told him to wait in the kitchen and not to run around.

Clan Leader Wanzhang got straight to the point. "Haihead's Mom, the situation is very clear to us. Our verdict is: firstly, Mei is married to Fifth Life, so she has to treat him well. Whether or not the old lady is around, she has to be good to him, keep him fed and clothed, and not beat or scold him. Secondly, as Mei is a Shen daughter-in-law, and Fifth Life cannot be counted on, Mei and Haihead must jointly care for the old lady until her death, and make sure she has everything she needs. Thirdly, it is Fifth Life's great good fortune to be married to a fine young woman like Mei, and you mustn't ask any more of her. Fourthly, Fifth Life will live with the old lady from now on, and Mei will pay for their living expenses, but otherwise will not be entangled with their lives."

Mei was delighted with this verdict, and Haihead and his wife were happy with it too. The old lady had thought all of her machinations would have ended with the clan leader taking her side and forcing Mei to give in. When that didn't happen, she burst into tears, only to have Wanrong smack the table and shout, "Stop that noise! If you keep raising a ruckus, I'll get a rope and tie you up." This scared the old lady into silence. Wanzhang said, "If you have an argument to make, let's hear it." But of course, the old lady had nothing to say, and so she just gaped in silence.

Haihead's wife pulled Mei aside. They merrily set the table and invited everyone to take a seat. Now that this matter, which had been troubling Shen Village for many years, had finally been resolved, everyone was feeling cheerful and drank a few more glasses than usual. Wanzhang couldn't hold his liquor and quickly got drunk. Wanrong and Wanhao carried him to Mei's bed, where he fell asleep. When everyone was done feasting, they got up to leave, telling Mei to keep an eye on Wanzhang and to send him home when he woke up.

Wanzhang regained consciousness at dusk and, finding himself in a strange bed, jerked upright. Mei, who had been sitting nearby, stood and fetched a teacup. "You're awake, Mr. Wanzhang. I'll pour you some tea." Wanzhang said, "Oh my, I really must apologize. I had too much to drink." Mei poured the tea and put it on the table to cool. Wanzhang said, "This has been hard on you." That was enough to make Mei's tears start flowing. "Living like this, I might as well be dead. My god, what kind of life is this!" The dam gave way, and all her sorrow flowed out at once. Wanzhang kept soothing her. The tea was cool enough to drink now, but as she was bringing it to him, she tripped over a little bench. Wanzhang reached out to catch her, and she clutched him tightly too.

Before long, everyone in Shen Village knew that Mei had become Wanzhang's lover. No one blamed her for it—in fact, because it was Wanzhang, they respected her all the more. Now that Mei was with Wanzhang, the old lady didn't dare to nag her anymore. When disputes happened, some people now chose to ask Mei for guidance instead. Whoever she decided was in the right, would then have the advantage. As for Mei, being with Wanzhang completely transformed her. She was radiant, always smiling, and even her walk became more charming. Her own father had once been a clan leader, and she'd grown up watching him resolve disputes. Now that she had to do it herself, she was able to find reasonable solutions to each situation that left everyone satisfied. Because she was fair in everything she did and lived up to her own words, never showing any prejudice or favoritism, she won the villagers' trust and admiration. People began addressing her respectfully as "Madame Fifth Life," even though she was only in her twenties.

Mei was now cheerful and carefree. She did as much weaving as before, but now she frequently invited people to visit her and check out the cloth. If they liked it, she let them have it, and wasn't too fussy about the price. They could pay as much or as little as they liked. Whenever there was a dispute between neighbors and they asked her to intervene, she put down her shuttle and headed straight there. Of course, resolving arguments is the sort of business where it's easy to offend people. Finally, the day came when disaster fell from the skies: Fifth Life went missing.

Rumors began spreading through Shen Village. Some said Mei had murdered her husband, others that she'd driven him away. There was talk of handing her over to the authorities. Madame Fifth Life hired people to search for him, but after five or six days, they hadn't turned up any signs.

Fifth Life had been hidden away, and the person who did this wanted to teach Mei a lesson. I've already described in detail the fate of the culprit's family. When he did this deed, his household was in the ascendant, like the sun at noon. All their misfortune began the year he died. He was gone by then, of course, and wouldn't see it. But for his family, it was a deluge.

THE RUMORS AROUND Fifth Life's disappearance entangled Wanzhang too. He went to Wanhao and suggested getting Stutter Yu Long to cast a spell.

After revealing that the scale-operator had set fire to the rice business, Stutter Yu Long gained a reputation in Shen Village as the most powerful sorcerer around, which raised his status quite a bit. When he got Wanzhang's invitation, he showed up the next day and began setting up at Madame Fifth Life's doorway. After three days of work, everything was in readiness. On the morning of the fourth day, a gong summoned the villagers to the vegetable patch in front of Fifth Life's house, which had been trodden flat. Yu Long upended a long bench on top of an eight-immortals table and stuck a sheet of white paper to it. Next, he waved his arms around and began casting his spell.

With his limbs swinging wildly, Yu Long chanted, "Spirits of the heavens and earth, shades from beyond the grave, answer my summons, lend us your wisdom. The deity Taishang Laojun commands you urgently." He crushed some ghost money and set it on fire, then gently waved it before the bench, so the tendrils of smoke drifted across the blank paper. Next, he brought a child over to bring the answer to light. Only someone who hadn't reached adulthood could have this revelation. No grown-up would be able to see this. The kid they found this time was a thirteen-year-old named Changfu, a laborer in Locust's household. Yu Long told Changfu to stare at the paper and, when he saw Fifth Life, to immediately say where he was. Changfu opened his eyes wide and stared, but nothing was discernible on the paper but smoke. Yu Long cried out, "Appear, Fifth Life!" He lashed his whip across Changfu's back. Changfu yelped in pain. "Do you see him?" Changfu said nothing, and Yu Long hit him again. After five or six lashes, Changfu said, "I see him! He's in a sorghum field a dozen li to the south of the village." "What's he doing?" "Just lying there. He looks bad—half his ass has rotted off."

Right away, the crowd exploded with cries of "Let's go, quick!" Madame Fifth Life turned pale and collapsed onto the ground, unable to speak.

Tall, strapping Locust bellowed, "Keep still. Changfu will lead the way, and we'll all go together." And so the rowdy crowd set off for the sorghum field.

With Changfu leading them, they spent the whole of lunchtime searching, but found nothing.

This time round, Stutter Yu Long had failed.

Changfu stood there limply. Locust said, "Did you say you saw him?" Changfu didn't reply, and Locust smacked him across the face so he fell to the ground, then mutely crawled to his feet and followed far behind the crowd as they trailed back to Shen Village.

Yu Long was smiling broadly, waiting expectantly for them to return with Fifth Life. Instead, Locust carried over a bucket full of shit, which he flung in front of Yu Long. "You dogfucker, you're talking nonsense. For two days we wined and dined you—you ought to vomit it all back up!" Yu Long stood by the shit, his face turning red and white. The villagers spat at him as they departed.

In fact, it was Locust who'd abducted Fifth Life. He'd been smiling on the inside the whole time he put on this show of rage, busy both onstage and behind the scenes. He did it to teach Mrs. Fifth Life a lesson. It pleased him to see this confident woman reduced to tears. Her anxiety and helplessness delighted him. This was the only way he could take the sting out of his rage at being publicly scolded by her after they'd clashed several times.

Darkness brushed across the sky. While no one was looking, Yu Long quickly packed his things and slunk away. He would never set foot in Shen Village again.

Two days later, Wanzhang's inquiries finally revealed that Fifth Life had been sent to a distant relative's house eighteen li to the northeast. Madame Fifth Life put out the word that she'd had someone do a reading—now she knew exactly where Fifth Life was, and he'd be back in a couple of days. If not, they would go and fetch him.

Late the following night, Fifth Life returned to Shen Village, and the rumors swirling around Madame Fifth Life evaporated just like that. Fifth Life refused to say a word, no matter how much he was questioned. Perhaps because of the shock he'd suffered, or perhaps because he'd caught a chill, he ended up ill in bed. Less than two months later, he was dead.

Fifth Life's death stunned Locust. He'd never imagined things would go this far. Now he was on tenterhooks, worried that Madame Fifth Life would come looking for him. If she took him to court, he might end up losing everything.

Madame Fifth Life didn't pursue the matter. She sold three mu of land and gave Fifth Life a grand send-off. Locust worked harder than anyone else to organize this funeral, running around and not sparing any effort. Although his behavior was as brash as ever, and his voice boomed just as loud, as soon as Madame Fifth Life's gaze swept across him, he felt a chill in his heart. For a very long time after Fifth Life's death, he did his best to stay away from her and avoid coming face-to-face.

Not long after his brother's passing, Haihead departed too. Right at the end, his son kept smiling—he didn't know how to cry. This son was the second person in the scale-operator's clan to have a severe developmental disability. Haihead's wife was pregnant at the time of his death. This posthumous son is now in his eighties, still alive and well despite being terribly hunched over, and in good spirits. The last time I went home for the New Year, I walked past the back of his house and saw him by the East Shan River, knife in hand, clearing a grove of withered bamboo. Seeing an unfamiliar person go by, he arched his back and effortfully lifted his head to look at me. It had been too many years, and he no longer recognized me. I said, "Sir, it's me, Fishy." His face cleared, and he smiled apologetically. "These old eyes of mine can't see much anymore. I'm practically blind." I offered him a cigarette, which he took happily and popped between his lips. I turned back after I'd walked quite a distance, and he was still gazing after me.

He had five sons. The first four all had very proper names, but the youngest had no name at all. They hadn't given him one, because it was clear as soon as he was born that he was severely developmentally disabled. They just called him Fifth Head, meaning the fifth child. The third person in the scale-operator's family to be so afflicted—and the final one, if the prophecy from a hundred years ago really is true. Fifth Head is a few years older than me, now in his forties. Each day, he walks cheerfully around Shen Village. When I was a kid, I would see him almost every day. The children gave him a hard time, but he still insisted on following behind us and playing with us, even if that meant getting bullied.

NOW THAT HAIHEAD and Fifth Life were dead, there were only widows and children left in the family. Haihead's wife had to raise a disabled son while pregnant with another, and there was really no way she could support herself. Madame Fifth Life said to her, "Why don't you and the old lady move in with me? We can all live together, and I'll help you with the kids." But the old lady refused. She still had an implacable hatred of Mei that couldn't be put into words. She accepted Mei's money to live on, but refused to set eyes on her, preferring to stay as far away as possible.

FIFTH LIFE'S DEATH caught the attention of a man named Zhang Diankun from Rui Village, fifteen li to the southeast of Shen Village. Forty-two days after Fifth Life's death, when the period of mourning was over, Zhang Diankun sent a matchmaker to Shen Village to seek the hand of Mei, who was then in her early thirties.

Mei rejected him immediately.

This refusal angered Zhang Diankun, who was a bit of a thug. He'd once had more than ten mu of land, as well as a very virtuous wife. Unfortunately, he'd been too fond of all the vices—eating, drinking, whoring, gambling— and soon after his marriage, he'd wagered away all his property. He got into an argument with his wife and lashed out harder than he'd meant to, then wouldn't let her see a doctor. A short time after, she died with hatred in her heart. Zhang Diankun continued swaggering around doing whatever he pleased for another two years, until he was felled by a serious illness. After he recovered, he suddenly felt it would be better to have a wife around. But what decent family would allow their daughter to marry such a wastrel? Then he heard that Fifth Life had died and thought to himself that surely he'd be a step up from a severely mentally disabled man, so it shouldn't be too difficult to marry the widow. Unexpectedly, however, Mei wouldn't give him the time of day.

Zhang Diankun went to see his old gambling buddy Thin Pock and asked him a lot of questions. He found out that Mei was both beautiful and talented, which only spurred him on. He and his cronies hatched a scheme: if she wouldn't marry him of her own free will, they would abduct her.

It was March 1927, and the warlord Sun Chuanfang was in retreat after his defeat in Nanjing. As his troops passed through Jiangbei, they conscripted or robbed everyone they came across. Close on their heels were the Nationalists, who were once again capturing all the Communists they could find. In Subei's Santai district, murder and mayhem was a regular occurrence. Society was in chaos. Never mind abduction, even outright murder often went unquestioned. Luckily, for centuries now, the villagers had essentially been self-regulating. They'd set off to work at sunrise and rest at sunset. Even now that the country lacked a functioning government, things were still fairly stable here. Given all the general confusion, though, kidnapping a widow wouldn't really be a big deal. In fact, as far as the widow's family was concerned, if she got taken but left her property behind, that might actually be for the best, and they probably wouldn't try to get her back. Zhang Diankun felt he had the tacit approval of society to seize this woman by force.

Either out of fear that Wanzhang would retaliate, or because he'd belatedly discovered a conscience, Zhang Diankun's associate Thin Pock revealed the plot to Mei ahead of time. When the eight strapping men burst into her home that night, they found no one there. Mei's home was at the southern edge of the village, far from any neighbors. If there was a struggle here, no one would notice. Zhang Diankun and his crew turned up every few nights, so Mei had to spend each night taking refuge in a different household, fearful and agonized.

Then one evening, when it wasn't quite dark and Mei hadn't left the house yet, six or seven men appeared on the road from the south. In a panic, Mei slipped out of the back door and climbed a mulberry tree in her backyard. From that height, she saw the tall, skinny man leading the pack push open her front door. Someone behind him called out, "Is she there, Diankun?" The skinny man walked in and looked around. "I saw her a minute ago, and ran to get you guys. How could she have disappeared so quickly?" The bride-snatchers split up to ransack the house and yard. When they didn't find her, they sat down in the living room. One of them went to the coop to nab a chicken, another found her flour and started making biscuits, and a third snipped some chives from the patch outside her front door to put into fried eggs. They found baijiu in one of the cupboards and poured it out into bowls. Thus provisioned, they began to eat, drink, and carouse. Some had too much booze and dozed off on Mei's bed. All this while she crouched on a high branch of the tree, perfectly motionless. The intruders reveled late into the night, before drunkenly stumbling away. Mei straightened up to watch them leave by moonlight, and only when they'd vanished into the distance did she climb down. Brushing away tears the whole time, she cleaned up the befouled crockery and bedding.

On a few occasions, Mei hired someone to stand guard outside her home with a club. Strangely enough, the bride-snatchers never showed up on these nights. Hapless, Mei could only face each terrifying day with trepidation. After a few months of this, she was completely exhausted.

One evening, the sun was still low in the sky, and Mei was working on a length of cloth that would become a winter outfit for Wanzhang. As she wove, someone suddenly burst in and cackled to see her there. "All right! You're not getting away this time." Seeing no one else outside, Mei brought out a stool and invited him to take a seat. It was the tall, skinny man she's seen before, Zhang Diankun. He'd come to carry out a recce on his own, and seeing Mei there, he'd decided to barge in rather than going to fetch his buddies.

As Mei chatted with him, she inched her seat closer and closer to his. Delighted by this, Zhang Diankun reached out to pinch her cheek. Mei looked down, grabbed the stool she was sitting on, and shoved it legs first against Diankun's throat, knocking him back and pinning him to the floor. As he lay there unable to move, she grabbed the wooden basin she fed the chickens from and smashed it down again and again. With the stool choking him, Diankun couldn't even beg for mercy. Mei screamed, "You thought you could snatch me? You really thought you could? I'd have beaten you to death in less than a month." She waited till his face turned purple, then slowly lifted the stool. It took him quite a while to catch his breath. She jabbed a finger at him and said, "Don't move. I'll go fetch someone."

As soon as she was gone, Zhang Diankun struggled to his feet and stumbled out the door.

The story of Zhang Diankun getting beaten up by the bride he'd come to snatch spread through every village for a dozen li around. Everyone now knew that Madame Fifth Life of Shen Village was a force to be reckoned with. After this, nobody would dream of trying anything with her. Instead, they treated her with much more respect. Many days later, Thin Pock came to tell Mei, "Zhang Diankun spent more than half a month in bed. He says every time he thinks of you, his legs start to tremble." Mei snorted with laughter and said, "That dogfucker."

MRS. WANZHANG HAD known about Mei and her husband for some time, but she chose not to ask any questions. After more than twenty years, Mei's curiosity got the better of her. She wanted to know what this woman looked like. She'd never been to Wanzhang's home before, but now she decided to.

While Wanzhang was in the county town taking care of some business, Mei took advantage of his absence to visit his home. Mrs. Wanzhang was from a wealthy family, and although her looks were fairly average, she carried herself with great dignity and treated everyone with kindness. When Mei appeared at her door, she very courteously offered her a seat and poured her a drink, then made small talk with exactly the right degree of formality. Mei tried her best to stay calm, but couldn't stop feeling uneasy. After a short while, she said goodbye. When Wanzhang came back, his wife told him simply, "Mrs. Fifth Life dropped in this morning, and we talked for a while. I tried to get her to stay for dinner, but she said she had to go."

Wanzhang said nothing, but after that day, he never set foot in Mei's house again. When they ran into each other in the presence of others, Wanzhang would nod a greeting at her, but never spoke. Mei knew it was her own rash behavior that had made Wanzhang leave her. She had no idea what was going through his mind, and even if he'd given her the chance to explain herself, she wouldn't have known where to start.

Seven years after Mei's lover Wanzhang stopped seeing her, he passed away.

In 1948, Shen Village had been liberated and was now due for land reform. Wanzhang said, "Sure, I'll give up my land, but I have a request. Ask the district leader to come here. I'd like to hand him the title deeds personally."

The district leader showed in Shen Village with two assistants, all three of them with Mauser pistols tucked into their belts. The village head struck a gong, summoning all the villagers to Wanzhang's house. Mei, now fifty-two years old, stepped inside for the second time. She said to Wanzhang, "Did you really give up your property?" He looked terrible. After staring at her for a long while, he finally said, "You got old too."

The crowd swarmed over.

Wanzhang had the title deeds in readiness, stacked up at the entrance of the ancestral hall.

"These were left to me by my ancestors, and today I will burn them to let my ancestors know what's happening." Wanzhang knelt down and kowtowed three times. His wife brought a lit taper from the kitchen and put it in his hand. Wanzhang touched the flame to the title deeds, and the wind whipped up the fire as they burned. Ash danced through the air and drifted into the distance.

The watching throng jabbered away in utter confusion. Some excitedly asked how and when the land would be split up, others timorously tried to find out more from those around them, not quite believing this was happening.

When all the title deeds were completely burned, Wanzhang fell to the ground with a crash.

Mrs. Wanzhang asked my grandfather to make two coffins: one for Wanzhang, and one for later. Every detail of the funeral was organized; Wanzhang was due to be buried four days after his passing. That morning, the mourners arrived in droves, and a grave had been dug in the cemetery. As for Mrs. Wanzhang, she was neatly dressed, lying dead in her bed.

The day after Mrs. Wanzhang's death, their son snuck out of Shen Village and never came back. In 1949, he left for Taiwan.

When my father was updating our family tree, he asked a clansman in Taiwan to find out what had happened to the son. It turned out Wanzhang's son was dead, and his grandson had died young, leaving two small boys behind. His wife had remarried, and her new husband was a low-ranking official in the Nationalist Kuomintang. When our clansman tracked her down and invited her to come back to Shen Village for a visit with her sons, the Kuomintang official yelled at him. His wife wasn't allowed to have any dealings with the

Mainland. As a result, our family tree only has Wanzhang and his son's names, but the line ends after that.

AFTER WANZHANG WAS buried, Madame Fifth Life sat by his grave for half a day. When she tried to get up to leave, she found herself unable to. She struggled for a while and finally had to grab onto his tombstone to heave herself to her feet. "Mr. Wanzhang, Mrs. Wanzhang, rest here and be well," she muttered to them.

In 1958, Shen Village was collectivized, and everyone had to "eat from the same pot of rice." All the food Madame Fifth Life had stockpiled was confiscated, and her cooking pots were taken too, so she was forced to eat in the cafeteria. The cafeteria soon closed down, and the famine arrived.

Her body started retaining fluids. She lay in bed suffering for several months. Then, in the winter of 1959, Madame Fifth Life passed away.

In her later years, she'd taken on an apprentice weaver named Tongqi, a loyal, honest boy who did nothing but work all day and barely spoke. I often saw Tongqi weaving. When the weather was good, he brought his loom out to the roadside near his home. We'd gather around him, forgetting all about the ragwort we were supposed to be picking. The weaver was always quite busy, because many households in Shen Village wanted him to weave fabric for them. This was especially true around the New Year, when everyone needed new outfits and would trade food or other valuable items for cloth. When I was a kid, most of my clothes came from fabric made by him.

When Madame Fifth Life died, they found her home pretty much empty, apart from the loom. Her former apprentice took this, then he hired laborers to tear down her house, piled together all the wood, and got a carpenter to turn it into her coffin. Madame Fifth Life's coffin was made by my eldest uncle, a man regarded by Grandpa as a useless carpenter. He worked with another carpenter, and by the time they were done, it was dark. They placed Madame Fifth Life's body in their creation. The weaver then hired someone else to dig a hole in the dark and lowered her into it. A scrappy funeral. Everyone was starving as they buried her, and barely had any energy, so the grave was shallow. No one tended to it afterward. After a year or two of weathering the elements, it had been completely wiped away, leaving no trace at all.

ENDINGS

WHEN THE BRICKLAYER DIED, HIS funeral was arranged by the Christians. They wrapped him in white cloth, and everyone left a flower by his bedside. There were a lot of them. They huddled around his body all night long, reading from the Bible.

A YEAR AFTER the bamboo-weaver's son got out of the hospital, he moved to the county town with his wife and son. Later, someone from the village spotted them. Apparently the whole family had become scavengers. They hoped to buy a house in town for their now-grown son.

THE TOFU-MAKER'S WIFE and daughter moved to a different village. The daughter was good to her mother, so the old lady lived a fairly decent life, although she was in poor health. She'd converted a few years before this and still got in touch with her Christian friends from Shen Village every once in a while. Their old house stood empty, and the yard was full of weeds. She didn't return even once. It was as if she'd completely forgotten she'd ever lived here.

THE LANTERN-MAKER WAS my grandfather. On his hundredth birthday, his daughter, my mother, got someone to construct paper houses and people and horses, and also some paper lanterns. She burned these on his grave, hoping to ease his existence in the underworld. She says she hasn't dreamed of him for seven or eight years now. Perhaps he's been reincarnated.

MY OTHER GRANDFATHER, the carpenter, left me some of his tools: an ax, a plane, a saw, a chisel, and so on. I brought them everywhere while I was working in Wuxi. Then I moved to Guangzhou and gave up carpentry, so I gave them to a fellow villager. This was twenty years ago, and I still regret it. I ought to have sent them back to the village instead, so they could have stayed in our family.

THE BARBER'S HOUSE is long gone. There used to be a large stone weight outside his front door, which he'd play around with when he had nothing better to do. On one visit home, I heard it had been taken by someone in the east of the village. I thought of acquiring it as a memento, but when this person heard I wanted to buy it, he started treating it as a precious object and refused to show it to anyone.

THE POT-MENDER'S HUT is still around. It's a bit sad to look at now—no windows front or back, just a tiny door facing south. This door is always shut, of course. There are graves all around the house, practically surrounding it. Buried here are his grandparents, his parents, and himself. Plus many others, who knows who they are. Perhaps strangers who thought the feng shui was good here and chose it for their final resting place.

BY THE ENTRANCE of the temple where the sculptor lived were two rose of Sharon shrubs, one tall and one short. Someone bought the tall one a year ago—I heard they paid two thousand yuan for it. The sculptor planted these shrubs in his youth. He must have had his reasons.

THE GARDENER COULDN'T find anything to do in Shen Village after his return, so he went to town and set up a stall, selling grilled cuttlefish. Business was all right for a while, but later tailed off. Next, he rented a space and started selling vegetable and flower seeds. People started calling him "gardener" again. This new venture wasn't particularly lucrative, but it made him happy.

THE BLACKSMITH'S SON Cao Hongrong is now eighty-one years old. He makes a living from farming and scavenging. I've heard he's got seventy or eighty thousand yuan stashed away. This has earned him the respect of almost all his relatives. Hongrong has always lived up to their image of him. He sometimes goes an entire month without touching a morsel of meat, but when his relatives have a wedding or funeral, he's sure to send a big portion.

THE JACK-OF-ALL-TRADES was what we called my uncle to make fun of him, because whatever he decided to do, he only dabbled in it and never put in the work to achieve anything. He didn't pay much attention to family matters either, just went around making merry all day long, frittering his life away. From when we were kids, Grandpa told us time and again not to be like him, leading a useless existence. That's why we never respected him. When I'd just finished writing this book, I was chatting with my father when the conversation turned to this uncle. When Grandma was seriously ill in the hospital, Dad went home to raise the medical fees, while Uncle stayed in the ward keeping her company. When the doctors said she needed a transfusion, Uncle gave her his blood rather than waiting for Dad to return. He donated one bag, then went back for a second round and fainted from blood loss. As soon as he revived, he called for the doctor and told him not to tell the family. My uncle's name is on the very front of our family tree: Qinglin. He was still alive the last time we updated it, so the date of his death hasn't been added yet.

THE TAILOR'S WIFE, Xu, lived on for fifty-six years after he was shot dead. At the age of seventy, she moved to another village to help her grandson raise his child. When the child got older, the grandson brought the boy to the city to work alongside him, leaving Xu all alone in the village. She broke her leg and couldn't move, so she just lay there in bed. They didn't find her until she'd been dead for three days.

THE TEACHER MINGJIU'S wife lost her mind after he died. Two years after this, she regained her senses. Abandoning her child, she got married again, to a farmer in Jiangnan. Her new husband was from a fairly well-off family who owned a two-story building. The only thing was, they often quarreled. One day in 1988, after a ferocious argument, she killed herself by drinking insecticide. This was a decade after Mingjiu's death.

ONE OF THE scale-operator's great-grandsons had severe developmental disabilities and spent his days wandering aimlessly around the village. He was the third generation to be afflicted in this way. No one in the generation after that was disabled, though all of them later moved to the county town.

THE WEAVER'S APPRENTICE was the most honest, loyal person in Shen Village. I heard that more than a decade ago, he was still persisting in making cloth on his large-scale loom. He eventually had to get with the times and started collecting empty bottles to support himself. He refused to get rid of the loom and often brought it out for a tune-up. After his death last year, his son immediately chopped the useless loom to pieces and burned them as firewood.

GLOSSARY

Agricultural collective 农业合作社—a system by which all the farmers shared resources and tasks, a precursor to the People's commune

Bagua reading 起卦—a traditional form of fortune-telling

Baijiu 白酒—a clear liquor usually made from sorghum

Big-character poster 大字报—large, handwritten posters, often used to denounce people during the Cultural Revolution

Big head Yuan 袁大头—a silver coin in circulation during the first half of the twentieth century, with President Yuan Shikai's head on it

Cadre 干部—a Communist Party administrator

Collectivization 成立合作社—the formation of farming cooperatives

Dongyue the Great 东岳大帝—the lord of Mount Tai, a deity in charge of all living things

Double Ninth Festival 重阳节—the ninth day of the ninth lunar month, a traditional holiday

Earth god 土地神—a folk deity responsible for the local land

Eight Immortals table 八仙桌—a square table large enough to seat eight; the name is a reference to the legend of the eight immortals

Fanshen 翻身—literally "to turn the body over," i.e., to adopt revolutionary ideas

General Xiangyu 项羽—a prominent warlord, 232–202 BC.

Great networking 大串联—a movement from 1966 to 1967 in which young people traveled across China to exchange revolutionary ideas

Household contract responsibility 家庭联产承包责任制—a system launched in the late 1970s in which individual households were made responsible for the profits and losses of production units

Land reform 土地改革—a system of forcibly reallocating land ownership during the 1950s

Li 里—a unit of distance equivalent to 500 meters

Mu 亩—a unit of area equivalent to one-fifteenth of a hectare

Nationalist/Kuomintang 国民党—a political party in the Republic of China that was eventually exiled from the Mainland to Taiwan

New Fourth Army 新四军—an army unit run by the Communist Party

Overturn the Qing and restore the Ming 反清复明—a movement during the Qing dynasty (1636–1912) aimed at overthrowing the Manchu rulers and bringing the previous Ming dynasty back to power

People's commune 公社化—first launched in 1958, a system of organizing farming households in which everything was shared and all agricultural activities were centrally assigned

Production brigade 生产队—a smaller organizational unit under the People's commune

Queue 辫子—a long braid worn by men that was compulsory during the Qing dynasty

Red Guards 红卫兵—a student-led paramilitary movement during the Cultural Revolution

Rightist 右派—an alleged enemy of Communism

Shijing 诗经—the oldest existing anthology of Chinese poetry, comprising over three hundred poems composed between the eleventh and seventh centuries BC.

Sun Yat-Sen 孙中山—1866–1925, a Nationalist revolutionary who was instrumental in overthrowing the Qing dynasty

Taiping Heavenly Kingdom 太平天国—a rebel state (1851–1964) opposed to the Qing dynasty

Tomb sweeping festival 清明节—a traditional holiday during which people tend to their family graves and make offerings to their departed relatives

Xinhai Revolution 辛亥革命—the 1911 overthrowing of the Qing dynasty, China's final imperial dynasty, leading to the establishment of the Republic of China

ABOUT THE AUTHOR

Shen Fuyu was born in Jiangsu, China, in 1970. At the age of eighteen, he left home and drifted around the country, taking up a variety of jobs—porter, clerk, and schoolteacher—and began his writing career. He graduated from the Department of Chinese Language and Literature of Nanjing University in 1996 and has been working as a journalist for twenty years. Having published more than a dozen books, Shen is a full-time writer now and lives in Paris.

ABOUT THE TRANSLATOR

Jeremy Tiang is a novelist, playwright, and literary translator from Chinese. His translations include novels by Yeng Pway Ngon, Yan Ge, Lo Yi-Chin, Zhang Yueran, Shuang Xuetao, Geling Yan, Chan Ho-Kei, and Li Er, as well as plays by Chen Si'an, Wei Yu-Chia, Quah Sy Ren, and Han Lao Da. His novel *State of Emergency* won the Singapore Literature Prize in 2018. Originally from Singapore, he lives in New York City.

It takes a village to get from a manuscript to the printed book in your hands. The team at Astra House would like to thank everyone who helped to publish *The Artisans*.

PUBLISHER
Ben Schrank

EDITORIAL
Alessandra Bastagli
Olivia Dontsov

CONTRACTS
Stefanie Ratzki

PUBLICITY
Rachael Small

MARKETING
Tiffany Gonzalez
Sarah Christensen Fu
Jordan Snowden

SALES
Jack W. Perry

DESIGN
Jacket: Rodrigo Corral Studio
Interior: Richard Oriolo
Jeanette Tran

PRODUCTION
Lisa Taylor
Alisa Trager
Rebecca Baumann

COPYEDITING
Ian Gibbs

COMPOSITION
Westchester Publishing Services

ABOUT ASTRA HOUSE

Astra House is dedicated to publishing authors across genres and from around the world. We value works that are authentic, ask new questions, present counter-narratives and original thinking, challenge our assumptions, and broaden and deepen our understanding of the world. Our mission is to advocate for authors who experience their subject deeply and personally, and who have a strong point of view; writers who represent multifaceted expressions of intellectual thought and personal experience, and who can introduce readers to new perspectives about their everyday lives as well as the lives of others.